Foundat in Caring for Children

Christine Hobart and Jill Frankel

Stanley Thornes (Publishers) Ltd

First published 2000 by
Stanley Thornes (Publishers) Ltd
Delta Place
27 Bath Road
Cheltenham
GL53 7TH
UK

ISBN 0 7487 4180 1

00 01 02 03 04 / 10 9 8 7 6 5 4 3 2 1

Illustrations by Angela Lumley; cartoons by Shaun Williams

Typeset by Northern Phototypesetting Company Ltd, Bolton
Printed and bound in Great Britain by Redwood Books, Trowbridge,
Wiltshire

Contents

CONTENTS

About the authors

The authors come from a background of nursery teaching and health visiting, and have worked together for many years training students to work with young children. They have written eight books encompassing most areas of the childcare and education curriculum.

ACKNOWLEDGEMENTS

The authors and publishers would like to thank the following people and organisations:

Angela Dare and Margaret O'Donovan for permission to use the charts and illustrations on pages 81, 115, 124, 133 and 164; West Thames College tutors and supervisors, for permission to adapt the handout on pages 250–1; Angela Dare and Victoria Hobart for reading and commenting on Chapter 5; Elisabeth Sadek for providing the accident form, the Job Description/Person Specification on page 279 and the Contract of Employment on page 283; Emma Breckenridge for reading and commenting on the manuscript; all the tutors on the pilot scheme who read various chapters and made such useful comments; Suzanne Pye and Susie Sainsbury for permission to take photographs at their school, the Gate Nursery School in Notting Hill, and to Leslie Frankel, the photographer; Miles Frankel, Jordan Gayle and Theo Tomking for letting us use their photographs; Montessori Centre International for access to their MCQ data bank.

Every effort has been made to contact copyright holders and we apologise if any have been overlooked.

Introduction

❦

This book has been written to cover all the units of the new **Foundation Award in Caring for Children**. With its emphasis on clear and simple explanations of all the key issues, it is intended for students needing to understand the basic principles of caring for children.

The book is intended as an introduction to working with children, and will help students develop a basic awareness of child development and of the basic skills required to meet children's needs. It will also help students' own personal development, and enable them to make an informed choice about their future career, training or education.

A number of features have been adopted in the book, each of which is designed to make learning easier:

Chapter introductions set the scene for what is to follow.

Case studies	help put the theory into context. Each is based on a life-like scenario, and is followed up by questions for group discussion or individual work.
Key points	are emphasised throughout. Margin boxes help point out the really important issues, and are ideal for helping in revision for each chapter.
Tasks	which provide simple activities for individual students to do. Each activity is designed to be relevant, and will contribute to the student's portfolio of evidence, required for assessment.
What do you think?	providing points to be thought through, or for small groups to discuss.
Test yourself	consisting of a number of short answer questions reviewing the chapter. Practising the questions will help students prepare for testing.
Glossary	coming at the end of each chapter, and at the end of the book. Key technical terms are explained in clear and simple language.
Clear and accessible style	helps to make the content more easily understood.

Throughout the book there are highly quality illustrations, all of which are relevant and informative. There are also many charts, diagrams and sample forms.

The female gender for the child has been used in every chapter. This was decided on the toss of a coin, as it was felt that this would be less confusing than changing gender every chapter!

Finally, it should be said that although the book is written for students of the Foundation Award in Caring for Children, it will also prove invaluable for other courses. In particular, students of the CACHE Certificate in Child Care and Education (CCE), the BTEC First in Care, NVQs in Early Years Care and Education at level 2 and GNVQs in Health and Social Care at Foundation and Intermediate level, will all find the book useful.

CHAPTER 1

Developing a professional approach to working with young children

This chapter includes:
- What you need to succeed in childcare
- Learning to work in a group
- Learning to work in a team
- Understanding childcare qualifications
- Action plans
- Glossary

KEY POINT

You will have a responsibility to respect the rights of the people with whom you work and behave in an appropriate way at all times.

If you are thinking of a career working with children, there are several questions you should ask yourself. Many would-be students feel it is enough to like children, to be 'good with kids', but there is a great deal more to childcare and child education than just enjoying being with children. You will be expected to behave in a **professional** manner. This means that you will have a responsibility to respect the rights of the people with whom you work and behave in an appropriate way at all times. This is particularly important for those working with young children, as the children are often unable to tell you what they want themselves and need to be protected and kept safe.

For further information on the material covered in this chapter, you could consult the following:

Hobart, C. and Frankel, J., *A Practical Guide to Working with Children*, *3rd edition*, Stanley Thornes (Publishers) Ltd, 1999

WHAT YOU NEED TO SUCCEED IN CHILDCARE

You should be able to answer 'Yes' to the following questions

1 Have you had experience working with children?
2 Are you in good health, and will you have the energy to complete the course?

3 Do you enjoy reading and writing and feel that you have the necessary skills to succeed on a course?

4 Do you have some interests and hobbies?

5 Do you have the sort of personality that allows you not only to get on with children, but also encourages them to learn and to feel secure with you?

6 Do you feel comfortable working with adults?

7 Are you able to accept helpful criticism?

Experience

It is useful to have spent some time with young children, who can be noisy, messy and occasionally quite hard to control. You will need put up with a high level of noise, enjoy messy play activities, be very patient, and be firm and consistent.

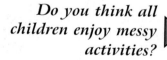

TASK

Many of you will have had some baby-sitting experience. It may have been within your family, or with children you did not know so well.

1 What did you enjoy about it the most?

2 What did you find the most difficult?

Do you think all children enjoy messy activities?

2

CASE STUDY

Janet

Janet, studying for her GCSEs, became involved in her local Church Sunday School. She helped look after a group of five- and six-year-olds for an hour of creative activities each week. One Sunday, the adult in charge of the group was called away to the telephone, just as a music session was beginning. Janet picked up a tambourine, and continued to sing with the group. Two of the children refused to join in, and started quarrelling over a toy. This upset the whole group and Janet felt she was losing control of the situation.

1   Should Janet have been left alone?
2   Why do you think the children behaved like this?
3   What could Janet have done to prevent this behaviour?
4   How should she have handled the situation once it developed?

What sort of music do your children enjoy? ▶

Health

Are you in good health? Caring for children is hard work as well as being satisfying. Young children develop many minor illnesses, and you will need to build up a resistance to coughs and colds very quickly. A good diet, plenty of rest, exercise and sleep will help you to stay healthy and cope with the infections to which you may be exposed when in close contact with children.

If you have severe back problems, **epilepsy** or a severe skin condition, it would be advisable to seek medical advice before starting a career in childcare.

What do YOU think?

Why do you think these medical conditions might make it difficult to work with children?

Knowledge

During your course, both in college and work experience, you will be gaining knowledge about children, their development and learning, and their needs. Knowledge plays an important part in preventing problems, for example, understanding that children who have a hearing loss might be slow in using speech and may need to be referred to a speech therapist at an early stage.

Knowledge helps you to understand the development of the children in your care, and how to read records and observations to pick up problems so as to make sure the child receives the necessary help and support.

You never stop learning. You will want to update your knowledge regularly by attending courses, reading professional magazines such as *Nursery World* and always being ready to question and challenge in a thoughtful and useful way.

Interests

Those working with young children need outside interests and hobbies, as not only can these interests be brought into the placements, but they will also make you a more interesting person. A love of music, enjoying reading, skill at craft activities, sporting activities, an understanding of art, an interest in animals: all these experiences and many more can be shared with the children.

KEY POINT

Those working with young children need outside interests and hobbies.

Personality

Caring for others can be tiring and stressful at times. You need to have the sort of personality that can rise above every day annoyances and difficulties, remaining cheerful, calm and approachable. Many shy people feel that they can get on well with children, whilst having difficulty talking with adults. You will have to work very closely with many adults, including colleagues, tutors, people in professional roles, and parents. Confidence in yourself is the key, whether you have a quiet calm manner, or a lively bubbly nature. A sense of humour is especially important when working with children, and with other people in a team.

TASK

List your interests and hobbies. Which ones do you think you might use in your work with children?

*Do you play an
instrument?*

*What outdoor game
would you feel confident
playing with school-aged
children?*

Disclosure of criminal background

If you have had a brush with the law in the past, you will need to discuss this with a tutor as soon as you apply for any childcare course. Anyone working with children has to have a possible criminal background checked by the Police Records Department as soon as they start work.

You may be required to complete a declaration of any criminal record or pending prosecution before you start the course. Some placements will require a police check to be carried out before accepting you as a student.

Communication

The ability to communicate is vitally important for any carer. This can take several forms: talking, listening, writing skills and body language. You have to be interested in people to communicate well with them. If a person fails to respond to other people's needs, it gets in the way of relationships.

The way that you communicate and talk to children, parents and other professional people should show them that you are a caring, knowledgeable and sensitive person, and able to state your views and ideas clearly. Your body language should show that you are interested and have **motivation**. Shrugging your shoulders and sulking is no substitute for calmly and clearly expressing your point of view over a disagreement. Maintaining eye-contact with children and adults will help maintain good relationships.

Accepting constructive criticism
As you are progressing through your course, you will be assessed regularly by your tutors. They have a responsibility to help you by feeding back to

What do YOU think?
Can you think of any examples when a person's failure to respond to your needs has spoilt your relationship?

Why do we find it difficult to accept criticism?

you where you may need to make progress. This should be accepted calmly and cheerfully in the spirit in which it is offered. Learning from and acting upon **constructive criticism** is part of your professional and personal development.

CASE STUDY

Tracey

Tracey, a young student on a childcare course, found it difficult to accept anyone in any way criticising her work in college or in her work experience placement. At the end of her second term, her tutor wrote on her report that 'Tracey finds it hard to accept constructive criticism.'

On reading this, Tracey became very upset, burst into tears and shouted that this was not true. Her tutor started to laugh, and Tracey saw the funny side, and signed the report as fair and true.

1 What do you take 'constructive criticism' to mean?
2 Why do some people find it hard to accept feedback from other people?
3 How do you react when part of your work is seen to be less than perfect?
4 What would the result be if you were never made to think about your strengths and weaknesses?

Personal development

During your college time and work experience placement, your interest in learning, enthusiasm and commitment will lead to your success. You should reach an understanding of what you can and cannot do during work experience. You must attend college and work experience placement regularly, and be punctual.

The well-being and safety of the children in your care has to be your main priority, and you should never behave in a way that might put the children in danger or at risk. No person is perfect in all respects, so understand and admit your weaknesses. Do not feel forced to take on responsibilities when you feel that you have not had the necessary knowledge and training to carry them out successfully. If, for example, you are asked to look after children on an outing, and feel unprepared for this, discuss it with your supervisor.

KEY POINT

The well-being and safety of the children in your care has to be your main priority, and you should never behave in a way that might put the children in danger or at risk.

CASE STUDY

Michelle

Michelle is doing her work experience placement in a Community Nursery. She is working with a group of ten two-year-olds and her supervisor wants her help in taking the children for a picnic in a local park. Michelle agrees, although she feels rather nervous at the thought of being responsible for so many children, even though two parents are coming as well.

After the picnic, the children run around playing with a ball and chasing each other. When it is time to go home, there are only nine children left. Michelle felt very agitated and upset and while the supervisor watched the other children, Michelle and the parents searched for the missing toddler. He was found thirty yards away, looking longingly at an ice-cream van on the main road leading into the park.

1 What might the consequences have been if the child was not found so quickly?
2 Was Michelle given too much responsibility?
3 Should Michelle have voiced her fears from the start, or would the nursery have thought she was just being unhelpful?
4 How could this incident have been prevented?

If you object on religious or moral grounds when asked to do some activity in your work experience placement, you must discuss this in an open way with your tutor and your supervisor. A common example of this is the celebration of some festivals, such as Christmas, to which some religious sects object.

It will be expected at all times that you show awareness and understanding of the total needs of children, parents and team members, regardless of race, class, culture, religion, sexual orientation, disability, gender and age, both individually and in groups.

Never show favouritism or special treatment towards some children in preference to others but always show respect and interest in the customs, values and beliefs of all the children with whom you are involved. This will help the children to have self-respect and confidence.

Complete the chart on page 9, showing your strengths and weaknesses.

TASK

Give examples of how you might put the needs of a group of children and those of an individual child before your own.

	Strengths	Weaknesses
Health record		
Interests/hobbies		
Personality		

Communication skills:
    written
 	
    oral		

Reliability		
Knowledge of various cultures		
Experience of working with children		
Ability to organise own work		

LEARNING TO WORK IN A GROUP

You are probably already a member of several groups. These would consist of:

- your family
- your friends
- the people you might meet in different interest groups, such as sport, religion, hobbies and so on
- the people you might meet working part-time.

In all these groups, you will be communicating, having fun, arguing and making decisions together.

Do your friends help you? ▶

You are now joining a new group in school or college and, at some stage, in your work experience placement. You need to understand how to behave in these groups, how to get on with many people from various backgrounds, how to communicate with your tutors and how to work successfully together within the group.

You know already, from your experience of school, how helpful it can be if any member of the group:

- asks sensible questions about the work
- offers to take notes for a friend who is absent
- gives information
- supports anyone having difficulty with the work
- encourages other people to take part.

What do YOU think?

1 Can you think of any other ways in which a person might contribute to or disrupt a group?
2 Some people seem to find it easy to settle into a new group, whereas others have more of a problem. Why do you think this is?
3 People who have difficulties settling into one group, often have problems in all groups. Why should this be so?

KEY POINT

You will find it easier to develop good relationships with the staff team if you take as full a part as possible in all activities, showing enthusiasm and a willingness to learn.

TASK

1 Have you had contact with all the people on the work experience placement team shown on the chart opposite?
2 Are there others at your placement not included on the chart?
3 With which people in the team do you have the closest contact?

You will also be aware of how damaging it can be to the learning of a group if a member:

- constantly interrupts
- chats to another person whilst the tutor is teaching
- does not listen to other people
- uses the class to promote their own ideas, and does not listen to the ideas of others.

LEARNING TO WORK IN A TEAM

Many of the skills that make you a useful member of the group are also needed when you start your work experience placement, and become a member of the childcare team. You will find it easier to develop good relationships with the staff team if you take as full a part as possible in all activities, showing enthusiasm and a willingness to learn. You will be expected to undertake any appropriate task asked of you. After a few days, you will be ready to show initiative, seeing tasks that need to be done without having to be directed and being sensitive to the needs of the placement and of the children.

Taking part in the social life of the placement is very important. Try to arrange to use the staff room at break times, so that the staff can see that you see yourself as one of them. You may find it scary at first but, with a little effort on your part, you will soon relax and become a member of the team.

support staff (caretaker / cleaner)
office staff
supervisor
visiting specialists e.g. doctor speech therapist health visitor social worker
THE STUDENT AND THE WORK EXPERIENCE PLACEMENT TEAM
other students
colleagues in room
parents
headteacher / nursery manager

Resolving conflicts

Whenever people work together, problems and conflicts are bound to arise. Working together to resolve conflicts can be a good thing, as it helps you to understand the people with whom you are working and better decisions are more likely to be made. If conflicts are not sorted out quickly, the children in your care may sense the atmosphere and may feel anxious and unhappy.

When you feel you have a problem with someone in the team, think about your feelings and attempt to tell others how you feel in a quiet, calm way and keep to the point. Being **assertive** rather than aggressive will allow others to see you as a sensible person.

How do you settle disagreements? ▶

The only way to resolve a conflict is to communicate and find out exactly what the problem is. Do not ignore it and hope it will disappear on its own. Talking things over will allow you to reach a decision, and this may involve some compromise on both sides.

To work well as part of a team you should:

- recognise the skills, knowledge and experience of the team members
- be willing to undertake appropriate tasks given to you
- ask for help and advice when necessary, but be careful not to be too demanding
- not ask questions about people's personal lives
- keep confidences
- try to co-operate with people
- be loyal to the team, and do not criticise them in public or behind their backs

- show enthusiasm. Make sure your body language is positive. Look people in the eye. Do not shrug your shoulders and turn away, even if something upsets you
- if there is a problem, present it in a clear and assertive manner at the right time. Never become aggressive
- accept responsibility for any mistake you may have made.

As you gain in confidence you will make good and lasting relationships with children and colleagues, and you are likely to thoroughly enjoy your time in your work experience placement.

What do YOU think?

Have you ever not owned up to a mistake you have made? Why did you find it difficult to admit you were wrong?

CASE STUDY

Greta

Greta, a 16-year-old student, arrives for the third day of her work experience in a nursery school, and is enjoying it very much. As she is meeting friends at the end of the day, she has dressed up more than usual, and is wearing high heels and items of chunky jewellery. The supervisor asks to have a word with her, and points out that she is unsuitably dressed for a hard day's work, that jewellery can be dangerous and high heels a hazard. She asks Greta to go home and change.

Greta feels angry and embarrassed, and responds by shouting at the supervisor and making some rude remarks about the clothing of the rest of the team. The supervisor takes her into the staff room, and tries to calm her down.

Greta bursts into tears and apologises. She explains that the journey home takes her half an hour, and costs £2. As a student, she is always short of money.

1 How should Greta have behaved?
2 How might the problem have been resolved, without Greta having to go home?
3 Could the problem have been avoided?
4 What long-term problems might result from this incident?
5 Do you think the supervisor handled the situation sensibly?

UNDERSTANDING CHILDCARE QUALIFICATIONS

There are many routes to obtaining a professional qualification to work with children. They are either college based, such as The Council for Awards in Children's Care and Education (CACHE) courses (the Diploma in Childcare and Education, and the Certificate in Childcare and Education) or gained during employment, such as the National Vocational Qualifications (NVQs). Many young people have a dream of working with children, and do not realise how long it might take to gain a professional qualification, or the various paths that can be followed.

Qualifications are set at various levels, from Level 1 to Level 5 (see page 15). The level of the course that you do first will depend on your age, your experience with children and your present qualifications.

There is not only one way to become a professional childcare and education worker. It will depend on:

- what courses are available in your area
- whether you can move nearer or travel to a suitable course
- your existing qualifications
- money.

The following case studies are just two examples, with both students having successfully completed the CACHE Foundation Award in Caring for Children (CFCC) course.

CASE STUDY

Karen

Karen progresses to the Certificate in Childcare and Education (CCE) course. This takes one year and, at the end of this course, her parents are unable to finance her further, so she finds employment in a local private nursery, where she is able to register for NVQ Level 3 in Childcare and Education. She takes advantage of in-service training and after four years employment, becomes manager of the nursery.

CASE STUDY

Sharon

Sharon progresses to the Diploma in Childcare and Education (DCE) course, which she successfully completes over two years. She gains a position in a daycare centre, and returns to college after two years to take the Advanced Diploma in Childcare and Education (ADCE) on a part-time basis. When this is completed she is able to register for teacher training at the local college, having saved up enough money during her employment to supplement her grant.

LEVEL 1	LEVEL 2	LEVEL 3	LEVEL 4	LEVEL 5
	CACHE Certificate in Childcare and Education	CACHE Diploma in Child Care and Education	CACHE Advanced Diploma in Childcare and Education	Degree Level — Teacher Training
	City and Guilds Progression Award in Early Years Care and Education	NVQ Level 3 in Early Years Care Education	NVQ Level 4 Playwork Development	Nurse Training
	City and Guilds Progression Award in Playwork	NVQ Level 3 Caring for Children and Young People	NVQ Level 4 Early Years Care Education	Social Work Training
		NVQ Level 3 Playwork		Early Years Degrees
CACHE Foundation Award in Caring for Children	NVQ Level 2 in Early Years Care and Education	**Specialist Awards** Certificate in Childminding Practice CACHE/NCMA		
Introductory courses	NVQ Level 2 in Playwork	Pre-school Learning Alliance/CACHE Diploma in Pre-school Practice		
	Pre-school Learning Alliance/Cache Certificate in Pre-school Practice	CACHE Specialist Teacher Assistant Award		

Professional Employment

CACHE Professional Development Awards

15

The following chart shows you the general areas of employment that are available to you working with children.

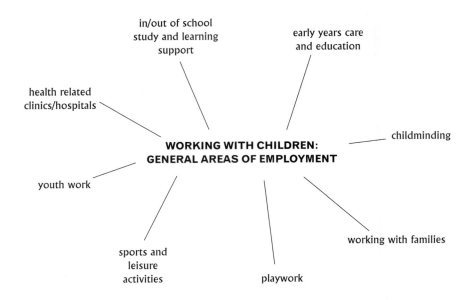

The following chart shows you what jobs are available to you working with children under supervision after you have completed a Level 2 qualification. The chart on page 17 shows you what jobs you can do after you have gained a Level 3 qualification.

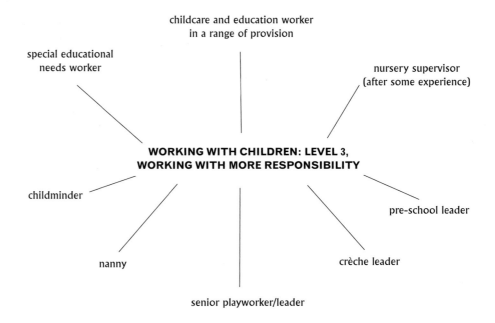

Recent information from CACHE shows that there are approximately 600,000 adults working with young children in the UK and Northern Ireland. They include:

- 120,000 pre-school workers
- 111,000 childminders
- 100,000 nannies
- 78,000 childcare and education workers in schools
- 56,000 childcare and education workers working in the private sector
- 30,000 out-of-school club workers
- 7,000 foster carers
- 1,000 childcare and education workers working in health centres and hospitals.

ACTION PLANS

Most people have dreams about their future. Some take positive steps to make sure these dreams come true. Action plans are very useful in helping you to see what is important so that you can achieve what you want. First of all, you need to name your long-term goal, and having done that you need to look at the stages you will have to go through to reach that goal. This may involve finding information, using books, talking to people who have achieved similar goals, and asking tutors for advice.

You will then need to think about these ideas and discussions and that should lead you into planning and setting deadlines for yourself so that you will succeed both on the course and in achieving your long-term goal.

Action plan

Name	Date

What have I learned from the course?

What do I want to do next?

What is my long-term goal?

Where do I go for advice and information?

What steps must I take to achieve my long-term goal?

Comments from tutor

Signature of student   **Signature of tutor**

Action plans can be written on a formal sheet provided for you (such as that on page 18) or in a style that you will find useful, using your own format. Some students prefer forms to fill in, whilst others prefer spider graphs or flow charts. You may have some other ideas.

✓ TEST YOURSELF

1   Name four essential talents you will need so you can work happily with children.
2   Describe three examples of body language.
3   Name three ways of communicating.
4   What is your first priority as a childcare worker?
5   Name three skills required by a member of a team.
6   Name two Level 3 childcare and education courses.

GLOSSARY

By the time you have finished this chapter you should understand the meaning of the following words:

assertive   dealing with difficult situations in a calm and non-threatening way whilst putting over your point of view
constructive criticism   criticism that helps you to improve your work, and that you are expected to accept
epilepsy   a condition caused by the disruption of electric impulses in the brain that might lead to having a fit
motivation   what makes you want to succeed or achieve
professional   working in a way that shows you have knowledge, behaviour and attitudes that show in good practice. It also means being reliable and keeping confidences.

Study skills

This chapter includes:
- Personal management
- Time management
- Resources and equipment
- Stress management
- Appeals and complaints
- Classroom techniques
- Learning resources
- Portfolio task planning
- Assessment procedures
- Glossary

To succeed on this course, increase your self-confidence and develop a **professional** attitude, you will need to find the time to study, and read books and magazines about childcare and education. You will also need to find out about and use other resources, such as videos and CD-ROMs, usually held in the learning resource centre. You will then be able to use what you have learnt in your work experience placement.

For further information on the material covered in this chapter, you could consult the following:

Hobart, C. and Frankel, J., **A-Z of Childcare**, Stanley Thornes (Publishers) Ltd, 1998

> ### KEY POINT
> **Discover as much as possible about the course and the work involved, before making any commitment.**

PERSONAL MANAGEMENT

Before starting a course of study, think about how you might manage your personal and social life, so that you are able to meet the new demands placed on you. Making plans to manage your more complicated life will help you to succeed on your course. It is a good idea to discover as much as possible about the course and the work involved, before making any commitment.

KEY POINT

Making good relationships with the group in college and in your work experience is important.

What do YOU think ?

As more of your time will be taken up with studying,

1 Who will be most affected by your new commitment to this course?
2 Who can give you support and encouragement?

What do YOU think ?

Suggest some ways of making friends within your group.

What leisure facilities do you have in your college or school? ▶

Relationships

Many students have found that it is easier to be successful on a course if they have the encouragement and support of their family and friends. Making good relationships with the group in college and in your work experience is also important.

Some students will enjoy their studies so much that other people in their lives may feel left out and left behind. It takes a great deal of tact to resolve this problem. There will be help available at most colleges, as tutors are familiar with this difficulty. Discuss your course with friends and family, as this will help them feel involved and they will enjoy your success.

During your course, you will be working closely in college with a group of people. You may find yourself with people from different backgrounds, of different ages, and with differing abilities. It may take you some time to settle in your group, but you will soon relax and enjoy the company of most of the people. Sharing ideas with everyone in the group will broaden your ideas and attitudes and help your learning and understanding.

Some groups will have a number of tutors teaching them, one of whom will act as personal tutor to the group. This tutor will be responsible for giving personal and group tutorial sessions. He or she will probably visit you in your work experience placement, discuss your progress and personal self-development and help you if you have any problems.

During your introduction to the college and the course, the roles and responsibilities of the tutors will be made clear. Get to know your college, and try to enter into some of the activities available to you.

TIME MANAGEMENT

You will find it easier to study and complete your course work if you manage your time well. Once you start a course you will have to fit in all its commitments as well as your family, friends, social and leisure activities, hobbies and interests and time for taking care of yourself in having enough rest, exercise and sleep. If one side of your life takes up too much of your time, pressure will be put on you and you may have to decide to put some things first and may even have to give up some of your other activities. Good time management means that you can be successful in college whilst enjoying your social life.

What do YOU think?

1 How did you spend a typical day before you started this course?
2 How will this change when you start the course?
3 Will you have to give up any interests or hobbies?

Good time keeping is valued in the world of work, and is especially important when working with young children. You will be expected to arrive punctually in college and in your work experience placement. You will need to have planned your journey, and allowed plenty of time to make sure that you do not let anyone down by arriving late.

Your attendance record will be monitored as no one will want to employ a person who is frequently absent or late, for whatever reason. If being late or absent is unavoidable, you must make contact as soon as possible,

KEY POINT

Good time keeping is valued in the world of work

What can make you late? ▶

explaining your problem, making sure that you keep in touch at regular intervals until you can return.

Missing a lot of time in college might mean that you find it difficult to keep up with your work. Talk over any problems with your personal tutor who may be able to help.

CASE STUDY

Charlene

Charlene is enjoying her work experience placement and the team thinks she is a real treasure. The children look forward to her coming. There is one major problem. Charlene is often late, and once she did not come at all, and did not telephone the placement or her tutor.

1 Suggest some possible reasons why Charlene is often late.
2 Why is it important to solve this problem?
3 Write an action plan to help Charlene overcome her difficulties.

Organising your time when studying

This is a key factor in making sure you succeed. You will probably spend much of your personal time in:

- organising notes, portfolios and files
- reading
- writing portfolio tasks
- planning and completing work undertaken in placement
- preparing individual and group presentations
- using the learning resource centre/library
- keeping a diary.

You will find keeping a diary really useful in helping you manage your time.

Remember to:

- keep *one* diary only, with *all* your appointments in it
- keep it with you all the time
- fill in all long-term information and arrangements as soon as you have the diary, for example holiday and placement dates and times, deadlines for assignments
- fill in new arrangements as soon as you make them, for example dates of appointments and meetings
- fill in information you may need when away from home, such as details of your next of kin, GP, bank, your national insurance number, work experience telephone number and name of supervisor, and any other important addresses and telephone numbers

- keep a copy of your college timetable in the diary
- keep the diary neat and up to date. You may decide to divide the day into three sections. Blank or cross out anything that has changed
- use a thick elastic band around the front cover and used pages, so that it opens at the current week
- paste an envelope in the back in which to keep tickets and appointment cards
- look at the diary every day, and at the end of the day, to see what is planned for tomorrow, and to allow you time to prepare yourself.

Are you well organised? ▶

What do YOU think?

In what ways is this diary different from any other one you have kept?

Placement diary

You may be asked by your tutor to keep a record of events and your experiences when you are in placement. This should be written up at the end of every day, whilst the details are still fresh in your mind. As this may be seen by other people do not include the actual names of the placement, the staff or the children. There should be nothing written in your record that you would not be happy for your tutor and your **supervisor** to read.

Managing your time

The way to make the best use of your time is to:

- record the dates for handing in work well in advance, and plan to finish each task ahead of time. If a problem occurs at the last minute, your work will not be delayed.
- keep up-to-date with all your work.
- file your work on a daily basis
- decide on the time of day that you are most awake and able to concentrate, and plan to study at this time
- note in your diary dates of any tests or deadlines so as to avoid planning major social events at these times if possible.

There will be less time for socialising once you have started the course, so you will want to make the most of it. You need to have time for yourself, and for your family and friends to make sure that they do not feel left out by your new life, and that you continue to enjoy your interests and hobbies. Try to make time for regular exercise as this will help to lessen stress. A life that is all work is a dull one, and the children in your work experience placement will benefit from your being well, energetic and enthusiastic.

RESOURCES AND EQUIPMENT FOR THE COURSE

There are some things you will need that are essential, and others that you might find useful.

Essential equipment

- pens and pencils
- felt tip pens, thick and thin for display work
- ruler
- rubber
- highlighter pens
- A4 paper, lined with punched holes
- A4 ring binders
- a strong bag or case to carry your work
- a diary
- a good general dictionary.

Suggestions for additional equipment
- scissors
- sticky tape
- glue or paste
- hole punch
- A4 plastic wallets
- a small notebook
- a stapler

Books

The college or school may give you a list of the essential books that you will need to buy or borrow to help you succeed on the course. It is a good idea to obtain these before the first day. Other books, perhaps on an optional list, you could order from libraries, or ask for them as presents from your family and friends. Books are often cheaper when ordered through the Internet. Jumble sales and charity shops are often a good source for cheap second hand books, as long as they are not too old. If you own the books yourself, you will be able to underline the passages of essential information or use a highlighter pen. Having done this, it will be easier for you to find what you need when you come to write your portfolio tasks.

Child care and education ideas are constantly changing and you will find it interesting to keep up with all the current opinions by reading professional magazines such as *Nursery World*, newspapers such as *The Guardian* and *The Independent*, watching television documentaries and listening to programmes on the radio.

Studying at home

Some of your study time may be away from college or school, and you will need to consider the following.

- Is there a room or a space where you can work without being interrupted?
- Is there a table or desk big enough for you to spread out your work undisturbed?
- Do you have shelving for your books and files?
- Do you have somewhere safe to keep your completed work?

Many students find it difficult to study at home, for many reasons, so you could look into the possibility of studying at a friend's house, or at your local library. Regular access to a computer would be helpful. Often college libraries can offer space and facilities for study.

Is there anything else you need to help you study? ▶

STRESS MANAGEMENT

As a student, you may often find yourself under stress at certain times. The main causes may be:

- too many demands on your time
- meeting assignment deadlines

- difficulty with the college work and meeting the expected standards
- being unclear about what tutors expect from you
- not feeling relaxed in your work experience
- frequent absences from college/school, leading to lack of information and inability to complete tasks
- tensions in your relationships with your **peer group**, tutors or supervisors
- coping with criticism
- personal problems unrelated to the course.

Sometimes students find it stressful if their families do not encourage them. The reasons for this may be that:

- the families wish them to work and earn money
- the families would prefer them to study a different course
- there may be stress within the family because of unemployment, bereavement or separation
- the relationship between the parents and the student is in conflict because, for example, the parents do not approve of the student's friends and lifestyle.

What do YOU think?

What other reasons might there be for a student feeling that his or her family does not encourage them on this course?

Signs of stress

Your stress level may be indicated by:

- headaches, or other aches and pains
- loss of appetite or wanting to eat too much
- not sleeping
- tiredness
- tearfulness
- lack of concentration
- inability to think clearly and make decisions
- feeling angry or losing your temper.

Managing stress

It is important to recognise and face up to the fact that you are stressed, and you need to know why. Think about the following ways to find a solution.

- Arrange to see your personal tutor to discuss your problems. He or she may assist you in devising an action plan to help you decide what to do, or what support you need.
- Arrange an appointment with your GP to discuss your symptoms and see what sources of help are available.
- Arrange an appointment with the student counsellor to consider counselling, to help you think about what is going on, and perhaps make changes in your lifestyle.

- Find out about assertiveness and relaxation techniques.
- Look again at how you are managing your time.
- Look at your lifestyle, including your diet and exercise programme.

List the causes of stress in this picture ▶

Remember that everyone gets stressed sometimes and it is perfectly normal to feel stress as a student. You are being judged all the time, both in college and in your work experience placement. Work experience requires a strong commitment and it is very tiring working with children, particularly at first.

CASE STUDY

Ellen

Ellen was in tears when she went to see her tutor. Her parents had just split up, her boyfriend was seen with her best friend, her mother was threatening to move her new boyfriend into the family home and Ellen had a terrible cold. She was one week late with her assignment, and had missed two days in her placement.

1 How might Ellen's tutor help her?
2 How might Ellen begin to sort out her problems?
3 Where might she seek some professional help?
4 Who else might she talk to?

How would you help a friend who was upset? ▶

APPEALS AND COMPLAINTS

Complaints usually occur when there has been a breakdown in communication between the student and the tutors. This does not happen often, but if it does your tutors will be as anxious as you to settle it as quickly as possible. Colleges/schools will have procedures to follow, and are likely to bring them to your attention during the introduction period. Other students from the student union are available to help you put your case.

If you feel you have grounds for an appeal, in the event that you fail any part of the course, CACHE operates an appeals procedure. Your tutors will let you know about CACHE's appeals procedure when you start the course. CACHE states that the appeals procedure must represent the principles of:

- natural justice
- fairness
- equity
- independence
- objectivity
- equal opportunities.

What do YOU think ❓

Look up the six terms opposite in your dictionary and, in groups of three or four, discuss the meaning of each, and suggest some examples.

CLASSROOM TECHNIQUES

To succeed on any course of study, you will need to understand some of the ways subjects are taught in the classroom. A good tutor will use a number of different approaches in most lessons.

Taking dictation

If your tutor needs to tell you some precise information, he or she might decide to dictate notes to you for a short period of time. This technique would not be used very often in most colleges or schools. You will need to have pen and paper and to sit where you can hear clearly and see the board, as the tutor may write certain words to make sure you spell them correctly. If you find it difficult to keep up with the pace, perhaps because of your style of writing, you should discuss it with the tutor.

Note-taking

During many classes your tutor will be addressing the whole class, explaining and introducing topics, encouraging questions, discussing new ideas and looking at controversial issues, such as the smacking debate. You will be expected to take notes of the most important points. Your tutor might explain what has to be covered in a particular topic, give the talk, and then confirm what has been covered in the lesson. On the other hand, your tutor might adopt a different approach by introducing an issue and then stating arguments for and against and trying to come to some conclusion. To take notes well you should:

- be on time
- have pens, paper and highlighters to hand
- sit where you can see and hear
- listen carefully, not allowing yourself to be distracted
- ask questions
- only write down the important points
- not try to write every word
- make a note of any important questions (and answers) asked at the end of the class
- always go over the notes the same day, so that you can correct, revise, add or take out information
- date and file your notes.

Filing work

One way of making sure that your course of study is a success is to be able to find your written work easily. All those notes that you so carefully wrote down, all those handouts given to you in class and those activities carried out in your work experience – all this needs to be carefully sorted and filed. All written work that you complete must be dated, titled and carry your name. Any work that is not completed needs to be finished before you file it.

There are several methods of filing your course work. You may choose one or both of the following methods.

1 Date order (chronological): each piece of work is added to the file in date order, with the date in the top right hand corner of the page.
2 Unit headings: this is a convenient method of filing but be careful not to view each unit on its own as they often link together. For example, the health and safety unit links in with the work experience unit.

Some students might find it useful to keep a list of contents at the front of the file for quick access. The use of dividers in different colours, with the name of each unit clearly shown is another useful way of finding what you need quickly.

Handouts

Sometimes your tutors will give out handouts describing various areas of the work and will either read them through in class with you, or expect you to study them on your own. This saves time in dictating important material. You can highlight any particular points that you or your tutors feel to be of vital interest, and this will help you later on when you might be writing a portfolio task. All handouts should be dated and filed with your course material.

Discussion in class

Sometimes your tutor will introduce a topic and then expect the group to spend some time give their own relevant ideas and experiences. This can be one of the best ways of understanding and learning.

It is not always easy at first to have the confidence to speak when you are in a group. You might be afraid that your ideas are not sensible, and that the rest of the group might reject or make fun of your remarks. To get the most from group discussion you should:

- listen to other people respectfully and not interrupt
- have pen and paper to jot down ideas as they occur to you
- indicate to the tutor that you wish to speak
- speak slowly and clearly
- try to avoid discussing your own personal experiences, particularly if it is going to cause you distress
- remember that nearly everybody feels nervous at first when contributing to a classroom discussion. It becomes easier with practice
- remember all opinions are important, including yours.

KEY POINT

Remember all opinions are important, including yours.

Presentations

You may be asked, during the course, to make a presentation to the group, either on your own or with two or three other students. You will need to be clear about the purpose of the presentation, what you wish to put across and how you are going to present the information. Remember to speak clearly and slowly enough so that the group has time to take in what you are saying. Face the group at all times, even if you are using visual aids, such as an overhead projector. Remember to:

- be yourself, and find your own style
- be positive
- accept that you will be nervous beforehand and try some relaxation techniques, such as deep breathing
- think about how you will speak, not too quietly nor too loudly, not too fast nor too slow
- avoid too many statistics. If necessary, put them in a handout and ask the tutor to photocopy it for you
- check any visual aids such as tape recorders beforehand, and practice using them first
- never apologise for your presentation
- try to rehearse with friends before the actual presentation.

It might be useful to look at just one member of the audience, perhaps someone you feel comfortable with, and direct your presentation to him or her.

Why do you think it is important to face the group during a presentation? ▶

Role play

Whilst on your course, you may be asked to take on the role of another person, so that you can begin to experience the feelings and emotions that someone might feel in a certain situation. This is unlikely to happen until the group has settled and the tutor knows you all well.

Your tutor will inform you very clearly as to what is expected of you. Usually, role play will be between two people, with a third one observing what is happening. The observer will then report back to the other two. On occasion, for example if you were pretending to be in a staff meeting, a larger group would be involved, and the rest of the class would observe. It is always important to have feedback, and for those taking part to have the opportunity to state how they felt. Taking on the role of others improves your ability to see other people's points of view. This ability is called 'empathy' and is different from feeling sympathetic, as it allows you to enter into the emotions of another person.

How comfortable would you feel if asked to role play an argument?

Exploring ideas together

On occasion your tutor may ask a group to discuss a particular topic with each student offering ideas and suggestions. All ideas are accepted however wild or extravagant they may seem at first.

Someone is generally chosen to record the ideas on a large sheet of paper, or on a board, whilst another person acts as Chairperson so as to keep some order in the proceedings. Everyone in the group is expected to take part in a positive fashion. The group or the tutor may decide to set a time limit to voice the ideas. The list is read back to the group on request and at the end of the first session.

The group will now look at the entire list, combining and improving ideas. They may discover gaps in the topic. Some ideas may be very similar. The tutor may now step in, and suggest other ideas. A general discussion will follow and the ideas will be looked at in a positive way. The value of this activity is that:

- it helps you to think about what you already know about a particular topic before taking on fresh ideas
- it allows the whole class to contribute without feeling silly or shy
- it allows free expression
- some students explore thoughts and ideas that they would not do on their own
- listing ideas is a useful exercise in organising one's own work
- working as a group on a topic helps you to develop the skills of teamwork
- it helps you to understand other students' views.

Are you prepared to offer ideas to a group? ▶

TASK

Watch a television programme during the week, highlighting a childcare or educational topic.
1 Take notes of the most important points
2 Make a summary of the programme.
3 Make a note of any conclusions reached.

Using worksheets with videos

As a student on a childcare course, you will need knowledge and understanding of many different children, from different backgrounds, with different needs, of different ages and in different settings. To add to your practical experience, your tutor may wish you to watch a number of videos. You will be expected to take notes on what you are watching, and sometimes complete worksheets. You may go on to discuss the video as a group. Always make a note of the title, date and publisher of the video, as you may wish to include it in your portfolio. You should file your video notes with your class notes.

Reading in class

Sometimes a tutor might ask you to read from a book or a handout in turn, and everyone will be expected to take part. If you think you are going to find this very difficult, speak to your tutor about it, and she is sure to listen sympathetically.

LEARNING RESOURCES

Every course of study will offer resources, such as books, CD ROMS and videos so that students may complete their work satisfactorily.

The learning resource centre

Learning resource centres have developed from traditional libraries that just carried books, to provide opportunities for students to study and research using all the current technology. In any learning resource centre you will find sections for:

- fiction books
- non-fiction books
- reference books
- magazines and newspapers
- information files, including press cuttings and handouts
- catalogues
- audio books, cassettes and videos
- computers, printers and CD ROMs.

At the start of your course you will be shown how to use the learning resource centre. You will learn how the books are set out on the shelves, and how to find the right books for your course, and given instruction in the **catalogue** system, which will cross-reference authors titles and subjects. The catalogue system might use index cards but the information will more likely be held on computers. The resource centre staff will probably help you search for material.

You will need to become familiar with the learning resource centre and be prepared to ask questions and use the skills of the professional staff if there is any area that is new to you. You will probably be spending a fair proportion of your time studying on your own preparing material for portfolio tasks.

The learning resource centre should be a quiet place of study. It is important that everyone respects this and uses other more appropriate areas of the college in which to socialise.

TASK

After your introduction to the learning resource centre,
1 Find out the numbers that belong to the following sections:
a) Education,
b) Health/care/welfare,
c) **Psychology.**
2 Find out if there are any magazines that relate directly to a) Nursery work, b) Education of young children, c) Parenting.

CASE STUDY

Leon

Leon is in the library, studying hard and working on a portfolio task. He shares his bedroom at home with a younger brother, and there is little space in the flat for quiet study.

Three girls enter the library in a group, sit at a table, pull out a few books, and then start to talk noisily. Leon asks them to be quiet, but they take no notice. The librarian asks them to leave the library, but they refuse, saying they have as much right there as anyone else and say that they are studying as a group.

1 What further steps might the librarian take?
2 Do you think the girls were in the right?
3 How will Leon manage to study if this problem is not solved?

Using information technology

Most of you will be familiar with computers, either from home or from school. You may find that information technology 'Key Skills' is part of your course and you will quickly appreciate the value of this skill in writing

Are you happy using a computer? ▶

portfolio tasks and reports and being able to help the children in your work experience. If you do not have a PC at home, you will be able to book sessions in the learning resource centre.

Access to the Internet, either at school, college or at home, will help you with your research. You will be able to find a wide range of up-to-date information. It will often give you a summary of books that you might want to read. Organisations such as the **NSPCC** and **Kidscape** will have web sites, and this is helpful in providing information quickly. Check what CD ROMs are available as these can be useful in your understanding of certain topics.

Using books for research

All textbooks have a list of chapters and lists of charts and illustrations. Some will also have **footnotes**, a **bibliography** and an **index**. When selecting a book, look at:

- the introduction. This may give you some idea what the book is about and at which level it is aimed
- the chapter headings. This will show the main topics covered
- the date of publication, which will tell you how up to date the work is
- the summary, which may give you some overview of the book
- appendices, which may appear at the end of the book, giving further information, often in chart form
- the index at the back of the book. If your topic is not mentioned in the chapter headings, you may find it here
- the bibliography. Some books will suggest further reading, as well as resources, references or useful addresses
- the charts, diagrams, graphs and illustrations which may be of help in your project.

You may not be able to find all that you require on a particular topic in your school or college learning resource centre. Join your local library where you will be able to order books and other resources for a small payment. Consider buying books in partnership with other members of your group and borrowing from people who have completed your course.

Other resources

Museums and exhibitions around the country offer resources and opportunities for extending your understanding and knowledge. Find out what is available in your local area and seize the opportunity to subscribe to any free mailing list. Your tutor may arrange some group visits and you will find that your learning will be greatly enriched.

Once a year, usually in September, the magazine *Nursery World* organises an exhibition of resources, books and equipment for under- twelves in London and once a year in another part of the country. This exhibition is particularly valuable as it keeps you up to date, offers a programme of talks on current childcare and education issues, and you get to meet a number of different people involved in working with young children.

Ask your tutor about local childcare exhibitions ▶

CASE STUDY

Mark

Mark is a committed student, succeeding at college and enjoying his placement. He always takes part in class discussions and has a pleasant personality. He has one fault – an inability to file his work in any order. At the end of each class, he stuffs all his notes and handouts into a supermarket carrier bag and when it is full, empties it into one of his drawers at home.

When he comes to write his first portfolio task he realises that he is unable to find the notes he needs.

1 How could this have been prevented?
2 What should Mark do to make sure he completes his task on time?
3 Who might help him?

PORTFOLIO TASK PLANNING

You will be assessed on your course by a series of tasks that you will be expected to complete by a given date. These may take the form of reports, presentations or projects. These tasks require careful long-term planning, research and recording.

Having been set a task, you need to be sure of:

- what you are required to do
- what information you need to complete the assignment
- where you will find this information
- the date of handing in the work.

Try to have a clear idea of how long the task will take, allowing time to read through the first draft and make any necessary alterations before handing it in. Your work needs to be presented as attractively as possible, preferably typed or word-processed, using double spacing on A4 paper, and securely bound. Neat and easy to read handwritten work is also acceptable.

You must be very careful when making notes from books or professional magazines to avoid the temptation to plagiarise. This means copying chunks of text from books and handouts and pretending it is your own work. This is very serious and your work will fail.

Reports

A report is a piece of writing on a specific subject. It may be long or short and will be limited to a precise number of words.

When writing a report on any subject, you need to be clear that you are:

- responding clearly to the instructions in the title
- referring to the relevant parts of the course
- showing a good understanding of the subject
- presenting a clear argument
- introducing evidence to support your argument
- attempting to present your work in a legible, easy to read style, with few spelling or grammatical errors.

Presentations and projects

Presentations include talks, interviews and role plays which have been prepared to perform in front of your group and tutors. They will show an understanding of work that you have done in some topic area. They need to be carefully planned and researched. This will increase your confidence in presenting work to a group. You may be asked to present a written copy of your presentation.

During your course, you may be called upon to produce posters, describe developmental ages and stages, organise a display, produce a booklet and conduct a short investigation into one of the Units.

Displays

Displays can be on the walls, on tables, on display screens, on low chests and cupboards. You will need to have clear aims for the displays and what they are for.

Displays can be a mixture of two-dimensional and **three-dimensional** work, objects, **resource books**, posters, and other materials or they can focus on just one of the above. They should be educational and not merely decorative.

To mount a display, you will need:

- wall space at a suitable level and table tops
- suitable mounting materials and tools for wall displays
- material for covering the tables.

Work looks better if it is mounted on paper. Choose a colour that complements or contrasts with the work. Light mounts make the work look darker, and dark mounts make the work look lighter, so you need to try out different ones before reaching a decision.

Using backing paper can change the colour of the display boards. If labelling is required, the writing should be done in lower case, with a capital letter at the beginning. The writing should be clear and well formed, and the following chart may help you with this task.

An example of lettering ▶

ASSESSMENT PROCEDURES

As a childcare student, you will be assessed in your college work during and at the end of the course. You will be expected to make progress in your personal development and, to some extent, in your practical work. You need to understand that your assessment starts from the first day of the course, and to be clear about what your tutors expect and what the college or school requires. CACHE candidates will be issued with an overview of their requirements and procedures.

Self-assessment
The chart on page 42 will help you to identify what you are like as a learner. It is important to know this because you are the one who has control over your learning, not the tutor.

Pre-course self-assessment

		YES	NO	Comment
1	I always check my work before I hand it in			
2	I try to complete each piece of work I am set			
3	I keep my file in order			
4	I am easily distracted by others			
5	I distract others			
6	I can identify the type of mistakes I often make			
7	I call a teacher over to help me if I get stuck			
8	I ask other students for help if I get stuck			
9	I concentrate well in class			
10	I get bored easily			
11	I avoid doing work I find difficult or boring			
12	I sometimes rush through work			
13	I plan what to write before I start writing			
14	If I run out of work, I ask for more			
15	I am prepared to do homework			
16	If I don't understand something I ask what it means			
17	I think about whether I am progressing in my work			
18	I keep my record of work up to date			
19	I feel confident that I am able to do the work			
20	I worry about my handwriting			

Complete the following chart towards the end of each term, before meeting your tutor to discuss your progress.

Self-assessment

Five things I have enjoyed this term.
Five things I have disliked this term.
Have I completed all my work on time?
Have I changed over the term?
What has helped me to learn?
What help do I need next term?
Comments

This page may be photocopied. © Stanley Thornes (Publishers) Ltd.

Short answer tests

Short answer tests are an opportunity for you to show what knowledge you have gained during the course. These tests are held under examination conditions and you will be given the date and times in advance by your tutor.

You will be given questions from the subjects you have studied in college. Some questions may ask for just one word answers, whilst others might require short sentences. Your tutors will prepare you for these tests.

Portfolios

The word 'portfolio' is used to describe the ring binder that contains evidence showing your ability to work competently and skilfully with children. Your tutor will tell you as you start the course how you should put the portfolio together. It is important to listen to your tutor, question anything you do not understand, and follow instructions carefully.

CACHE states that, 'The portfolio is a file of your work for each of the units in the Award. This is an important part of your assessment and will be presented for External Moderation towards the end of your course. You may also find it useful to present to potential employers or course tutors if you are interested in further study when you have completed this Award. It is therefore really important that the document is presented to your highest standard.'

You will need a hard-backed ring binder to keep your work in and dividers for the different sections would make your work easier to read.

- Each Unit Portfolio Task should be in a separate section and should be clearly indicated.
- Your work may be neatly handwritten, word-processed or typed.
- There should be a contents/index page to show where the different Unit Portfolio Tasks can be found.
- You need to include your personal details and a sheet is provided. This should include your name, personal identification number, study centre, placement details including ages of children, size of group, number of staff and number of days attended for work experience.

When providing details about your work experience placement you must not give personal details of the children and their families or of the staff you work with, as you are in a position of trust. You must also not talk about the children or their families outside the work experience placement.

It is probably a sensible idea to place the portfolio tasks in a separate ring binder, so that it will be easier for the External Moderator to assess your work.

✓ TEST YOURSELF

1   What information do you need to have when starting a course?
2   Name four pieces of essential equipment.
3   How can you gain information, other than by reading books?
4   Name four signs of stress.
5   Describe two ways of managing stress.
6   Describe two ways of filing work.
7   What are some of the advantages of exploring ideas together?

GLOSSARY

By the time you have finished this chapter you should understand the meaning of the following words:

catalogue system	a way of storing information about books and resources, usually alphabetically
confidentiality	keeping to yourself information about children and their families
bibliography	a list of books and articles that have been used in a book or in your own work
footnotes	notes at the bottom of pages
index	what is contained in a book or in your own work, in alphabetical order
Kidscape	an organisation founded to prevent child abuse and neglect

NSPCC the National Society for the Prevention of Cruelty to Children, a charity that helps protect children from abuse and neglect

peer group friends

psychology the study of the behaviour of an individual

resource books books used for your work

supervisor a qualified person who will support you in placement, assess your progress and write a report

three-dimensional an object having length, width and depth, such as a cube as opposed to a two-dimensional object that only has length and width, such as a photograph or a drawing.

3

Children in society

This chapter includes:
- Government strategies
- Children's rights
- The Children Act, 1989
- Equal opportunities
- Anti-discriminatory practice
- Working with parents
- The role of the responsible citizen
- Child protection
- Glossary

KEY POINT

The society we live in is always changing.

The **society** we live in is always changing and these changes will affect the children who live in it. For example, a generation ago, children had a great deal more freedom to play outside the home as there was little fear of being taken away by strangers, or of being run over by a car. Children would walk to school or travel alone on buses and trains.

Schools had more say in what they taught. Nowadays they are made to follow a National Curriculum, and children are tested regularly to assess that they are reaching a good standard.

There is more awareness that we are living in a society made up from many and various religions and cultures, and that all children and adults should enjoy equality of opportunity. Families are different today. It is no longer assumed that all children live at home with a married mother and father.

TASK

1 Describe how society has changed in your lifetime.
2 Speak to the oldest person you know, and ask them about the changes they have seen.

For further information on the material covered in this chapter, you could consult the following:

Hobart, C. and Frankel, J., **Good Practice in Child Protection**, Stanley Thornes (Publishers) Ltd, 1998

Malik, H., **A Practical Guide to Equal Opportunities**, Stanley Thornes (Publishers) Ltd, 1998

Why should we encourage children to walk to school?

GOVERNMENT STRATEGIES

The government has outlined plans to reduce the number of children living in poverty. Part of this strategy includes financial support, such as the Working Families Tax Credit, which will give many poor working families an increase in their income. Another plan promises more childcare for those who need it, so that **lone parent**s are able to take a job or resume a career. The 'Sure Start' programme aims to help poor families who are at a disadvantage in our society. The chart on page 49 shows you other ways in which the government is helping. The diagram on page 50 shows the many pressures there may be on the family.

CASE STUDY

Sherrill

Sherrill has recently left her violent partner and moved to a new area with her three young children, aged 3, 4 and 7 years. She is claiming income support and child benefit, and has found places for the children at the local school and at a nursery school. She desperately wants to return to work, but has no qualifications and few skills.

1 What further help might be available for Sherrill and her children now?
2 What help might be available if she finds employment?

Government plans to reduce the number of children living in poverty

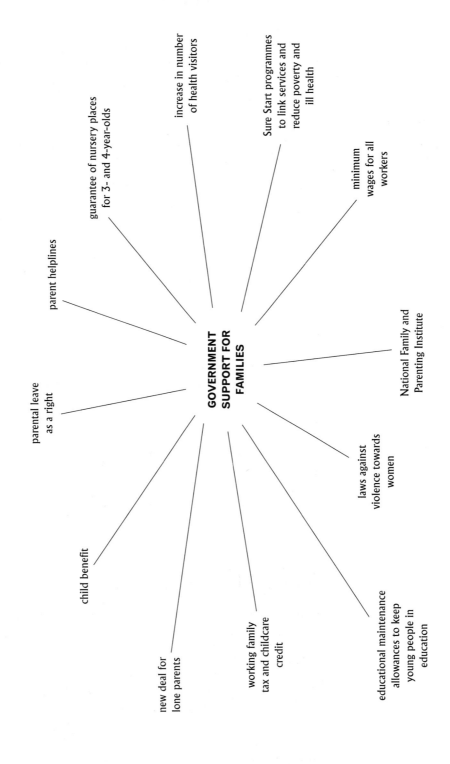

increase in number of health visitors

Sure Start programmes to link services and reduce poverty and ill health

guarantee of nursery places for 3- and 4-year-olds

minimum wages for all workers

parent helplines

GOVERNMENT SUPPORT FOR FAMILIES

National Family and Parenting Institute

parental leave as a right

laws against violence towards women

child benefit

new deal for lone parents

working family tax and childcare credit

educational maintenance allowances to keep young people in education

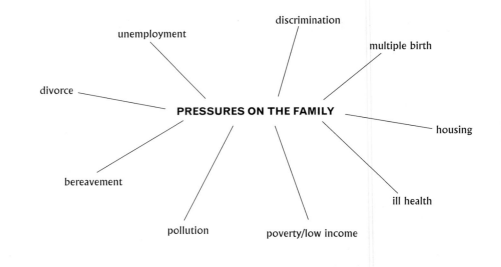

Do you know where your local job centre is? ▶

CHILDREN'S RIGHTS

Everyone has rights, including children, but because they are young they are more likely than adults to have their rights forgotten or ignored. All children, regardless of their background, need and have the right to the following.

1 Physical care, including safety, good health and a nourishing diet
2 Intellectual stimulation, including education through play to develop language and learning skills
3 Emotional care, resulting from warm caring constant relationships
4 Social relationships, developing friendships, mixing with other children and adults from many different backgrounds, and learning to value people for what they are.

KEY POINT

We need to understand the rights of children and respect them.

In November 1959, the United Nations issued a document declaring the rights of the child. This was **motivated** by the dreadful **plight** of some children due to wars and famine: children left without parents, family and homes. These rights are set out as follows.

1 The right to equality, regardless of race, colour, religion, sex or nationality.
2 The right to healthy mental and physical development.
3 The right to a name and a nationality.
4 The right to sufficient food, housing and medical care.
5 The right to special care, if handicapped.
6 The right to love, understanding and care.
7 The right to free education, play and recreation.
8 The right to medical aid in the event of disasters and emergencies.
9 The right to protection from cruelty, neglect and exploitation.
10 The right to protection from persecution and to an upbringing in the spirit of world-wide brotherhood and peace.

TASK

Identify two countries where it would not be possible at this time for children to have all these rights. Why not?

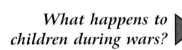
What happens to children during wars?

Thirty years later, in 1989, further points were added, including:

• the right of every child to a standard of living adequate for the child's physical, mental, spiritual, moral and social development.

THE CHILDREN ACT, 1989

The Children Act became law on 14 October 1991. It has had a major impact on the law relating to children, affecting all children and their families. The emphasis of this law was that parents should have responsibilities for their

TASK

In this country, some children are still living in poverty.
1 What do you think children in this country should have as a right?
2 Name three important things that would make children's lives better.

Under The Children Act, 1989, children come first

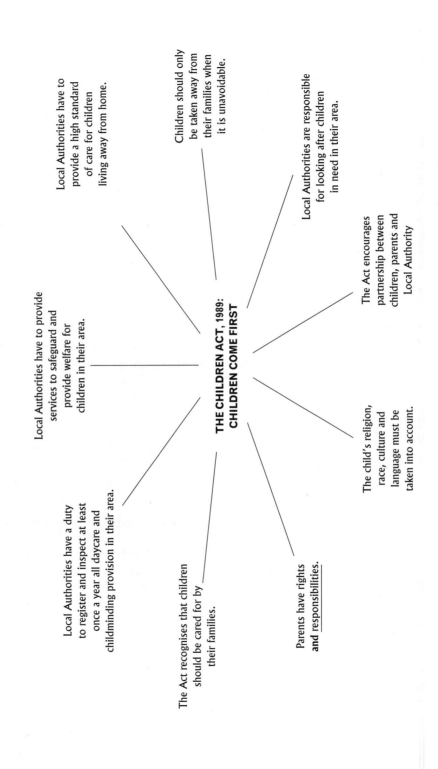

Local Authorities have to provide a high standard of care for children living away from home.

Children should only be taken away from their families when it is unavoidable.

Local Authorities have to provide services to safeguard and provide welfare for children in their area.

Local Authorities are responsible for looking after children in need in their area.

THE CHILDREN ACT, 1989: CHILDREN COME FIRST

The Act encourages partnership between children, parents and Local Authority

Local Authorities have a duty to register and inspect at least once a year all daycare and childminding provision in their area.

The Act recognises that children should be cared for by their families.

The child's religion, race, culture and language must be taken into account.

Parents have rights **and responsibilities.**

children, rather than rights over them. The Children Act acknowledged the importance of the wishes of the child. The rights of parents over children become less as the child grows older. For example, once you are sixteen you can choose your own doctor.

Local authorities have a responsibility to make sure there is a good standard of care in all types of daycare for children under eight, by means of registration and inspection of the care provided. Inspection must be carried out at least once a year. The Department of Health and the Department for Education and Employment have agreed what is good practice for all children in daycare:

- the child's welfare and development is of **paramount** importance
- the child should be respected as an individual and treated in such a way as to meet his or her particular needs
- the parents' first hand knowledge and **parental responsibility** for their child should be recognised and respected
- values arising from different racial, cultural, religious and language backgrounds should be recognised and respected
- childcare and education workers should work in ways that show they understand that parents are the most important caregivers and educators of their child
- parents should be told about available services and be able to choose what is best for them and their child.

EQUAL OPPORTUNITIES

Anyone working with children needs to understand the importance of equal opportunities and **anti-discriminatory** practice. This understanding of equal opportunities should form the basis of your practical work.

Why are equal opportunities important?

No member of society should be discriminated against because of his or her race, gender, **class**, culture, age, religion, disability, or sexual orientation. This is especially important for those people working with young children, as the younger you are, the harder it is to challenge **prejudice**. Children need to feel confident about themselves, and be sure that they are valued. If they do not feel good about themselves, they find it difficult to learn.

In your work experience placement, you may meet children from various backgrounds and cultures, with many different views of the world, possibly speaking different languages. There may be anti-racist and anti-sexist policies available for you to read. The needs of children with disabilities to have access to equal opportunities is slowly being recognised and this should lead to all these children being included in all activities in the placement.

*How would you make
children feel cared for?* ▶

*Do you recognise the
language these children
are using?* ▶

Gender

In your work experience placement, it is important that all the activities are made available to all boys and girls. You might find that some parents and some people you are working with still expect to see the girls in the home corner and the boys using the large bricks. If this happens, opportunities for learning are being limited. There is no reason why boys should not grow up to be nurses and girls to be engineers. Attitudes are learnt very young, in the home, from the **media** and from school influences, but this is all the more reason why the placement should challenge **stereotype**s. The pressure later on in life for children to behave in a certain way is very strong, and it is most important that the children experience equal opportunities in their play at the youngest age. Boys should be allowed to dress up as brides, if they want to, and girls should be encouraged to let off steam by running around outside yelling loudly.

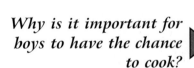

Why is it important for boys to have the chance to cook?

TASK

With your supervisor's permission, send the girls outside to use the wheeled toys, while the boys have access to the home corner undisturbed. Write down the children's reactions.

Children know if they are boys or girls, and most four-year-old boys will play together in groups, whilst girls of this age will usually choose another girl as 'best friend' and play mainly with her. You should not seek to split up these friendships but occasionally it is helpful to encourage the children towards activities they might not choose themselves.

TASK

Collect some photographs or pictures showing adults in varied roles, such as women pilots or male nannies.

Adults as role models

The children will see you as a role model. If you are a female student, you must make sure you take part in all the activities, particularly in outside play such as ball games and assault courses, big block construction and woodwork. The male student should be able to join in with confidence in the caring roles in the home corner, cooking, dressing up, and having quiet moments on a one-to-one basis with a child. The pictures on the wall and in the book corner should show women and men in a variety of roles, such as female doctors and male nurses. The text in the books should express a wide variety of settings and roles for both sexes.

In some placements, boys seem to demand the attention of the adults with rough and noisy play. You need to be aware of this, and make sure you value the contribution of both boys and girls.

Watch your use of language with the children. Make sure that you sometimes comment on how smart a boy might look, and how well a girl has planned a building with the large blocks.

Why is it important to give girls the chance to build models? ▶

Race

We live in a **multi-racial society**, and on your course and in work experience placements you may meet students and children from many different **ethnic groups**. If you are a student in a college that does not provide this experience, it is even more important that you are sensitive to multicultural issues and anti-racist policies. A young white female student taking her course in a young white female environment in a quiet country area needs to be aware and responsive to the wider society. In areas where students are working only with white English children, there is a responsibility to bring to them knowledge and understanding of the multi-racial world

Many work experience placements will have an anti-racist policy and you should make sure you read it. Your supervisor will explain any parts you do not understand, and how they use the policy to help prevent racism. Many students find it difficult at first to challenge racism, whether from adults or from children, and may need to discuss ways of dealing with this issue with their supervisor and college tutors.

Children need to have a good understanding of all cultures. The book corner should have a good selection of books, some of them in languages other than English. All should have **positive images** of people and children from all over the world. The home corner should have kitchen equipment and dolls from as many different cultures as possible. Staff and students must understand the use of the different household equipment, such as woks and rice steamers.

Dressing-up clothes from many countries should be included. Music and musical instruments from all over the world enrich the classroom. Listening carefully to the children talking about their experiences will help you to become more knowledgeable. Many placements involve parents in reading to the children, making music with them and cooking different foods. This all helps the children feel valued.

Many placements will celebrate a variety of different festivals, as described later in this chapter.

Religion

In college and in your work experience placement you will probably come across many different beliefs and religions. Tolerance, acceptance, and a willingness to learn from others are essential, so that you can develop awareness and sensitivity to the needs of children in your care.

Knowledge of different religious customs and festivals is important to those working with young children. As a student, you should make yourself aware of the various religions that the families may have. Children will not always be able to give you details concerning beliefs, diet, dress and festivals. It is far wiser to involve the parents and community leaders.

TASK

Look at the books in your local children's library.
1 Do you think any of them are racist?
2 Why?
3 Name three books you would be happy to use in your placement.

KEY POINT

Knowledge of different religious customs and festivals is important to those working with young children.

TASK

Find out from your supervisor what religions are represented in the placement. What differences might there be in dress, diet, holy days and celebrations?

Most religions have many different groups within them. For example, Christians can belong to the Methodist Church, the High Anglican, the Roman Catholic and so on. Jews can obey all the rules laid down from ancient times, whilst others just observe the festivals. Muslims may follow all the teachings of Mohammed and observe the times of prayer, whilst others are not so strict. Some families who see themselves as Christian may only use the Church for christenings, weddings and funerals, rarely going to services at other times. Other Christians may attend Church every week, and see Sunday as a day of rest and prayer.

Whilst attempting to meet the needs of all religions, it is important to remember that some children will come from an atheist (unbelieving) background. They should not feel left out or unable to identify with their carers. Whatever religious celebrations are taking place, there should be an emphasis on caring for others.

CASE STUDY

Jayshree

One of the parents asks Jayshree, a childcare student, if there were any birthdays being celebrated that week. When Jayshree says that it would be Andrew's birthday on Thursday, the parent says, 'Well, I won't bring Hannah in that day then'. On being asked why, the parent explains that the family are Jehovah's witnesses and that they did not believe in celebrating a special day for anyone.

1 How should Jayshree respond to the parent?
2 How do you think the placement should handle this in the short term?
3 What do you think should happen when there is another birthday?

Class

In the UK, we are very aware of people's backgrounds, and we are often judged by the way we speak, what we wear, the jobs we do and where we live. Some people may be looked down on if they appear to be more disadvantaged than most of the others in the group.

There are no laws to prevent discrimination on grounds of class. It is known that children from higher income groups have easier access to higher education.

Social disadvantage

In the placement, you may be working with children from many different backgrounds. Children from all classes may be equally intelligent, but a very deprived home life can have an effect on all areas of a child's development. For instance, children from lower social groups are known to have more accidents and worse health than those who have more advantages.

You may find you are meeting for the first time children from different backgrounds from their own. Working with socially deprived children may arouse distress and anger that a wealthy country such as ours still has families living without enough money to provide a decent standard of living. Some placements will try to help the children by offering special educational programmes. Working with very wealthy families can also be upsetting, if the children seem to have many different people looking after them and are expected to achieve at school to the exclusion of all else.

Age discrimination

Young students will gain a great deal from the life experience of older students. Sometimes a young student with personal problems might find it easier to confide in an older student in the group than in a parent or a tutor. The experiences that parents are having with their own children will help students to understand the rights and responsibilities of all parents.

Sometimes, mature students find study skills difficult at first, and may lack confidence in organising their work and in writing essays. This is where students who have just left school can be of help, not in doing the

Find out if there are any children in your placement who are being offered special help.

What do old people gain from visits by young children?

59

actual work, but in giving support that will lead to confidence. All students need to value each other irrespective of age, and appreciate the perspectives that different generations bring to the work.

As a young student, you might find it hard to accept criticism even from your own parents, but in the work experience placement it is an important part of the supervisor's role to use his or her knowledge and experience to help you to progress. You will come to value and respect his or her advice, providing the supervisor realises that you are not a child, but a student, and as such a valuable member of the team.

Sexual orientation

You may meet colleagues and parents who are in gay and lesbian homosexual relationships, so you need to have considered the subject of sexual orientation, and how it will affect your work.

In the placement it is important to provide positive self-images for children from all family backgrounds and to encourage caring attitudes, helping them to understand that people choose different people to be special to them. They will learn to value the choices made by their own family. All children will see that their homes and families are valued as highly as others.

Disability

If you have a student with a disability in your group at college or school, you will be able to learn at first hand that it is the person who matters, not the disability. With some people, the disability might be obvious, but it might take you a little while to discover that your new friend has dyslexia. If you have a special need or disability, sharing your experiences with the group at a time when you feel safe and comfortable will be helpful to them as well as to yourself.

You may find children with disabilities in your work experience placement. Such disabilities are not always physical, but may be seen in emotional, social, intellectual or language development.

ANTI-DISCRIMINATORY PRACTICE

Since the Children Act 1989, anti-discriminatory practice is required by law in all establishments where there are children. The child's religious, racial origin, cultural and language background must be taken into account. This practice should help to promote positive images and give children confidence. Challenging **prejudice** is a major responsibility for all childcare and education workers.

When you are in your work experience placement:

- present positive images in your choice of books and use of equipment

- present yourself as a good **role model**
- admit what you do not know, and be prepared to ask for help and advice
- challenge all offensive remarks, whether from children or from adults, or whether directed against yourself or others
- answer children's questions honestly, with explanations they can understand
- make sure you pronounce and spell all the children's names correctly
- make sure you know and pronounce the names of the clothes the children wear
- understand the different skin and hair care needs of all the children
- encourage children to have positive feelings about their skin tone, hair texture and facial features
- make sure you understand the importance of a varied diet, that will appeal to all the children and does not go against any cultural or religious **taboos**.
- challenge stereotypes. You may be watching a television programme with the children that shows girls as quiet and inferior to boys. You will need to discuss this, pointing out that the females often show more leadership, and can be just as assertive as the males.
- involve all children in all activities
- encourage all children to be assertive and to stand up for themselves.

Festivals

There are a great many religious and cultural festivals to celebrate, from all over the world, and quite a few have become a part of all our lives, particularly those of our young children.

It is important, because of our multicultural society, to know about festivals celebrated by all the ethnic and religious groups in the country, as well as the dominant Christian ones of Christmas and Easter and events such as Guy Fawkes and Halloween.

Children from all groups should feel that their culture and religion is respected by their peers. Groups of children from just one culture should also have the opportunity to know about other cultures and understand that we live in a multicultural society. Where possible, parents should be involved in advising and organising festival celebrations.

Primary schools use festivals as themes which cover many different parts of the National Curriculum as is shown by the celebration of Divali on page 64.

Before celebrating any festival there should be plenty of resources and information about the festival. There will be a need for clothes, music, food, books and other equipment.

Festivals encourage children to dance and to play instruments. They may be involved in the making of masks, clothes, art and craft work and cooking. They are large social events, with the whole group and the parents working and planning together, learning new songs and poems.

What do YOU think?

Many children are severely burnt by fireworks. Do you think private firework parties should be banned?

61

Religious and cultural festivals

Autumn term	Spring term	Summer term
Harvest Festival	Rastafarian Christmas	May Day
Rosh Hashana (Jewish New Year)	Chinese New Year	Dragon Boast Festival
Yom Kippur (Day of Atonement)	Shrove Tuesday	Carnival
	Ash Wednesday	Raksha Bandhan (Festival of Sisters)
Sukkot (Jewish Harvest Festival)	Mothering Sunday	Father's Day
Ethiopian New Year (Rastafarian)	Passover	American Independence Day
	St Patrick's Day	
All Souls Day	St David's Day	Wesak
Divali (Festival of Light)	St George's Day	Pentecost
Guy Fawkes	Lent	Whitsuntide
Remembrance Sunday	Easter	Festival of Hungry Ghosts (Chinese)
Thanksgiving	Saraswati Puja	Birthday of Haile Selassie
St Andrew's Day	Holi (Festival of Colour)	
Birthday of guru Nanak Dev Ji (Sikh)	Baisakhi	Birthday of Muhammad
Chanukah (Jewish) Festival of Light)	Martin Luther King Day	Janamashtami
	Lantern Festival (Chinese)	Shavuot
Advent	April Fool's Day	World Environment Day
Christmas		
Kwanzaa		Raskha Bandhan

Times of Ramadan and Eid-ul-Fitr vary each year as they are determined by the phases of the moon.

Do you think Halloween should be celebrated? ▶

Remember that some families may not wish their children to take part in festivals, either due to their own religion or to their very strong anti-religious beliefs. If you do have children who are not going to take part respect their wish not to be involved.

Any clothes or equipment lent by parents must be handled carefully, but parents must be made aware that accidents can happen. If you have one or two children to represent the culture or religion you are celebrating, be careful not to continually single them out as you may embarrass them.

There is a risk of stereotyping if you celebrate festivals too extravagantly, and concentrate on the exotic side of their beliefs or culture. Respecting other cultures should be an every day event, not a once-a-year wonder.

Celebrating Divali

Social and moral
Celebrate the festival together.
Make a rangoli, cook together – learn to share and cooperate.
Hear the story of the victory of good over evil.
Discuss making new beginnings.

Music and movement
Listen and dance to Indian music.
Play appropriate instruments.

Language
Make a 'take home' book with the children to discuss with parents.
Learn songs and rhymes.
Tell the story and discuss.
Write in Gujarati and Bengali. Listen to tapes in several languages.
Write Divali cards.

Art and craft/Aesthetic appreciation
Make big rangoli patterns for display.
Make Divali cards, using small rangoli patterns to take home.
Portray the story in 3D.
Block print rangoli patterns.
Make divas from Plasticine or clay.
Make mehndi pattern on hands.
Make paper chains and hanging garlands.
Make candles.
Make shadow puppets.

DIVALI

Mathematics
Make shapes and patterns.
Sequence the Divali story.
Discuss time past, present and tomorrow.

Science and technology
Observe changes that occur in cooking (onion bhaja, chapatti, sweets, biscuits, vegetables).
Observe effect of oxygen on burning. Observe light and dark; and light and shadow.
Make a lighthouse.

Environmental studies
If possible, visit a temple.
Provide appropriate dressing-up clothes.
Hold a sari day.
Use relevant utensils and equipment in the home corner.

Sensory
Be aware of the smell and taste of food.
Be aware of the smell of incense sticks.
Be aware of light and dark.

WORKING WITH PARENTS

As you have decided on a career with children you will have realised how important it is to make good relationships with the parents of the children in your care. The words 'parent' or 'parent/carer' are used to describe all primary carers, whether they are the child's biological parents, foster parents, adoptive parents, grandparents or others having responsibility for the child.

For some time it has been acknowledged that the support and hopes of parents play a vital part in the school life of the children. All the research shows the importance of parental involvement and therefore parents need to be kept well informed about their child's development and behaviour and understand how their children are taught. The child will benefit most when parent, child and carer are all working together.

Parents spend a great deal of time with their children and will know their strengths and weaknesses, predict their needs and will have made many decisions about their children in the early years. Therefore, it is sensible to work with the parents for the benefit of the child. It will make the child more secure to see parents and carer working together.

> ## KEY POINT
>
> **The child will benefit most when parent, child and carer are all working together.**

CASE STUDY

Jessie

Jessie is in her work experience placement and feels that she is progressing well. She is upset and shocked when her supervisor asks her to wait after work and tells her that she has had some complaints from parents about Jessie's manner. They have found it difficult to talk to her and complain that she is unfriendly.

1 Why might the parents have found Jessie unfriendly?
2 How can the supervisor help Jessie to make better relationships?
3 How can Jessie improve her **body language**?
4 Why is it important for Jessie to overcome this problem?
5 Might Jessie seek help from someone else?

Why women work

It is important that you respect the decision of people to return to work, even if their children are very young. Many women today wish to combine careers with bringing up children. Some women are leaving it later to start a family, and are usually quite well established in their careers. They are able to afford to pay for help with the children. Younger women, perhaps not so advanced in their careers, often feel that it is worth making other sacrifices, such as giving up holidays and going out to the cinema or a restaurant, to pay for childcare.

Increasing numbers of women are returning to work after having their children. Research shows that two-thirds of mothers go back to work within eleven months of having a baby and that they are returning to work sooner after giving birth. Eighty-one per cent go back within 28 weeks and of these, 20,000 women a year in the UK return to work after less than 14 weeks maternity leave.

Many women need to work to keep their standard of living, whilst for others it is important not to interrupt their careers for too long a period. Some employers have schemes to help women employees to balance work and family commitments by providing flexible working hours, job shares, time off if their children are ill, and workplace nurseries.

Understanding various cultures and child rearing practices

Children are brought up in many different types of families. These include:

- the nuclear family — a small family of parents and children, with no other family members living with them
- the extended family —the parents, children and other family members who may live with the family or close by, and who are in frequent contact with each other
- the lone parent family, sometimes known as single or one parent family — the mother or father plus children. Roughly 90 per cent of these households are headed by the mother and 10 per cent by the father. Of the women, about 60 per cent are divorced or separated, 23 per cent are single and 7 per cent widowed.
- the 'reconstituted family' —parents have divorced or separated and re-married or are living with new partners and perhaps the partner's children
- a homosexual partnerships: two men or two women living together with the children of a previous heterosexual partnership or, in some lesbian relationships, their own children. The couple may adopt children. All the research carried out since the sixties shows no differences in the social and emotional development of children living in these households, or to their sexual orientation.

Other family types include communes, where many groups of people live together and support each other, and travellers, such as 'New Agers' and Romanies.

Various child rearing practices

Children's needs and parents wishes may come from a cultural or religious source or for medical reasons or quite simply, that is what the parents want for

What do YOU think?

Do you think fathers should take more responsibility for looking after their young children at home? Do you know any fathers who have given up work to look after the children?

KEY POINT

Children are brought up in many different types of families.

KEY POINT

Parents' wishes and child-rearing practices must be respected.

their child. Parents' wishes and child-rearing practices must be respected and every effort made to comply with them.

There should be agreement and understanding about matters relating to:

- food, its preparation and eating, and any special diet
- personal hygiene
- skin and hair care, for example creams and combs suitable for some African-Caribbean children
- the question of clothing during play, for example, maintaining modesty in physical play, covering very curly or braided hair for sand play, or protecting against strong sunlight
- periods of rest and sleep, for example routines and **comfort objects**.

Do not assume that because a family is part of a particular cultural group, they follow all the practices of that culture. Some may observe all the customs of the group, whilst others pick and choose.

When you are in contact with parents in your work experience, make sure you:

- respect all parents as individuals, and learn from them different ways of child rearing
- contribute to a welcoming and relaxed atmosphere, encouraging parents to settle their children in and to spend time with them whenever they wish
- remember the parents are the experts on their own individual children
- never gossip about parents to other parents.

You may be at a placement near to where you live, and be familiar with some of the parents. You should discuss this with your supervisor, as it might have a bearing on confidential matters.

THE ROLE OF THE RESPONSIBLE CITIZEN

During one lifetime, a person plays many roles, many of them at the same time. For example, a woman may be:

- a mother
- a daughter
- a sister
- a grandmother
- a grand daughter
- an aunt
- a niece
- a wife.

She may also be

- a friend
- a doctor

- a counsellor
- a student
- a teacher
- a dancer
- a swimmer
- a cook

and so on.

Some roles are decided for you. You cannot help being a daughter or a son. Some roles are formal and these are often linked to the job you choose, such as a carer or member of Parliament. Other roles are less formal, depending upon the interests of the moment, and on your personality.

A baby has to learn his or her role in the family. This takes place by **socialisation**: the way we learn the rules of behaviour that the family expects of us. It is by learning these codes of behaviour that we become accepted into a group.

At a certain age, a person is expected to become responsible and to follow certain rules of behaviour, and to act within the laws of the country.

In many societies, there are initiation ceremonies into adulthood, usually around the age of 13. For example, Jewish children are expected to read a portion from Judaic law, and to address the congregation in the synagogue at the age of thirteen, and are then expected to take an adult and responsible role in their community. In the Sikh community, young people aged between 14 and 16 often seek admission to the Khalsa. This involves showing that they are trying to live the Sikh way of life.

In the UK, as can be seen from the chart on page 69, the age of taking on responsibility for oneself varies, and can be changed by law. For example, the age of consent for homosexual sex has recently been lowered from 21 to 18, and the eighteenth birthday is now seen as the one when you come of age, rather than at 21 as it was a few years ago.

Students in a class session in a college came up with the following definition: 'Becoming a responsible citizen means that:

- you accept the rules of the society, and obey the law
- you take part in the life of your community, being aware of the more vulnerable groups, such as children, the disabled and the elderly
- you use your vote to influence decision making.

It is not being responsible if you:

- use substances that may cause your body harm, such as tobacco
- frequently become drunk and unable to control your behaviour
- have a child that you are not able to support, financially and emotionally
- have sex that is not safe
- get into unnecessary debt by buying non-essentials you cannot afford.'

TASK

What expectations of behaviour would you have of the following?

1 A pilot
2 A nurse
3 A minister of religion
4 A two-year-old child.

What do YOU think?

Do you agree with the above two paragraphs? Perhaps you can think of some extra points.

The law and young people

From birth	• you have to be registered by day 42. • you can have a passport. • you can have a savings account or premium bonds in your name.
At 5 years	• you are of compulsory school age.
At 7 years	• you can draw money from a savings account in your name.
At 10 years	• you can be convicted of a criminal offence if it is proved you know the difference between right and wrong.
At 12 years	• you can buy a pet animal.
At 13 years	• you can be employed part time under very regulated conditions.
At 14 years	• you can be held responsible for a crime. • you can go into a pub *but* not drink alcohol there.
At 16 years	• you can get a National Insurance Number. • you can buy premium bonds. • you can buy cigarettes or tobacco. • you can leave school on the last Friday in June of the school year you are 16. • you can choose your own doctor. • you can consent to medical, surgical and dental treatment. • you can work full time. • you can consent to heterosexual intercourse. • if you are a boy you can join the Armed Forces with parental consent. • you can marry with parental consent. • you can probably leave home without parental consent but may be subject to a local authority care order or wardship. • you can drink wine and beer in a restaurant.
At 17 years	you can: • hold a driving licence. • if a girl, join the Armed Forces at 17½ years with parental consent. • appear in an adult court if charged with an offence.
At 18 years	you can: • leave home without parental consent. • get married without parental consent. • vote in elections. • get tattooed. • enter a betting shop and bet. • change your name.

▶

	• make a will. • own property. • sit on a jury. • sue and be sued. • be a blood donor. • buy alcohol. • see your birth certificate if you are adopted. • a man can have sex with another man provided they are both over 18. There are no laws governing sex between women.
At 21 years	• you can stand as a candidate in an election. • you can hold a licence to sell alcohol. • you can adopt a child.

As a childcare and education worker, part of your role will be helping children to become responsible citizens. To help them to understand how important it is to obey the law and the rules of the society we live in, you might:

- help them to express their feelings, so that they can say how they feel rather than shouting and fighting
- help them to understand that rules are for the good of the group, and that the wishes of the individual cannot always be met
- explain the rules in a clear way, so that the children understand why they have been made.

As children mature, they will be expected to take part in the life of their community. The school might:

- celebrate festivals of various groups and cultures, showing respect for those different from your own
- create an environment that displays positive images of all cultures, by having toys, music, dance, dressing-up clothes, equipment, books and posters from around the world
- involve representatives of the local community in visiting your school or nursery, such as the police, firefighters and leaders of local ethnic groups
- arrange visits, such as visiting hospitals, residential homes and other places where the children might have the opportunity of meeting people with whom they might not normally come into contact
- teach the children to take care of their environment, by not throwing litter about, and generally taking a pride in the appearance of the school
- discuss current issues with the children, at the appropriate level for their age, so that they understand the debates to do with, for example, global warming or the devastating effects of war, famine and natural disasters.

Most schools and nurseries today are run in a democratic way. This means that the staff, the governors and the parents all have a say in how the estab-

TASK

1 In your placement, who sits on the Board of Governors/Management Committee?
2 Who do they represent?
3 How does this come about?

KEY POINT

The welfare of the child is always your first responsibility.

lishment is run. In a small way, the group that you are working with might be allowed to decide some issues in a democratic fashion. For example, they might be allowed to have some say in new equipment for the outside area, or to choose a colour scheme for a newly decorated classroom. Most secondary schools have School Councils, and the older students have a chance to vote for delegates.

CHILD PROTECTION

The whole of society has a duty to protect children. The welfare of the child is always your first responsibility. The NSPCC estimate that 150 – 200 children die each year in England and Wales following incidents of abuse or neglect. Thousands more suffer emotional and psychological problems because of ill treatment by their parents or those looking after them. More than 20,000 children a year tell ChildLine they have been physically or sexually abused.

If you, or someone close to you, suffered any form of abuse or neglect, you might find this section difficult to discuss in a group. Speak to your tutor about it, and he or she may be able to advise you where you can get help, should you feel the need for it.

Definitions of abuse and neglect

Child abuse is sometimes difficult to define, but a clear understanding is necessary so that you may act with confidence when working with children. Abuse and neglect include physical abuse and injury, emotional abuse and sexual abuse, but all these areas overlap and interconnect and a child is often subjected to more than one form of abuse.

Physical abuse and injury
Physical abuse is the deliberate non-accidental use of physical force and violence, resulting in hurting, injuring or death. It includes poisoning.

Physical neglect
Physical neglect is the failure by the parents/carers to feed, shelter, keep safe, keep clean and provide medical care for a child.

Educational neglect
Educational neglect is the failure to meet the child's need for stimulation by not providing any opportunities for play and education to encourage language and intellectual development.

Emotional neglect
Emotional neglect is withdrawing or not providing love, affection and emotional consistency for the child, not providing an environment of warmth, interest and care.

Sexual abuse
Sexual abuse is involving young children and adolescents in sexual activities that they do not understand, and to which they are unable to give their consent. It would include inappropriate touches, incest and intercourse as well as showing pornographic videos and photographs.

Emotional abuse
Emotional abuse is the exposure of children to constant criticism and hostility. It is always linked to emotional neglect.

Failure to thrive
A failure to thrive is the failure of a baby or child to achieve his or her expected weight or height with no obvious medical or physical cause. It is often associated with a poor relationship with the parent/carer.

Munchausen Syndrome by Proxy
Munchausen Syndrome by Proxy is a psychological condition, where the parent/carer pretends a child is ill, seeking different medical opinions and bringing about symptoms in the child to deceive the doctors. The child may be harmed to support the parent's claim.

Recognition of abuse and neglect
As a person who cares for children in a professional manner, you need to be able to recognise the signs of abuse and neglect. The following indicators should ring alarm bells:

- all bruises on the head or face of a small baby
- bruises on the cheeks of a toddler
- bald patches on the head
- cigarette burns
- two black eyes
- any neck injury
- finger tip bruising
- bruises on genitalia
- adult bite marks
- scratches
- scalds on the child's feet and legs, caused by 'dunking' in very hot water
- splash burns

What do YOU think?
It can happen that child abuse is not deliberate cruelty but something that happens when adults lose control and cannot stop themselves. Do you think that an adult who deliberately abuses children is more at fault than an adult who loses control?

- babies unable to move any limb
- bruises on soft tissue
- injury to ear lobes
- bruising of lips, gums or a torn frenulum (the piece of tissue that attaches the lips to the gums).

You must report any concerns, worries or suspicions to your supervisor.

Most children will suffer accidental injuries from time to time. Deciding what is accidental and what is deliberate can be very difficult, even for experienced doctors who mainly look after children (paediatricians). Many signs that might lead you to think that abuse has taken place might be explained. For example, bald patches might occur if a child frequently pulls and twists the hair as a comfort habit.

Fingertip bruising

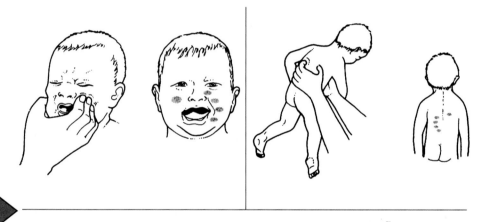

Examples of fingertip bruising and thumb marks ▶

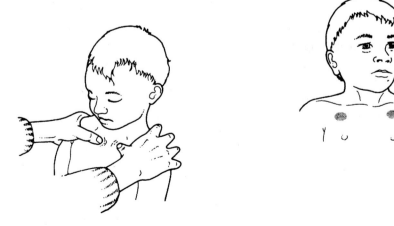

Thumb marks just below the collar bone

KEY POINT

A baby who is shaken vigorously suffers similar damage to the brain as being dropped onto concrete.

Shaking babies and young children

Shaking a child can cause serious injury, even death, and many people are ignorant of the effects of such shaking. A baby who is shaken vigorously suffers similar damage to the brain as being dropped onto concrete. A baby's head is large compared to the rest of the body and the neck muscles are not yet strong enough to support it. Shaking the head with great force will cause tiny blood vessels to tear and bleed inside the brain. This can lead to loss of sight and hearing, fits, brain damage or death. Shaking can also cause serious harm to older children. Signs to cause concern would be a child arriving at your establishment, looking very tired and floppy, miserable, not interested in feeding and unable to settle. This may also indicate the start of infection, but your establishment will immediately contact the parents and seek medical advice

Changes in behaviour

Abuse and neglect may cause a change of behaviour. This will vary a great deal according to the age of the child. You may see the child:

- not want to be touched
- not wanting to form close relationships with adults and other children
- be upset when other children cry
- appear to be frightened of the parent/carer
- losing confidence in what she does
- display self-destructive behaviour such as hair pulling and head banging
- be aggressive
- begin to over-eat or to refuse food.
- be afraid of new situations
- show comfort seeking behaviour, such as thumb-sucking, excessive **masturbation** and rocking to and fro.

The child may also show:

- speech disorders, such as stammering and stuttering
- delay in all-round development
- a willingness to please
- low **self-esteem**
- nightmares and changes in sleep patterns
- wetting and soiling after the child has become clean and dry
- temper tantrums which are not normal behaviour in an older child
- inability to concentrate for more than a few minutes.

Changes in behaviour are not necessarily due to abuse or neglect. Children go through many difficult stages in their normal development. It is only when there are many changes in behaviour that the possibility of abuse can be considered.

What other signs in a child might be mistaken for abuse?

Signs of neglect

A child who is underweight, small for her age, with flabby muscles and a dry wrinkled skin may be suffering from neglect. The child may arrive at school or nursery and immediately demand food, displaying an enormous appetite during the day. If personal hygiene needs are not being met, the child may appear dirty and uncared for, smell of urine, have unbrushed hair and teeth, and wear dirty clothing that does not fit her.

The younger child may suffer from severe nappy rash and/or **cradle cap** that never seems to be treated. She may appear constantly tired, with frequent colds and coughs, stomach upsets and rashes. The parents may appear reluctant to seek any medical help. The child frequently arrives and is collected late. It may have been noticed that the parents do not show any affection, warmth and interest in the child. They may seem to expect too much of the child. All these concerns must be discussed with your supervisor.

Child protection procedures

Local Authorities issue all establishments involved in caring and educating children with guidelines of the procedures to be followed in cases of suspected abuse or neglect. All establishments should have a child protection policy

An investigation has to take place once abuse or neglect is suspected. The case will be referred to Social Services who will investigate the matter, and a child protection conference may take place. Following this a child may be placed on the child protection register and a plan to protect the child and help and support the family will be drawn up.

CASE STUDY

George

George is 18, and lives next door to a family of four who moved in to the area two months ago. The children are aged 5 and 3. They appear to be a loving stable family. The last two nights George has heard cries and screams coming from the house, once for over an hour. He has not seen the mother or the children since.

1 What possible explanations might there be?
2 What action might George take?
3 Who might he inform?
4 What might the consequences be for George, the children and the parents?

The smacking debate

During the last few years, there has been much discussion on whether to smack children or not. The UK is one of the last countries in Europe to allow parents and carers to smack children whenever they feel like it. Hitting anyone else is a criminal assault.

Some people are for smacking and some are against. The End Physical Punishment of Children (EPOCH) was set up in 1989. It now has sixty organisations linked to its campaign, including the NSPCC, the National Children's Bureau, and Save the Children. All the major children's charities support EPOCH's 'commitment to non-violence in parenting, childcare and education'.

The *Gulbenkian Foundation Report on Children and Violence* in 1995 proposed a national charter of non-violence. Sir William Utting who chaired the commission was quoted as saying 'Hitting people is wrong. Hitting children teaches them that violence is the most effective means of getting your own way. We must develop a culture which disapproves of all forms of violence. All the lessons of my working life point to the fact that violence breeds misery. It does not resolve it.'

The opposing arguments are often presented by parents, who insist that 'smacking never did me any harm'. They may quote the Bible, saying that if you 'spare the rod, you spoil the child'. Many parents feel they have the right to discipline their children any way they wish.

Anne Davis, a childminder and spokesperson of 'Families for Discipline', won the right to smack in a legal battle against Sutton Borough Council after they threatened to de-register her for refusing to sign a form agreeing not to use any physical discipline on children in her care (1995).

What do YOU think?

Were you smacked as a child? Do you think it did you any harm?

When looking after other people's children, it is never right to use force or physical punishment, whether the parents request it or not. There would never be any reason why a childcare and education worker should hit a child.

In your working career, you will sometimes come across parents who choose to use physical punishment to discipline their children. You must use your judgement as to when you feel it is necessary to intervene.

Many parents, who see themselves as 'anti-smackers', may have on occasion lost control and slapped their child. They know it is not the way they want to behave, and often feel guilty about it afterwards. Young people, who are not parents, might find this hard to understand.

'Discipline' is frequently thought to be of a physical type. Parents sometimes need help in understanding that there are other ways of managing children's behaviour

There have been many changes in our society in the last twenty or so years. There is a better understanding of how to protect children and to make sure their rights are respected. The government is seeking to support families where there are children and are committed to reduce poverty during the next few years. Equality of opportunity is now written into all the laws concerning children, and anti-discriminatory practice is taught on all childcare and education courses at all levels.

✓ TEST YOURSELF

1 Name four basic rights that apply to children.
2 Give two reasons why equal opportunities are important in childcare and educational practice.
3 Give two reasons why some mothers chose to work.
4 Name three reasons why it is important to work closely with parents.
5 Name four different types of families.
6 Name four signs that might lead you to suspect that a child has been physically abused.

GLOSSARY

By the time you have finished this chapter you should understand the meaning of the following words:

anti-discriminatory practice   making sure that no one is discriminated against, that all resources, language and behaviour in the school/nursery is appropriate

body language   where your face and the way you use your body show what you are thinking, without having to talk

class   one way of looking at a society is to put people into different groups according to their education, job, accent, income and housing

comfort object   an object, often a blanket or a soft toy, which a child carries around as a comforter, and usually takes to bed

cradle cap   a crusty brown patch seen on babies' heads. It can be dry or greasy

ethnic groups   refers to racial groups

lone parent   (may also be referred to as 'single parent') one person living alone with his or her children

masturbation   playing with the genitals to achieve sexual pleasure. A common practice in children of both sexes, causing no harm to health or development

motivated   inspired to succeed for a reason

multi-racial society   a society that includes many races

paramount   of the utmost importance

parental responsibility   the rights, duties, powers, responsibilities and authority, which by law a parent of a child has in relation to the child and his or her property.

plight   a desperate state, often used to describe the state people are in who are suffering from famine, earthquakes, flood or homelessness

positive images   developing an environment that shows **all** people in a positive way, shown in posters, dressing up clothes, books, equipment and the attitude of the staff

prejudice   a set of beliefs, usually strongly held, that leads to discrimination against a particular group

role model   a person looked to by others as a good example in a particular situation

self-esteem   confidence in oneself as a worthwhile person. This is essential to learning and achievement

socialisation   the way the family, at first, and later other people influences the child to behave in an acceptable way

society   the customs and organisation of a community

stereotype   generalisations about a particular group for example, believing that all boys are more aggressive than girls

taboo   a practice forbidden and regarded as totally unacceptable by any society. For example, in our society one taboo would be incest. In an Islamic society, blasphemy against Mohammed is taboo.

Human growth and development

This chapter includes:
- Areas of development
- Development throughout life
- Growth
- Health checks
- Factors that affect growth and development
- Glossary

A good understanding of how children develop and grow is necessary for all people working with children. Unless you understand normal development and growth, you will not be able to recognise those children outside the normal range: children who are either delayed or advanced in their development.

There is an essential difference between development and growth. Development refers to gaining skills, becoming mature, and being able to live independently within society. Growth can be measured: weight, height, shoe size, hat size and so on.

For further information on the material covered in this chapter, you could consult the following:

Beaver, M., Brewster, J., Jones, P., Keene, A., Neaum, S. and Tallack, J., **Babies and Young Children, Book 1: Early Years Development, 2nd edition,** Stanley Thornes (Publishers) Ltd, 1999

AREAS OF DEVELOPMENT

Children develop at different rates, and you may find that one of the children you care for might be advanced physically, being well co-ordinated and able to hop and jump at an early age, whereas others might be talking earlier than you would expect. Children vary in the age they gain a skill, but all development takes place in stages, that is to say one skill has to be learnt before the child can go to the next one. For example, a child learning to walk always goes through the following stages:

> **KEY POINT**
>
> **There is an essential difference between development and growth.**

> **KEY POINT**
>
> **Children vary in the age they gain a skill, but all development takes place in stages.**

- gaining head control
- sitting with support
- sitting without support
- pulling to stand
- walking with support
- gaining balance and walking.

Some children walk at ten months or even earlier, others may wait until eighteen months or later, whilst the majority walk between twelve and fifteen months. This is all within a normal range of development as recognised by doctors and scientists. These normal ranges are called **developmental norms**.

What is the difference between development and growth?

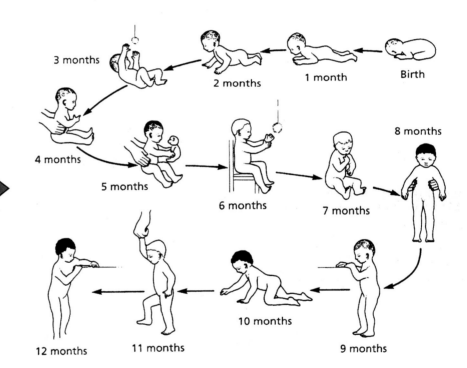

The main areas of development are physical, intellectual, language, emotional, and social development, (PILES). Babies and young children learn through the five senses of sight, hearing, touch, taste and smell. As children grow older the senses of sight and hearing become more important. Nevertheless, it is important to give children opportunities to use all the senses and encourage them to taste different foods, smell many different smells and to feel both soft and harsh textures.

81

What other smells might a small child enjoy? ▶

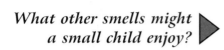

TASK

When in your work experience placement, list five activities that involve gross motor skills, and five that use fine motor skills.

Physical development

Physical development describes the gaining of two kinds of physical skills called gross motor skills and fine motor skills.

- Gross motor skills are those using the whole body, of running, sitting and throwing, all of which are to do with movement.
- Fine motor skills, also called **manipulative skills**, are those using the hands and the eyes together such as feeding, threading and picking up objects, which are dependent on using the hands and on using the hands together with the eyes (**hand-eye co-ordination**).

Gaining physical skills depends on the opportunity for practice and the encouragement of the parent/carer. The development of gross motor skills starts with head control and works down the body, the child learning to sit, perhaps crawl, pull up and walk. She learns to balance and then to hop and skip.

Intellectual (cognitive) development

Intellectual development, sometimes called cognitive development. describes the way in which we learn to think. It includes being able to concentrate, remember, recall and understand information. As children develop intellectually, they are able to think logically and creatively and to relate past learning to solving present problems. There are many theories that show how this takes place. It would seem that learning happens in stages in a particular sequence, so it is important to recognise these stages (see pages 292–6).

There is an on-going debate as to whether intelligence is inherited, or if the influence of the environment is more important. This is known as the 'nature versus nurture' issue.

What area of development does this photograph show?

Learning is helped by the child having opportunities to:

- look at adults and children interacting together
- look at children interacting with other children
- observe and explore their world
- extend their language
- use their senses to the full.

Language development

Human beings are the only animals that can talk fluently to each other and can read and write. Being able to communicate well is essential to happiness and achievement. The discovery of children brought up by animals (**feral** children) has shown us that practice and exposure to language is essential from birth, and that without language it is not possible to grow and develop satisfactorily.

What else might children play with outside? ▶

Do you know which Disney film is based on a feral child? ▶

Communication includes:

- eye gazing in babies
- facial expressions
- gestures
- body language
- reading and writing
- understanding spoken language
- speech
- listening.

In all countries and cultures, language development follows the same sequence.

In all countries and cultures, language development follows the same sequence. A good knowledge of language development will help childcare and education workers to identify a child whose language is **immature** or delayed, know how to help a child themselves, and when to suggest the parents seek help. Children find it simple to learn a second language at a young age.

Children whose home language is not English have the enormous advantage of growing up speaking two languages fluently. When they first attend nursery or school they may need some support and additional help. Be careful not to assume that delay in learning English shows a delay in other areas of development. Fluency in the home language will help them to become fluent in English later on.

What do YOU think?

Why do you think it is an advantage to be able to speak more than one language fluently?

Emotional development

During your career, you will come to realise how important it is to have good relationships with children, helping them to become strong emotionally, and to reach adulthood, confident in themselves and their achievements.

From the moment of birth, the baby begins the process of attachment, bonding with the mother at the same time as the mother bonds with the baby.

From the moment of birth, the baby begins the process of **attachment**, **bonding** with the mother at the same time as the mother bonds with the baby. This love and mutual trust is the basis of emotional development, allowing the child to continue to make loving and trusting relationships with other members of the family and later with the outside world. Childcare and education workers often have a part to play in giving young parents reassurance and helping them to bond with their baby.

There will be times in the lives of children when parents and carers need to be particularly sensitive. Settling a child successfully into the nursery often needs careful handling. The birth of a new baby may lead to feelings of jealousy and rejection in the older child. Problems within the child's family, such as divorce, unemployment, death or addiction may distress the child and slow down emotional development, causing her to behave in an immature way. Understanding the stages of emotional development is necessary so as to help children to become confident and able to make good relationships with adults and children.

What might prevent a mother bonding with her baby? ▶

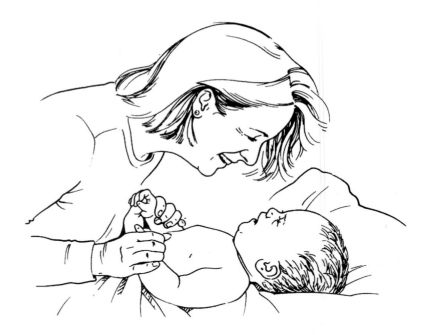

A child's own image of herself also develops gradually. If you show a child under 15 months a photograph of herself or a reflection in the mirror, she is unlikely to recognise herself. As the child matures, she realises that she is a separate person from her mother and this will probably result in testing the mother in many different ways!

Social development

A human being is born without any social skills, and becoming a social being is learnt at first in the family, and then in the outside world. Feral children who are brought up by animals in the wild, or those children locked away with no human contact, not only do not develop socially, they often do not develop physical skills, such as walking. They do not have any recognisable language. The existence of these children shows that all children need human contact to develop normally so that they can take their place in society. Social development takes place alongside emotional development (see pages 292–6).

There are other areas in which a child develops outside the main five described above.

Moral development

Moral development starts with the understanding of right and wrong, and the beginning of a conscience. Toddlers will try and please their parents (sometimes!) by being obedient. At around 5 years, children begin to understand rules when they are playing games, and develop a sense of fairness.

> ### TASK
> In your work experience placement, which children seem to be the most popular? Why do you think this is so?

> ### TASK
> What board games do young children play that help them to understand rules?

Children will lie when they have done something wrong, usually to escape punishment. This often makes them feel guilty and this unpleasant feeling will only go away when they have confessed to their wrongdoing. In later childhood, sensitivity develops to other people's feelings and values, and moral behaviour is valued for its own sake, not just because it stops you getting into trouble.

Spiritual development

This is often linked to a belief, usually in a form of God. It values the unworldly ways of living, rather than the consumer society we are all familiar with today. Spiritual development often starts in children in their awareness of the wonder of the natural world, and it is important that you point out to young children the beauty of the world around them.

Creative development

Creativity is bringing something original into being. It means being able to invent and research and select a wide range of materials tools and instruments. It also includes imagination, feelings and ideas that lead to an understanding of art, music, drama, dance, stories and imaginative play. It has been said that all human being are creative, but if creativity is not valued in young children it can be suppressed and die. To develop creativity in children, the childcare and education worker needs to provide a wide range of creative activities.

> ### KEY POINT
> **It is important that you point out to young children the beauty of the world around them.**

> ### KEY POINT
> **If creativity is not valued in young children it can be suppressed and die.**

Are you creative? In what way? ▶

DEVELOPMENT THROUGHOUT LIFE

It is possible to describe the stages of life that we all follow as:

- babyhood — the first 12 months
- the toddler — 1 to 2 years
- the pre-schooler — 2 to 5 years
- the primary-school-aged child — 5 to 12 years
- adolescence — 12 to 18 years
- young adulthood — 18 to 35 years
- middle age — 35 to 60 years
- active retirement years — 60 to 80 years
- old age — 80 upwards

Babyhood

Babies are attractive and provide their parents/carers with constant rewards. A baby who is loved and given as much attention as she demands will give you many smiles and cuddles. Caring for babies takes much time and energy.

The first twelve months of life is the time when development is fastest. The newborn has little awareness of what is going on around her, beyond feeling safe in her mother's arms or less secure when put in her cot. She is sensitive to pain, to touch and to pressure, resulting in various reflexes (an instinctive movement, over which the baby has no control). The most common reflexes are:

- rooting (turning head to search for milk if the cheek is touched)
- sucking and swallowing
- grasping a finger or object placed in the palm of the hand (and being unable to let go)
- walking reflex; a supported baby will make walking movements during the first few weeks of life, when held upright on a flat surface
- the Moro reflex; if the baby is not held securely and the head is allowed to drop, she will open her arms wide and then pull them back across her chest. Her fingers will fan out. This reflex can also be seen if the baby is alarmed by a sudden loud noise.

By six weeks, most babies are smiling, showing that they are responding to an adult or child, usually during a conversation where there is eye contact. This is a good time to introduce mobiles and rattles. The mobiles that will interest her most will have horizontal pictures, so that she can gaze at them when lying on her back in a cot or supported in a bouncing cradle. Bright colours add interest and some mobiles have a musical attachment.

Many toys are taken to the baby's mouth, so that she can learn with one of the most sensitive parts of her body the shape, size, weight and texture of the object. This should not be stopped, but checks must be made for

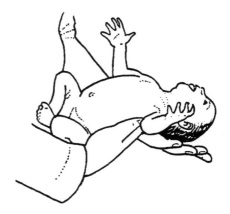

The Moro reflex: what causes the baby to react in this way?

safety. Every object needs to be hard-wearing, well made, non-poisonous, with no sharp edges, washable and should be too large to swallow.

The most important **stimulus** is still the holding and cuddling given to the baby by parents, family and carer. Singing and talking to the baby will aid emotional, intellectual and language development. At first the baby will smile and look intently. Be sure to take turns and listen to the baby when she begins to use her voice. After changing the baby's nappy, allow time for her to play with hands and feet without her clothes on. Most babies enjoy their bathtimes, getting pleasure from the warmth of the water and the freedom to kick and splash. This helps the baby's all-round development.

> **KEY POINT**
>
> **The most important stimulus is still the holding and cuddling given to the baby by parents, family and carer.**

At around 6 weeks, babies can be seen occasionally moving their hands towards objects in their sight and sometimes accidentally succeeding in touching them. At 3 months, the baby discovers her hands and begins to play with her fingers. By 6 months, babies can reach out for an object and grasp it. At first, toys such as an activity centre, which hang just within the baby's reach, will help develop this skill.

Once the baby is able to sit up, supported by cushions, other toys may be offered. An exciting assortment of objects gathered together for her to explore will encourage her all-round development. Bricks can be built into towers and knocked down. Objects can be banged together.

> **KEY POINT**
>
> **Singing to a baby comes naturally to most adults.**

Singing to a baby comes naturally to most adults. From action songs to finger rhymes, from nursery rhymes to lullabies, the baby will get pleasure from them all and enjoy a sense of security and comfort, as well as helping her to recognise different sounds. At this age too, the baby will start to enjoy books. Sitting with an adult and looking at pictures of familiar objects can start as young as six months, and help intellectual and emotional development.

What types of books are suitable for a baby? ▶

A baby will show her personality from the start. She may be calm or excitable, easy or difficult to feed or to settle for sleep, need constant attention or be content on her own, cry rarely or a great deal or show a mixture of all of these behaviours.

Some babies appear not to mind who handles and cares for them and will welcome new people and new experiences. Other babies are slower and more reluctant to accept change and you might have to be patient until they are more familiar with a new carer. A few babies are extremely difficult and will cry loudly at every change. Many babies will show a mixture of these responses.

> ## KEY POINT
>
> **Small babies need warm consistent care that promotes emotional security.**

Small babies need warm **consistent care** that promotes emotional security. Curiously enough, it may be easier to settle a very young baby with a carer than one of 7 months or so. At this age, babies start to miss their mothers and become very aware of strangers, and with some babies this may continue for some time. Between 7 and 15 months, babies feel 'stranger anxiety': becoming anxious in the company of strangers and strange places, and 'separation anxiety': not wishing to be separated from their mother.

Babies are learning and developing as soon as they are born, quickly learning to recognise the smell, taste, voice, feel and face of the mother, and using all their senses to make sure they survive. In addition to love, protection, shelter and food the baby also needs stimulation. At first, the mother provides all the stimulation the baby requires through gentle handling and stroking, speaking in a soft voice and feeding. As the baby

Should the toddler be made to go to the other adult? ▶

develops, the interaction between the mother and the baby becomes increasingly important. As routines become established, there is time to play when feeding, bathing and changing nappies. Many babies are spending longer parts of the day awake, and they are fun to play with. The baby should not be left alone for long periods.

The toddler

Toddlers are challenging and will often use the toys and activities provided by you in a very different way, but this is acceptable as learning is still taking place. Toddlers should be given every opportunity to explore within a safe environment.

Some will be walking confidently by their first birthday, whilst others may need encouragement to get started and develop balance and co-ordination.

Stairs should be protected by gates, but these could be removed on occasion so as to show the toddler how to climb up the stairs and, more importantly, how to crawl down. Strong supermarket cartons, which are sturdy and large enough for toddlers to climb in, encourage skills of getting in and out of objects, co-ordination and balance.

During the first year, babies start to practice handling small objects, reaching and grasping, holding and letting go, moving objects from hand to hand, passing objects, poking and pointing with one finger, and picking up objects with finger and thumb.

> ### KEY POINT
> **Toddlers should be given every opportunity to explore within a safe environment.**

91

What other items of equipment help to keep baby safe?

There are many materials that will help toddlers develop manipulative skills and hand-eye co-ordination, such as:

- bricks for building towers that can be knocked down
- stacking cups and beakers
- small tins and cartons that can be found in any house
- posting boxes
- hammer sets
- dolls that are easily undressed
- simple inset jigsaws.

Outings to parks where the playground will have swings, see-saws, climbing frames and rocking toys are enjoyable and help balance and co-ordination as well as strengthening arm and leg muscles.

Ball play, pull-along toys and small scale climbing and sliding equipment encourage physical skills. Other toys and equipment a toddler will enjoy include:

- wheeled toys to sit on and move with the feet
- rockers
- tunnels and boxes to climb in and out.

Playing with stacking beakers, posting boxes, barrels, bricks and small model toys with be good for her manipulative skills. Child-sized tea sets and cooking and cleaning equipment encourage her to imitate you, and this type of play leads to more creative and imaginative play.

The contents of the lower kitchen cupboards, where it is sensible to store only safe sturdy equipment such as saucepans, plastic storage containers, baking tins and wooden spoons, can be played with as well as small bouncy balls, Duplo, large threading toys and screw toys. Play dough, crayons and finger paints can be used.

Intellectual development

Children learn at an amazing rate, and during the first year the baby has learnt, among other things, to move around, to understand a great deal of what is said, to speak a few words, to know people whom she sees regularly, and to recognise food she enjoys. The next year shows an increase in learning as the toddler uses more language.

The toddler spends an increasingly large amount of time in exploring and experimenting. She will enjoy looking at books, listening to and taking part in songs and rhymes, learning that objects have names as do parts of the body, and realising that by using language her needs are met without having to point and cry. Children's minds develop at different rates and in different ways, and they often seem obsessed in doing some things over and over again, such as wrapping things up, making 'nests', taking toys around and around and arranging objects in straight lines over and over again.

One good way of helping language development is to find the time to sit down with a toddler with a book or a toy, and have an enjoyable conversation, making sure you take the time to listen to what she says, and to add to her vocabulary.

Emotional development

During the first year, the baby has progressed emotionally from total dependency to an understanding that there are some things she is able to do on her own and this increases during the second year. You will need to have patience as the toddler tries to help with her own care or with the housework.

> **TASK**
>
> Learn a number of songs and finger rhymes to use with babies and toddlers.

CASE STUDY

Sabina

Sabina entered the day nursery when she was just over a year. She has a good appetite and enjoys her food Her mother has always allowed her to feed herself with her fingers, and not worried about the mess. Celeste, the student childcare and education worker, is unhappy about the mess involved, especially as Sabina needs all her clothes changed after each meal and the floor needs mopping. This is often seen as Celeste's job.

1 Should Celeste be concerned?
2 Should the nursery be concerned?
3 Should the parents be consulted?

Tantrums can be caused by the toddler being bored, frustrated, hot or cold, hungry or feeling anxious. Sometimes she just cannot cope with her angry feelings. It is often possible to avoid having arguments, but if these do take place, toddlers are easy to distract. Some feelings are so strong and over-powering that you just have to wait until the storm has passed and then cuddle and comfort her, as she may well be frightened by the strength of these emotions.

A great deal depends on the developing personality of the child as to how happy or sad she may be. Comfort objects, such as a loved teddy or a piece of blanket, may play a large part in her life and no attempt should be made to remove them. It is best to have as few rules as possible and to make sure that the environment is safe and offers security. Toddlers still need the love and support of a familiar adult and find new emotional demands difficult to deal with. You need to be aware of this when first making a relationship with a child of this age and take it slowly and sensitively.

Why are comfort objects important at this stage? ▶

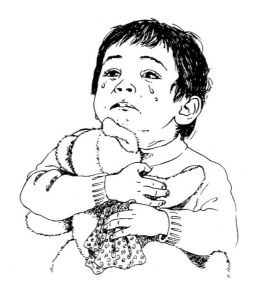

This is the age when toddlers really get into messy play. This allows toddlers to express their frustrations and is relaxing and soothing. Parents do not always find it easy to organise this in the home but painting and water play can take place outside. Water-based paints and markers that wash out of clothing can be bought. Parents should be asked to bring children to the nursery in clothing that is tough and easily washed. The garden offers opportunities for messy play, such as making mud pies and digging for worms.

Social development

During the second year as the child begins to understand more, she has to learn how to fit happily into the household and the larger outside

94

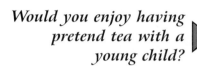

environment and a whole set of rules has to be learnt about acceptable behaviour. At this stage she will mostly play on her own, but the presence of a familiar adult provides reassurance and security. The toddler is not interested in playing co-operatively with other children. She has just learnt the meaning of 'mine', and the concept of sharing does not usually occur until the third year.

> **KEY POINT**
>
> The presence of a familiar adult provides reassurance and security.

Would you enjoy having pretend tea with a young child?

> **KEY POINT**
>
> Very young children learn mainly through their senses.

Taking toddlers to the park, shopping, visiting friends, parent and toddler groups, drop-in centres, the local library and visits to the clinic where other small children are likely to be found will let her play alongside other children. Providing small scale household equipment, such as brooms, tea-sets and telephones, will encourage **domestic play** and the beginning of role play.

The pre-school child

By the age of 3, most children will be attending either a nursery or a pre-school. Three- and four-year-olds are generally happy outgoing little people, who enjoy life and want to please adults and get on with other children. Between the ages of 3 and 5 years, physical skills that were learnt previously will be improved. Skills such as hopping, skipping, crossing the legs when seated, catching and throwing balls will all be in evidence in most four-year-olds. Some four-year-olds can ride a two-wheeler bicycle, often needing stabilisers. They can climb, run and jump on one or both feet. They enjoy all physical activities, and should have the opportunity of playing outside as often as they wish so as to practise these skills.

Most pre-schoolers enjoy eating with adults, using cutlery mostly correctly, and are less fussy about their food. They can manage some fastenings, such as buttons, but shoelaces will probably be beyond most of them. They are able to build with construction toys, the younger ones using Duplo and the older ones coping with Lego. By the time they are 5, most will be able to colour in pictures within the lines and have enough control of a pencil to write their name and do recognisable drawings.

What are the advantages of large floor jigsaws? ▶

There is a spurt in intellectual development between 3 and 5 years. The five-year-old will recognise shapes, know their colours, count and do basic mathematical sums, and some may even have begun to read. Their language is now fully developed, with an increasing vocabulary the more they are read and talked to. Grammatically, the language is now more correct and they are using full sentences. Most children know how old they are, and can repeat their name, address, birthday and telephone number. They understand relationships in the family. They can talk about past experiences, and retell stories. This is the time when children ask continual questions, and you will need patience to answer them satisfactorily. A sense of humour develops, and from 4 years much pleasure is found in jokes and nonsense rhymes.

They are full of wonder and curiosity, and usually a delight to be with. Socially, they will be friends with both boys and girls. They are friendly to adults and children alike, and some need to be taught not to run up to every stranger they meet. By the time they are 5, a sense of fair play is developing, they have learnt to share and they understand rules, playing games usually in a co-operative way. They are becoming more and more independent, being able to look after their toilet needs for themselves and to dress and undress. They now choose their own friends, no longer having to rely on their parents to choose friends for them. They become upset if their friends are distressed, showing caring attitudes.

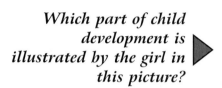

Which part of child development is illustrated by the girl in this picture?

All areas of pre-schoolers' development will be helped and extended by the activities outlined in Chapter 9.

The school child

Once a child starts school full-time she will be increasingly independent and her friends (peer group) will become more important. At 5 years old, most children will be able to dress and undress themselves, clean their teeth, comb their hair, wash themselves and attend to all their toilet needs. By 6 or 7, they can usually make themselves a snack, skip with a rope and ride a two-wheeler bike skilfully. Ball skills develop and often take up a large part of their leisure time.

Children of 5 start learning to write, and this skill is developed and improved all through their school days. Tying shoelaces and colouring in perfectly are indicators of better control (hand-eye co-ordination).

Physical skills continue to improve and develop. Muscles become stronger and outside play can become more energetic. Team games help social development. Swimming is learnt. Regular sporting activities and exercise encourage these skills and lay down interest in later life for keeping fit and healthy.

Should playing team games be compulsory? ▶

Starting school will obviously encourage intellectual development as the young child is keen to learn and ask many questions about events outside her family. A good school and an interested family will help to keep these interests alive throughout childhood. By 8 years of age, most children will be able to read quite well, write short stories, will have some mathematical skills, tell the time and perhaps start to learn a musical instrument, act in a play, and paint and draw. Between the ages of 8 and 12 children begin to think in a more abstract way. They do not need to have, for example, actual counters in front of them to calculate numbers.

Being able to think logically becomes increasingly developed throughout the school years. Their language and vocabulary is often as good as an adult's. This will depend to some extent on the language abilities of the family and the other adults they mix with.

Some children, when they first start school will find the noise level, the number of children, and the size of the school and the playground rather frightening. Having to go the lavatory on her own may be an unpleasant experience, especially if she is not kept clean. If your work experience is in a reception class, you will need to look out for those children who might find the first weeks at school scary. If a child is not collected on time, for some reason, perhaps you could wait with her and take her mind off it by reading her a story.

When children first start school, their development may appear to go backwards. They might become fussy about food, demand help with putting on outside clothes and play with toys that are old and familiar. This is just an adjustment to having to be a 'big girl' whilst at school, and a perfectly normal stage of development. A full school day is physically tiring, and this might also affect her behaviour.

How can schools prevent fighting in the playground?

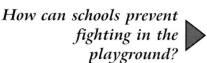

On some days, she may be full of news and expect her parent's undivided attention as she relates the exciting events of the day. At other times, perhaps after a day when things have not gone so well, she may be silent and sullen, and just want to flop down on the couch and watch the television.

How much TV should children be allowed to watch?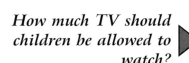

At 5 years of age, she begins to have her own private world separate from her family. Sometimes this leads to increasing fights and squabbles with younger brothers and sisters as she needs her own privacy and a place to think. From about the age of 8, this growing independence should be encouraged and her parents and carers need to let go gradually, trusting her to make her own mistakes within a framework of respect, and valuing her as a more independent person. School-age children become more aware of their special identity and gender, due to the influence of their friends.

CASE STUDY

In your work experience placement there is an African-Caribbean child, aged five. You set up a painting activity for him. You are surprised when you see that the picture he has painted of himself has a white skin.

1 Why do you think he has painted himself like this?
2 What immediate response would you make?
3 Should you discuss this with your supervisor?

Adolescence

Adolescence describes the period of time from puberty, at about 12 years of age, to adulthood. This is a time of physical change and growth. Up until now, boys and girls of the same age are quite similar in height, weight and strength, but at puberty differences become obvious. As girls reach puberty before boys, for a year or so they are often taller and stronger, but once the boys catch up, their growth spurt is even more apparent. Boys develop larger muscles and less fat than girls. This gives them greater speed and strength of movement. They are superior in sports that demand strength and speed. Both boys and girls may develop spots, sometimes leading to acne, due to over-active hormones.

What do YOU think?

It is said that boys of 11 often have not reached the same intellectual level of girls of the same age. Do you think this is so, and if so why?

As well as a physical growth spurt there is also an increase in intellectual ability. It is thought that, because girls reach puberty before boys, they often do better in exams and tests at 11 years of age. Abstract thought becomes more complex and boys and girls go on to higher education in about the same numbers. As there is more equality of opportunity these days, girls have more opportunity to study traditional 'male' subjects such as mathematics, physics and technology. The wider world beckons, and adolescents become interested in the local community and in national and international affairs. They can develop an intense interest in religion or politics.

This period is a time of change in emotional behaviour. By testing their feelings against authority, such as their parents or the school, adolescents find out their true identity and discover their own codes of behaviour. Parents often find it difficult to cope with the mood swings of their children, loving and caring one day, difficult and argumentative the next.

This can be a difficult time for all concerned, but most issues are resolved during this period.

It is a time when an interest in sex begins. Friends become even more important and have a great influence on general behaviour. Adolescents can become depressed quite easily and can lose confidence in themselves, becoming shy and embarrassed. Eating disorders often start during this time.

Adulthood

Adulthood is the time from completing education until death. Young adulthood includes making lasting relationships, often leading to marriage and children. Young adults find out what job or career they want to follow and during the next forty or so years until retirement, work takes up a great deal of their time.

Around about the age of 40, there is sometimes a change of career, due to new interests or **redundancy**. The adult's own children are now growing up and are more independent. It can be a time of security and contentment when they feel they have achieved their goals. On the other hand, some adults miss having their children around, and feel dissatisfied with their lives. The forties and fifties can be a time of change. This can be threatening and upsetting, but usually leads to deeper satisfaction in the end, with the discovery of new talents and skills.

What do YOU think?

Why are some adults in their forties and fifties dissatisfied with their lives? What can they do about it?

The elderly

Becoming old is a state that most people do not look forward to. It is often looked upon as time of poor health and little money. This is not true of everyone. Many old people remain energetic, mentally active and have a great enjoyment of life well into their eighties. The rate at which people age depends on:

- inherited factors
- approach to life
- state of health.

To delay the effects of ageing, old people should:

- keep physically active
- keep mentally active
- have a balanced wholesome diet
- avoid overweight
- take care of their feet
- maintain a good social life
- keep warm
- avoid stress
- have regular dental and eyesight check ups.

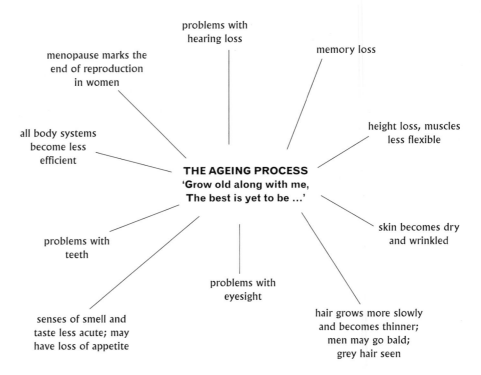

problems with
hearing loss

memory loss

menopause marks the
end of reproduction
in women

height loss, muscles
less flexible

all body systems
become less
efficient

THE AGEING PROCESS
'Grow old along with me,
The best is yet to be ...'

skin becomes dry
and wrinkled

problems with
teeth

problems with
eyesight

hair grows more slowly
and becomes thinner;
men may go bald;
grey hair seen

senses of smell and
taste less acute; may
have loss of appetite

How elderly people feel about themselves depends a great deal on the support they receive from their family and friends, how much money they have, if their memory is not letting them down, and whether they can still walk and have full control of their bladder so that they are still able to live independently. There is often reluctance about being looked after in a residential or nursing home, and most old people fight against this as long as they can.

In the richer countries of the world, we are all living longer and longer. Every decade the life expectancy goes up. Perhaps the worst thing that old people face is loneliness, as their friends die, and they find it more difficult to go out and about. Their immediate family may have moved away, or have many commitments that prevent them from visiting as often as they would like.

CASE STUDY

Fay

Fay is 93 and lives alone. Her husband died thirty years ago, and she has made an independent life for herself. Her daughter lives quite near and now that she has retired is able to help with the chores and the shopping and visits often.

Fay still works voluntarily at the local hospital three mornings helping with the teas and the library books.

1 Why do you think Fay is still living an active life?
2 How might her life change in the next 2 to 3 years?

What do YOU think?

This poem shows very clearly that young people look at older people and do not realise that old people have once been young and have lived a full and active life. Do we stereotype old people, instead of treating them as individuals? Do you know an old person to whom you are close?

The following poem is written by Phyllis McCormack, and titled 'What Do You See?'

What do you see? What do you see?
Are you thinking when you're looking at me,
A crabbit old woman, not very wise,
Uncertain of habit with far away eyes;
Who dribbles her food and makes no reply
When you say in a loud voice, 'I do wish you'd try';
Who seems not to notice the things that you do,
And forever is losing a stocking or shoe;
Who quite unresisting, lets you do as you will,
With bathing and feeding, the long day to fill;
Is that what you're thinking, is that what you see?
Then open your eyes, you're not looking at me;
I'll tell you who I am as I sit here so still:
As I move at your bidding, as I eat at your will;
I'm a small child of ten with a father and mother,
Brothers and sisters who love one another;
A young girl of sixteen with wings on her feet,
Dreaming that soon now a lover she'll meet;
A bride soon at twenty, my heart gives a leap,
Remembering the vows that I promised to keep;
At twenty-five now I have young of my own
Who need me to build a secure, happy home;
A woman of thirty, my young now grown fast,
Bound to each other with ties that should last;
At forty my young sons will soon all be gone,
But my man is beside me to see I don't mourn;
At fifty, once more babies play round my knee,
Again we know children, my loved one and me;
Dark days are upon me, my husband is dead,
I look at the future, I shudder with dread;
For my young are all busy with young of their own
And I think of the years and the love that I've known;
I'm an old woman now and nature is cruel,
'Tis her jest to make old age look like a fool;
The body it crumbles, grace and vigour depart,
There is now a stone where I once had a heart.
But inside this old carcass a young girl still dwells,
And now and again my battered heart swells,
I remember the joys, I remember the pain,
I'm loving and living life over again;
I think of the years all too few, gone too fast
And accept the stark fact that nothing can last,
So, open your eyes, open and see
Not a crabbit old woman, look closer – see me.

GROWTH

Physical development is often linked with growth, which can be measured; and relates to an increase in weight, height and head circumference. How much you grow depends partly on the size of your parents, and partly on the way you live. Better diet has resulted in taller and heavier people in most parts of the developed world. Babies are measured at birth, and this is used as a starting point for measuring their growth in the future.

A child grows rapidly in the first three years of life. The fastest growth occurs in the three months before birth. Birth weight and length vary greatly among healthy newborn babies. This depends mainly on:

- the length of the pregnancy
- the mother's health and diet during pregnancy
- the characteristics of parents (heredity)
- race
- single or **multiple births**.

The newborn baby will lose weight in the first few days of life. Most babies double their birth weight by 6 months and treble it by 1 year.

Growth in height is fastest in the first year and then begins to slow down. Changes in growth patterns for bone, muscle and fat change the chubby, short-limbed, large-headed baby into the thinner, wiry school child. Later, children broaden out, boys at the shoulders, girls at the hips.

After the rapid growth of the first years, height and weight increase more slowly in middle childhood. The start of puberty is linked to a sudden spurt in growth. Girls mature faster than boys and usually stop growing by about 16 years. In boys, the growth spurt is later and often continues after 18 years.

Growth in adolescence is linked with the sex hormones: oestrogen in girls and testosterone in boys. The following physical changes take place:

- the development of the testes and penis in boys
- the growth and enlargement of the breasts in girls
- increase in size and strength
- the voice becomes lower, especially in boys
- the growth of body hair
- girls change shape as they start to menstruate (periods start).

Once adulthood has been reached, most adults usually do not grow taller. Weight might go up and down all through adult life, depending on pregnancy, hormones, lifestyle, diet, income and emotional factors. In older people, bones can become less dense, and they may lose height.

HEALTH CHECKS

In Britain, a Health visitor will visit every baby from birth and will regularly carry out growth and development checks. The baby is examined to make sure she is developing and growing normally, and any problems can be picked up early and help sought.

The chart on page 106 shows the tests carried out from birth to 16 years.

FACTORS THAT AFFECT GROWTH AND DEVELOPMENT

There are many factors that may affect growth and development. Look around you at your group. You will see many different shapes and sizes, abilities and talents.

Physical growth and development

The size you become as an adult depends on many things. These may be inherited from your parents, or due to the environment you live in, how well off your family is financially, or your general health, and so on.

Before birth (ante-natal)

Even before a baby is born, there will be influences that will eventually affect her physical growth and development such as:

- the diet of the mother, even for some months before the baby is conceived
- whether the baby is of a single or multiple birth
- the inheritance from her parents which determines her height and eventual shape
- some infections during the pregnancy, such as rubella (German measles)
- any illness of the mother, such as **diabetes**
- the mother smoking, drinking or taking any other drugs
- the length of the pregnancy. Some babies are born before nine months and may experience problems
- the placenta (afterbirth) not working efficiently. The baby does not receive enough food in the womb.

Health checks from birth to 16 years

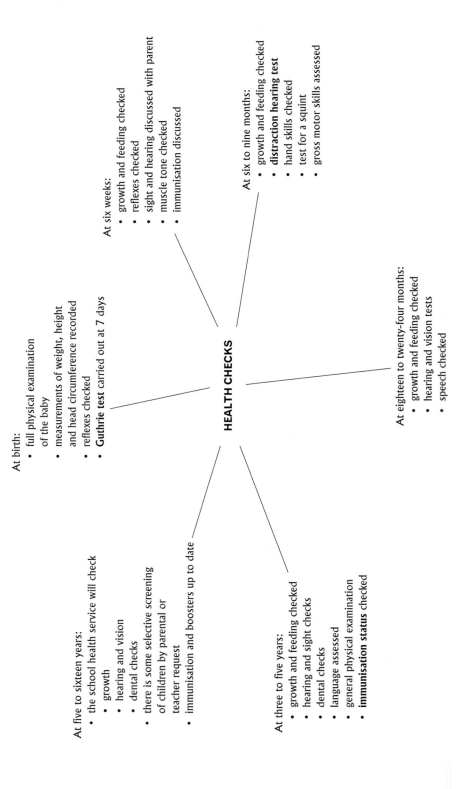

HEALTH CHECKS

At birth:
- full physical examination of the baby
- measurements of weight, height and head circumference recorded
- reflexes checked
- **Guthrie test** carried out at 7 days

At six weeks:
- growth and feeding checked
- reflexes checked
- sight and hearing discussed with parent
- muscle tone checked
- immunisation discussed

At six to nine months:
- growth and feeding checked
- **distraction hearing test**
- hand skills checked
- test for a squint
- gross motor skills assessed

At eighteen to twenty-four months:
- growth and feeding checked
- hearing and vision tests
- speech checked

At three to five years:
- growth and feeding checked
- hearing and sight checks
- dental checks
- language assessed
- general physical examination
- **immunisation status** checked

At five to sixteen years:
- the school health service will check
  - growth
  - hearing and vision
  - dental checks
- there is some selective screening of children by parental or teacher request
- immunisation and boosters up to date

At birth (peri-natal)

Childbirth today is very safe, but there can be complications. During the birth, the baby may become distressed because of:

- a lack of oxygen (anoxia) which can be the main cause of brain damage
- anaesthetics or pain killers given too close to the birth which can cause breathing difficulties
- a long labour, perhaps because the baby is lying in an unusual position, such as feet first, which may result in a shocked baby or anoxia
- birth weight. Some babies are small or 'light for dates'.

After the birth (post-natal)

The baby may be born quite normally, but some influences may be present during childhood that may affect her growth and development.

These may be:

- poverty, leading to a poor diet and lack of good housing
- lack of exercise
- lack of space and the opportunity in which to exercise and practice physical skills
- passive smoking
- neglect and/or abuse
- pollution
- frequent accidents perhaps leading to stays in hospital
- lack of rest and sleep
- hormonal imbalance
- frequent illness.

Many children may experience one or more or these factors, yet grow up perfectly healthy and of normal size.

Other areas of development

Intellectual, language, emotional and social development will also be influenced by the same factors that affect physical development and growth. In addition, intellectual and language development will be influenced by:

- the amount of stimulation in the home and in the school. A home with books and a quiet place to study will help children to do well at school. A poor school with low expectations of its pupils will not lead to high levels of success, whereas a school that expects all its pupils to succeed will have students that do well
- inherited intellectual ability
- the child being given the opportunity to discuss complex issues with her parents
- the parents and carers showing an interest in and encouraging children's achievements.

Social and emotional development will be influenced by:
- the quality of bonding and attachment in the early years
- the amount of love and consistent care in the home
- a sociable home where friends are welcome
- the income of the family
- the amount of abuse or violence in the home
- experience of the outside world
- the child's peer group.

In this country, most children grow up well and strong, sometimes in spite of difficulties during their childhood, their birth and in the womb. Understanding how children develop and grow is a key aspect of a childcare and education worker's skills, as from this understanding you will be able to extend and promote development in all the areas.

<table>
<tr><td>KEY POINT</td></tr>
<tr><td>Understanding how children develop and grow is a key aspect of a childcare and education worker's skills.</td></tr>
</table>

✔ TEST YOURSELF

1 Name the five main areas of development.
2 Give three ways in which you can help the social development of a child aged 18 months.
3 Name four physical skills that most five-year-olds have achieved.
4 Name three factors that might affect growth.
5 List four signs of ageing.
6 Name three factors that might influence development before birth.

GLOSSARY

By the time you have finished this chapter you should understand the meaning of the following words:

attachment feeling affection, often devotion to another, which is always returned, and is often between parent and child

bonding becoming emotionally attached to one person, and usually describes the attachment of the mother to the baby and of the baby to the mother

consistent care children should be cared for in a way that does not change very much, and is the same each day, so that the child feels safe and secure. When the child is very young there should not be too many changes in carers

developmental norms normal development as recognised by doctors and scientists. Patterns of development that most children follow in sequence

diabetes   the body is unable to produce insulin, the hormone that controls the amount of sugar released into the bloodstream

distraction hearing test   a hearing test carried out at seven months. The baby's attention is distracted by a person in front of them, while someone behind makes a number of sounds. The baby's awareness of these sounds is noted

domestic play   pretending to make cups of tea and doing domestic chores, often taking place in the home corner or in the home

feral   refers to animals in the wild, often cats that have been left to die. On occasion this has happened to children who have been cared for by animals

Guthrie test   routine blood test carried out within days of birth for all babies in the UK

hand-eye co-ordination   the way that sight and hands are used together to complete a task, for example threading a needle

immature   behaving or speaking in a younger way than one would expect for the age

immunisation status   a record showing how many immunisations a child has had

manipulative skills   all skills that require the hands

multiple birth   the birth of two or more children being born at the same time. This is more common today because of fertilisation treatment.

puberty   the shift from childhood to adolescence, involving many changes in the body and in mood swings

redundancy   loss of employment due to a business closing down or cutting down on staff. There is often a payment to the employee

stimulus   a situation or action that needs a response. For example, the smell and sight of dinner will make a hungry child run to the table eager for her food.

Food and nutrition

This chapter includes:
- A healthy diet
- Feeding babies
- The dietary needs of children
- Adolescent appetites
- Special diets
- Social, emotional and cultural influences on diet
- Food hygiene
- Mealtimes
- Glossary

KEY POINT

To be and remain healthy you need to have a wholesome balanced diet.

Nutrition is the study of food, and how it is used in the body. To be and remain healthy you need to have a wholesome balanced diet. To provide a balanced diet, you need to know what the body requires, and this will depend on the age, sex, and how much exercise is taken. You will need some understanding of what is contained in different types of food. The body needs energy to keep alive, to breathe, to grow and to keep warm. This energy comes from food. The more active the person, the more energy will be used.

For further information on the material covered in this chapter, you could consult the following:

Dare, A. and O'Donovan, M., *A Practical Guide to Child Nutrition*, Stanley Thornes (Publishers) Ltd, 1996

Eating patterns are established at a very early age. Part of your role in caring for children will include providing food and drinks, educating them in eating healthily, understanding the main rules of nutrition, and being a good role model by setting a good example when you are eating with the children.

A HEALTHY DIET

Food consists of substances known as nutrients. Without food we could not exist. The main nutrients in food and drink are:

- carbohydrates
- **fibre**

- proteins
- fats
- vitamins
- minerals
- water.

Proteins, carbohydrates, fats and water are present in large amounts in our food and are known as macro-nutrients. Vitamins and minerals are only present in small amounts and are known as micro-nutrients.

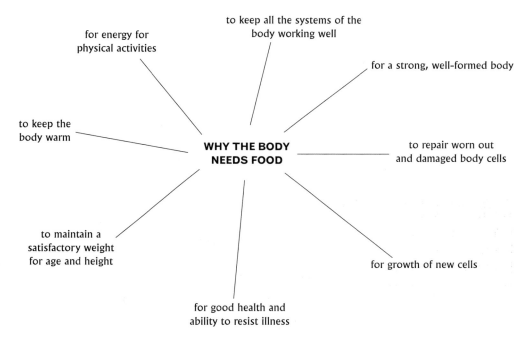

to keep all the systems of the body working well

for energy for physical activities

for a strong, well-formed body

to keep the body warm

WHY THE BODY NEEDS FOOD

to repair worn out and damaged body cells

to maintain a satisfactory weight for age and height

for growth of new cells

for good health and ability to resist illness

Macro-nutrients consist of the following.

- Carbohydrates, which are sugars and starches, provide the body with the main source of energy for immediate use. They are found, for example, in potatoes, flour, pasta, rice and sweet foods. Excess of these, particularly sweet foods, can lead to weight gain. When more is eaten than the body can use it is changed into body fat and stored.
- Fibre is a type of carbohydrate that we need in our diet, but which we do not digest. Fibre helps the food to pass through the body more quickly and protects the body from some diseases.
- Protein is needed for growth and repair of the body, and forms a large part of the body's muscle tissue. It is particularly important for children, so as to build brain and muscle tissue. Protein is found in meats, fish, poultry, dairy foods and vegetables. The animal protein provides all the chemical elements (amino acids) necessary for growth and repair of the body. Vegetable proteins by themselves do not provide all the amino acids necessary, and have to be mixed. Pulses, cereals, nuts and grains all need to be eaten by vegetarians.

- Fats provide energy for the body in a more concentrated form than carbohydrates, and weight for weight contains more calories. Fats are needed to maintain the body's cell structures, and provide warmth. They are found in meat, eggs, oils, and dairy produce. Fat found in animals is high in saturated fats (those fats that become solid at room temperature) and if too much is eaten can be linked with heart disease. Fats found in plants are liquid at room temperature and are found in oils made from seeds and fruits, such as olives and corn. We all need to eat some fat, but if adults eat too much it turns into body fat. Children must have a certain amount of fat in their diet to make sure they are getting the fat-soluble vitamins that can be stored in the body which are vitamins A, D, E and K.

KEY POINT

Children must have a certain amount of fat in their diet to make sure they are getting the fat-soluble vitamins.

Which do you prefer to eat?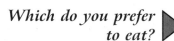

KEY POINT

Water is essential for life.

- Water is essential for life. Your body consists of 70 to 80 per cent water, or two-thirds of the body weight. It helps to get rid of the poisons produced in the body. We need water to replace that lost from the body in sweat, urine, breathing and solid body waste. Water that is lost from the body must be replaced and children should be encouraged to drink several glasses of water a day. More people in the world are ill or die because of a lack of clean water, rather than from a lack of food.

Micro-nutrients consist of the following.

- Vitamins are needed to help your body work correctly, and help to control the body systems, such as the circulation of blood, digestion, and so on (see page 113).
- Minerals help to control the body chemistry, such as the production of blood cells, and are also used in growth and repair (see page 114).

Lack of vitamins and minerals can cause deficiency diseases, for example, a lack of iron may result in anaemia.

Vitamins needed by the body

Vitamin	Main source	Function	Notes
Fat soluble vitamins that can be stored in the body			
A	Carrots, spinach, fish liver oils, tomatoes, butter, cheese	Good vision, healthy skin	Avoid excess if pregnant
D	Oily fish, liver, cod liver oil, egg yolk Added to margarine and milk	Healthy bones and teeth	Can be made in the skin if it is exposed to sunlight
E	Vegetable oils, egg yolk, cereals, nuts, seeds	Aids healing and blood clotting	Poorly understood at present
K	Leafy green vegetables, liver, whole grains	Essential for blood clotting	
Water soluble vitamins that cannot be stored in the body and must be eaten every day			
B 1, 2, 5, 6, 12	Yeast, rice, fish, meat, green vegetables, beans, eggs	Healthy nerves and muscles Needed for making red blood cells	
C	Citrus fruits, green vegetables	Needed to help hold body cells together For healthy skin and tissue Helps healing	

Minerals needed by the body

Mineral	Main source	Function	Notes
Calcium	Milk, cheese, fish, yoghurt, eggs, pulses, hard water	Needed for healthy bones and teeth	Works with vitamin D
Fluoride	Found in water in some areas Added to water, toothpaste	Helps tooth enamel to resist decay	—
Iodine	Water, seafish, shellfish Added to salt	Helps efficient working of the thyroid gland	—
Iron	Red meat, liver, eggs, cocoa, green vegetables, apricots	Needed for the production of red blood cells	Helped by vitamin C
Phosphorus	Most foods, especially fish, eggs, meat, fruit and vegetables	Needed for healthy bones and teeth Helps to absorb carbohydrate	—
Potassium	Leafy vegetables, fruit, liver, meat, milk, cereals	Helps to maintain fluid balance Needed for nerve and muscle activity	—
Sodium Chloride	Salt, fish, meat, bread, bacon, processed foods	Needed for the production of body fluids, blood, sweat and tears	Salt should NOT be added to food for babies and young children

A balanced diet

A balanced diet consists of a variety of foods from all the nutrients shown in the table on page 114. Care must be taken not to overeat, particularly saturated fats and sugars, but to eat sufficient to meet your needs. The more energetic you are, the more calories (units of energy) you will burn up, and the more food you will need. Energy is required by all living things to maintain the changes and chemical reactions that occur in the body (metabolism).

Foods that have little water and a high proportion of fat or carbohydrate have a high energy value. Children need more kilocalories because their bodies are growing and they use a lot of energy. The kilocalories required will vary according to age, gender, size, physical activity and climate.

The following chart from *A Practical Guide to Child Nutrition* by Angela Dare and Margaret O'Donovan clearly shows how a balanced diet promotes health and development.

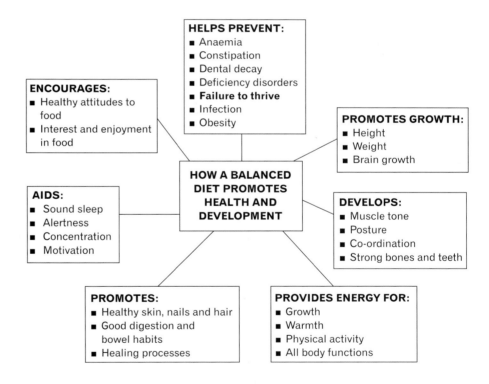

A variety of fresh foods daily in adequate amounts, from the following food groups, should be offered to children every day:

- bread, cereal, rice and pasta
- vegetables and fruits
- fats and sugars
- milk, yoghurt and cheese
- meat, poultry, fish, eggs, beans and pulses.

To allow for their healthy growth and development, children have different food needs to adults. No single food can supply all the nutrients required by a child.

Milk is an important food for children as it contains all the major nutrients needed, except for iron and vitamin C. Drinking too much milk may reduce the appetite for other important foods.

Children need a certain amount of fat in their diet to provide energy and the necessary vitamins. It is as well to offer less fat from animal sources, and more vegetable fat, such as frying food with oil instead of butter. Too much animal fat in the diet may lead to heart problems in later life.

Water is an important nutrient and should be offered several times a day, instead of sugared drinks.

Fibre is necessary in preventing constipation. Fibre is found in brown rice, wholemeal bread or pasta, baked beans, pulses, potato skins, fruit and vegetables. Small children find it difficult to digest a great deal of fibre and should never be given a high-fibre diet, but it can be offered in small amounts as a snack.

Fruit and vegetables are good sources of vitamins, minerals and fibre especially when eaten raw. A variety is necessary, as they all contain different vitamins. It is recommended that everyone eats at least five portions of fresh, frozen or tinned fruit and vegetables every day.

Breads and cereals, especially whole grain products, are an important source of vitamin B and iron, and supply some protein.

Nuts provide protein but can be a safety hazard for young children, because of the risk of choking. Parents need to be asked if a child has an allergy to nuts including peanut butter. Some children may be allergic to other foods, such as strawberries and shellfish.

There is a view that some children, particularly the younger ones, or children who are unwell, benefit if they eat little and often. Snacks should be offered if children are hungry, but try to discourage children from snacking less than two hours before a meal as it might spoil their appetite for the main meal. Examples of wholesome, enjoyable snacks are:

- water, milk and fresh fruit juices (diluted with water to prevent tooth enamel rotting)
- fresh fruit
- dried fruit such as apricots (a good source of iron), prunes and figs
- vegetable sticks, such as carrots, celery and cucumber
- houmous
- yoghurt
- crackers, oatmeal biscuits or rice cakes.

There are concerns about the use of food additives. These are usually chemicals that are added to food to stop it from going bad, and help it to look and taste good. It is thought that some additives may contribute to **hyper-activity** and allergies. Parents should advise you if they wish you to exclude certain foods from their child's diet. Many processed foods and drinks contain many additives, including salt and sugar. Looking at the labels will inform you of the amount and type of additives used in the product.

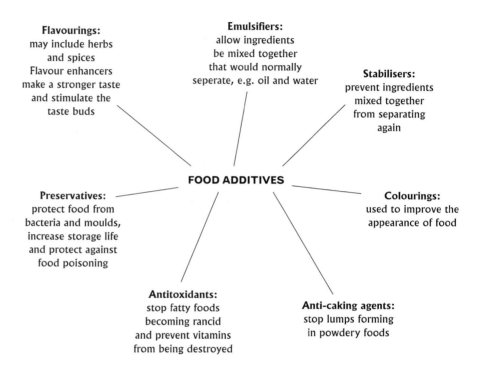

Flavourings:
may include herbs and spices
Flavour enhancers make a stronger taste and stimulate the taste buds

Emulsifiers:
allow ingredients be mixed together that would normally seperate, e.g. oil and water

Stabilisers:
prevent ingredients mixed together from separating again

FOOD ADDITIVES

Colourings:
used to improve the appearance of food

Preservatives:
protect food from bacteria and moulds, increase storage life and protect against food poisoning

Antitoxidants:
stop fatty foods becoming rancid and prevent vitamins from being destroyed

Anti-caking agents:
stop lumps forming in powdery foods

Use sugar in moderation, as sugar can lead to tooth decay and over-weight (obesity). If you are cooking with the children, try to cook something other than cakes and biscuits. Salt should be used sparingly in cooking, and should not be put on the table for children to help themselves.

It is quite common these days for families to be vegetarian, and exclude meat and perhaps fish from the diet. There are various types of vegetarians, some of whom eat quite restricted diets:

- lacto-ovo-vegetarians eat plant foods, dairy products and eggs; this is the usual vegetarian diet
- lacto vegetarians eat plant foods and dairy products, but no eggs
- vegans eat no animal product of any kind
- fruitarians eat only fruit, including nuts and seeds
- some people eat a Zen macro-biotic diet, based on whole grain cereals and pulses.

Problems rarely arise with the first two diets. A vegan diet is adequate with a supplement of vitamin B12. The last two diets are not adequate for babies and children.

Some schools and daycare centres provide food for the children that is bought in from outside caterers. It is often the cheapest deal, but does not always contain all the nutrients a healthy diet requires.

Did you enjoy school dinners?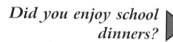

Organic food

During the last few years, there have been many food scares. **BSE** (bovine spongiform encephalitis), **GMF** (genetically modified foods), pesticides and herbicides have made the general public aware that not all food might be good for us. The sales and the availability of organic produce have increased enormously during the past few years.

'Organic' is a legally protected term, and organic food production is tightly regulated. Organic farmers avoid the use of chemical fertilisers and pesticides. They grow a balanced mixture of crops, encouraging insects and other wild life to destroy pests in healthy soil. Animals are not given antibiotics and other drugs, and are allowed to roam in fields with plenty of space. Organic food should carry the symbol of the soil association and is guaranteed free of genetically modified organisms (GMs).

The popularity of organic food has grown out of the fear of contamination and the over consumption of antibiotics and growth hormones via the food chain. There has been no incidence of BSE on organic farms. Many private nurseries are now advertising the fact that they provide organic food for the children as a positive selling point.

FEEDING BABIES

Babies' first food is milk. This can be breast milk or formula (dried cows' milk, enriched with vitamins, and given in a bottle).

Breast feeding

After a baby is born, mothers have to decide whether to breast- or bottle-feed their babies. Both have advantages and disadvantages. It is very important that the baby's food needs are met, as the first year of life is a time of very rapid growth and development. A baby who is not getting enough food may suffer developmental delay and restricted growth, resulting in failure to thrive.

The advantages of breast-feeding are:

- it is designed for the baby
- it meets the complete nutritional needs of the baby
- there is less risk of infection
- it plays a part in preventing allergies
- it contains **antibodies** to help fight infection
- it is cheap
- it is less work, once it is established
- the baby has close contact with the mother.

The disadvantages of breast-feeding are:

- fathers play a less active part in feeding the baby
- it may cause sore nipples
- it may cause inflammation of the breast, linked to infection (mastitis)
- it is difficult to know how much the baby has taken.
- it may be difficult to establish
- it may limit the mother's diet
- mothers may resent restriction to their freedom.

Mothers returning to work may wish to continue to breast-feed either by using **expressed breast milk**, or returning to the home or nursery during the day. The desire to do this must be respected, but it can be stressful as babies do not necessarily match timetables or recognise lunch breaks. Mothers will make sure there is plenty of expressed breast milk in the freezer, for carers to use in an emergency.

Bottle feeds

Formula milk is usually made from cows' milk, where the protein and fat levels have been altered and vitamins and minerals added. An approximate guide to calculating the amount of formula milk required by a baby is 75 ml of fully re-constituted feed for every 500 gm. of a baby's weight (2½ fluid ounces per pound body weight) in twenty-four hours. The total is divided into the number of bottles the baby is likely to take in that time.

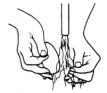

1 Check that the formula has not passed its sell-by date. Read the instructions on the tin. Ensure the tin has been kept in a cool, dry cupboard

2 Boil some **fresh** water and allow to cool

3 Wash hands and nails thoroughly.

Preparing the bottle feed ▶

4 Take required equipment from sterilising tank and rinse with cool, boiled water

5 Fill bottle, or a jug if making a large quantity, to the required level with water.

6 Measure the exact amount of powder using the scoop provided. Level with a knife. **Do not pack down**.

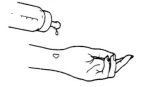

7 Add the powder to the measured water in the bottle or jug.

8 Screw cap on bottle and shake, or mix well in the jug and pour into sterilised bottles.

9 If not using immediately, **cool quickly** and store in the fridge. If using immediately, test temperature on the inside of your wrist.

10 Babies will take cold milk but they prefer warm food (as from the breast). If you wish to warm the milk, place bottle in a jug of hot water. **Never keep warm for longer than 45 minutes** to reduce chances of bacteria breeding.

Note Whenever the bottle is left for short periods, or stored in the fridge, cover with the cap provided.

Like a breast-fed baby, the baby should be allowed to dictate its feeding requirements to allow for changes in appetite and growth.

Studies have shown that bottle-fed babies are frequently given feeds that are over or under concentrated, so always read and follow the instructions on the packet, as manufacturers often develop and change their products. The advantages of bottle-feeding are:

- it lets the father take part in feeding the baby
- it gives the mother more freedom. She may find it easier to return to work
- it is easy to see how much the baby has taken
- it avoids the risk of sore nipples or inflammation of the breast.

The disadvantages of bottle-feeding are:

- there is an increased risk of infection
- it is expensive
- there is a risk of not measuring the formula correctly, so that it may be too concentrated or too liquid
- it is less easy to establish bonding especially if the baby is handed to too many people to be fed
- it may result in choking, if the bottle is put in the baby's mouth whilst she is lying down and left alone
- some babies may be allergic to cow's milk
- the formula may be too hot if care is not taken.

All equipment (bottles, teats, bottle tops, scoops) used for bottle-feeding should be sterile as germs thrive on milk. Sterilisation of this equipment usually involves using a chemical agent such as Milton, a particular disinfectant for keeping bottles free from germs that cause disease. Bottles and equipment may also be boiled, but have to be kept under the boiling water for at least ten minutes. You should always make sure you have washed your hands before preparing bottles.

2 Rinse everything thoroughly in clean running water.

The procedure for sterilising feeding equipment ▶

1 Wash the bottles, teats and other equipment in hot water and detergent. Use a bottle brush for the inside of bottles. **Do not rub salt on the teats**. Squeeze boiled water through the teats.

3 Fill the steriliser with clean, cold water. Add chemical solution. If in a tablet form, allow to dissolve.

4 Put the bottles, teats and other equipment (nothing metal) into the water. Ensure everything is covered completely by the water, with no bubbles. If necessary, weight down. Leave for the required time according to manufacturer's instructions.

Apart from making completely sure that the feed is germ free, it is equally important to know how to hold the baby when giving a feed. Both the adult and the baby need to be comfortable and to look at each other, and the adult should speak softly and encouragingly to the baby from time to time. Never leave the baby on her own with a bottle (prop feeding). This is very dangerous as the baby might choke.

Weaning

It is recommended that babies should be introduced to solid food (weaning) between the age of 4 to 6 months, by which age the baby's digestive system is more able to cope with a variety of food. The milk diet alone might not be satisfying a baby, and she might be waking hungry during the night.

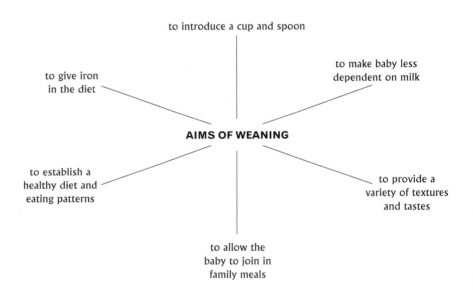

By six months, the reserves of iron that the baby has taken in during the pregnancy have run out, and milk on its own does not provide enough for her. She will need some iron rich foods such as lentils, apricots, and green leaf vegetables. For the first two weeks, just one teaspoonful of pureed vegetables a day is enough. This should be offered after a feed as she is less likely to refuse it.

For the next six to eight weeks gradually introduce solids three times a day before, during or after milk feeds. These first solid foods should be soft and lump free (pureed), as the baby cannot chew and finds it difficult to swallow and digest lumps.

From 6 months, solid food becomes important for growth and the prevention of anaemia (a blood disorder, where there is a lack of red blood cells). From this age, foods that can be held by the baby (finger foods) and food that is no longer pureed but just mashed may be introduced. Finger foods could include pieces of carrot and apple, crusts of bread or rice biscuits. It is also thought that if solid food is not introduced by 6 months an important developmental stage may be missed, resulting in chewing difficulties and food refusal. Babies should have their own plate and spoon. This equipment does not have to be sterilised, but should be kept very clean.

CASE STUDY

Sylvia

It was snack time in a small private nursery. The children were given juice to drink, and the work experience student, Sylvia, handed a plate of biscuits around. Theo, aged 6 months, thoroughly enjoyed his biscuit – a new experience for him. Sylvia told Theo's mother how much the baby had enjoyed his snack time. On hearing that Theo had eaten a biscuit, his mother was furious as she did not want her baby to have anything to eat in the nursery that she had not provided herself, and thought she had made this clear to the staff.

1 Why do you think the mother was angry about the baby having a biscuit?
2 How might this situation have been prevented?
3 Who was at fault?
4 What should Sylvia check next time she is handing out snacks?

KEY POINT

The first foods should not have salt or sugar added to them.

The first foods should not have salt or sugar added to them, as the kidneys cannot digest salt, and too much sugar can lead to a craving for sweet food and eventual tooth decay. Any cereal containing gluten (a protein found in cereals, such as wheat, barley, oats and rye) should be avoided until the baby is at least 7 months, as there is a danger of allergy to gluten.

Eggs that are well cooked can be introduced towards the end of the first year. Never give soft boiled eggs to a baby because of the risk of salmonella food poisoning. After six months, as the quantity of solid food is increased, the amount of milk offered may be gradually reduced. The fluid should be replaced with cooled boiled water, given in a cup.

The weaning plan on page 124 is from *A Practical Guide to Working with Babies* (2nd edition) by Angela Dare and Margaret O'Donovan.

A suggested weaning plan

Age/months	4 months	4½ months	5–6 months	6–7 months	7–8 months	9–12 months
On waking	Breast- or bottle-feed	Breast- or bottle-feed	Breast- or bottle-feed	Breast- or bottle-feed	Breast- or bottle-feed	Breast- or bottle-feed/cup
Breakfast	1–2 teaspoons baby rice mixed with milk from feed or with water; breast- or bottle-feed	2 teaspoons baby rice mixed with milk from feed or with water; breast- or bottle-feed	Baby rice or cereal mixed with milk from feed or with water or pureed banana; breast- or bottle-feed	Cereal mixed with milk from feed or water; fruit, toast fingers spread with unsalted butter	Cereal, fish or fruit; toast fingers; milk	Cereal and milk; fish, yoghurt or fruit; toast and milk
Lunch	Breast- or bottle-feed	1–2 teaspoons pureed or sieved vegetables, or vegetables and chicken; breast- or bottle-feed	Pureed or sieved meat or fish and vegetables, or proprietary food; followed by 2 teaspoons pureed fruit or prepared baby dessert; drink of cooled, boiled water or well-diluted juice (from cup)	Finely minced meat or mashed fish, with mashed vegetables; mashed banana or stewed fruit or milk pudding; drink of cooled boiled water or well-diluted juice in a cup	Mashed fish, minced meat or cheese with vegetables; milk pudding or stewed fruit; drink	Well-chopped meat, liver or fish or cheese with mashed vegetables; milk pudding or fruit fingers; drink
Tea	Breast- or bottle-feed	Breast- or bottle-feed	Pureed fruit or baby dessert; breast- or bottle-feed	Toast with cheese or savoury spread; breast- or bottle-feed	Bread and butter sandwiches with savoury spread or seedless jam; sponge finger or biscuit; milk drink	Fish, cheese or pasta; sandwiches; fruit; milk drink
Late evening	Breast- or bottle-feed	Breast- or bottle-feed	Breast- or bottle-feed, if necessary			

All mealtimes, especially those for a baby, should take place in a quiet, calm atmosphere. New tastes should be encouraged without ever forcing them upon her. If the baby dislikes something on a Monday, she may well enjoy it the following Friday. It is always worthwhile re-introducing foods, as the baby's tastes become more mature. Babies should be encouraged to enjoy their food, allowed to help by holding a spoon, given finger foods, and no fuss should be made if there is any mess.

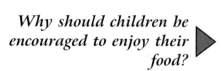

Why should children be encouraged to enjoy their food?

THE DIETARY NEEDS OF CHILDREN

The first three years of life are a period of rapid growth. Protein is needed to support this growth and allow the bones and the brain to develop properly. Children also require a high intake of calories to provide energy for physical activity. If the calories needed for energy are not provided by carbohydrates and fat, then protein will be used to provide energy rather than being used for growth.

The Department of Health recommends one pint of whole milk daily for children under 5 years, particularly for its fat and vitamin content. This can be offered in a variety of ways: in puddings, custard, yoghurt and cheese, as well as on cereal or as a drink. Sugar should never be added to children's food and drinks, and foods containing a great deal of sugar such as biscuits, pastries and jams should be offered only occasionally in small quantities.

Salt is not needed when preparing and cooking food for children as a high intake of salt is linked with high blood pressure in later life. Many processed foods, such as ready-made meals, cooked meats and many canned foods contain high levels of salt and/or sugar, and should be avoided in children's diets.

ADOLESCENT APPETITES

Adolescence is a time of rapid growth and, for many, great physical activity. There is an increased need for protein for growth and carbohydrate and some fat for energy. Adolescents like to take control of what they eat, and are greatly influenced by their friends. If they move away from home to attend a college, they may find it difficult to make ends meet, and some have little knowledge of nutrition. For many young people, having a good time and spending their money on entertainment and drink can lead to them having a very poor diet.

Has your taste in food changed since you were in primary school?

For girls, once they have their first period, there is an increased need for iron in the diet as regular loss of blood can lead to anaemia.

Eating disorders

Most eating disorders start in adolescence, although some younger children have been known to lose their appetites. Making children, particularly girls, conscious of their size, can often lead to an eating disorder. The two most common are anorexia nervosa and bulimia.

A person who has anorexia nervosa often sees herself as hugely overweight and has a great fear of getting fat. She rarely eats, unless forced to do so, and often feel sick at the very thought of food. It is sometimes seen to be a form of control in less than happy teenagers, a way of taking control of their own lives. It is also seen in girls who have succeeded at a very young age, pushed by their parents to take up a sport or a career, and might be a way of getting back at the parents.

CASE STUDY

Sarah

Sarah is a student on a childcare course. She is doing well and enjoying working with the children. Some concern is felt among her friends as she seems to be getting thinner and is never seen in the college canteen. She has hinted that there are some problems in her home life but is unwilling to talk about them. She has confided in her best friend that she is looking for a room to rent.

1 Should Sarah's friends be concerned about her?
2 How might they help her?
3 Should they tell her personal tutor?
4 What professional help might be available?

Anorexia nervosa is not an illness that gets better without help. Once the pattern has been established it is very hard to start eating again. It is rather like an addiction to alcohol or drugs and professional help is needed. A small percentage of young people die and many never fully recover. Some children who have very poor appetites are found to have mothers who have been anorexic.

Bulimia nervosa is often harder to recognise, as the person will eat in public and then vomit up the contents of their stomach in private. Bulimics often binge on their own, and then make themselves sick. Unlike anorexics, they enjoy food, but are equally fearful of becoming fat.

It might be thought that the image of the supermodel has influenced these young people. The media has also been blamed, by promoting very thin people as the yardstick for beauty.

What do YOU think?
Are there any disadvantages to being overweight when working with young children?

SPECIAL DIETS

Some children that you may care for may be on a special diet, particularly if you are placed in a special school. Special diets are worked out by the doctor and dietician according to the individual needs of the child. The chart on page 128 shows some common disorders that require special diets. Nurseries and schools have to work closely with parents in order to provide the correct diet for the child. You will be told during your work experience placement if a child is on a special diet. It is important that you find out as much as you can about the condition and encourage and support the child on a special diet. Under no circumstances must you give the child anything that she is not allowed. You will need to tell your supervisor if the whole meal provided is not eaten.

KEY POINT
It is important that you find out as much as you can about the condition and encourage and support the child on a special diet.

Common disorders that require a special diet

Condition	Description	Diet
Coeliac disease	Sensitivity to gluten, a protein found in wheat, rye, barley and oats. Child fails to thrive	Exclude all foods containing gluten. Can eat fresh fruit and vegetables, fish, meat and dairy produce
Cystic fibrosis	An inherited condition, sticky thick mucus is found in the lungs and digestive system. Interferes with the digestion of food	Tablets given to help the digestion. Needs a high protein, high calorie diet
Diabetes	The body fails to produce enough insulin to control the amount of sugar in the body	Regular meals, diet carefully balanced and controlled. May need a snack before exercise, should be observed closely
Obesity	Overweight for height and age	Plan, offer and encourage a healthy balanced diet. Discourage over-eating. Encourage daily exercise
Anaemia	Lack of iron in the diet. Can also be caused by severe blood loss	A diet high in red meat, liver, eggs, cocoa, green vegetables, apricots, helped by taking Vitamin C at the same time
Cows' milk allergy: • to protein • lactose (milk sugar) intolerance	Associated with family history of allergy. Can result in wheezing, diarrhoea, vomiting, rashes, abdominal pain and tiredness	Special formula milk for babies. Substitute milks for older children. Avoid cows' milk, cheese and yoghurt

Some children, not suffering from any particular disorder, may be restricted in their diet in certain foods. For example, children who may have frequent chesty illnesses, might be rationed in their intake of milk, and offered fruit juice instead.

Parents of children who are very active may wish to reduce the amount of additives their children eat and drink, as it is thought that some additives contribute to **hyperactivity**. Make a point of asking your supervisor if there are any children in the group who have their diet limited.

SOCIAL, EMOTIONAL AND CULTURAL INFLUENCES ON DIET

Social factors

There was little realised about the influence that diet had on the well-being and health of the individual before the 1900s. When there was a drive to recruit soldiers for the Boer War, nearly half were judged to be unfit to fight. The reason was poverty: the families were too poor to give their children adequate nourishing food. The Government of the time acted by bringing in a number of infant and child health measures such as school meals, school milk, school medicals and infant clinics.

During the Second World War (1939–45) food was very scarce and was rationed. The government of the day encouraged people to grow as many vegetables as they could in their gardens. Sweets, fats and meat were rationed. An average four-year-old living in the 1940s ate more bread and vegetables, and milk, tea and water were the usual drinks. This diet is similar to the one recommended today. In addition, children were more active. There was no television and no computers. With few cars on the road, the children could play outside in the street, and there was little fear of being run over or being taken away.

These days, the main factor that prevents children eating healthy and wholesome food is poverty. On income support, it is not possible to eat the recommended diet. Fish, fruit and vegetables are expensive. Poverty often leads to shopping at expensive small shops, rather than taking a car to a supermarket, where it is possible to bulk buy and take advantage of special offers.

Cooking is seldom taught in schools these days, and many young families are uncertain as to what makes a healthy balanced diet. Parents often work, and the family relies on processed convenience foods. The art of cooking may not be handed down from one generation to the next.

CASE STUDY

Patricia

Patricia is a young qualified nanny, having recently gained her Diploma in Childcare and Education. She has spent four years in College and is enjoying her first job, looking after a baby, a toddler and a six-year-old. Her employer has gone back to work, leaving Patricia caring for the children from eight o'clock to six o'clock. There is one problem: she has never learnt how to cook. She understands how important it is to give the children a wholesome balanced diet, and for the first week feeds them on salads, fresh fruit, sandwiches and cold meat. The six-year-old gets fed up with this diet and complains to his parents.

1 Why do you think Patricia never learnt to cook?
2 What can Patricia do about learning to cook?
3 How might the parent help Patricia?

Emotional factors

For the majority of parents/carers, offering food is a way of expressing love. Toddlers soon learn the power they have if they refuse to eat. It is a sure-fire way to wind up her parent/carer. No child has ever starved to death by refusing one or two meals, and the sensible person will learn to ignore food refusal, and just remove the plate in a calm manner.

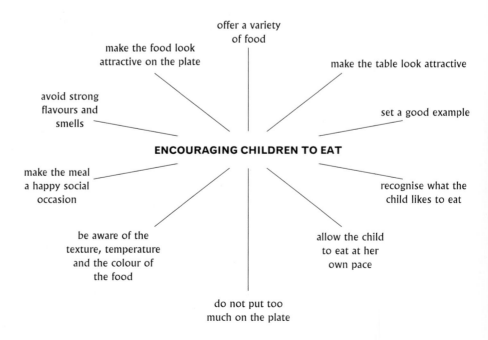

offer a variety of food

make the food look attractive on the plate

make the table look attractive

avoid strong flavours and smells

set a good example

ENCOURAGING CHILDREN TO EAT

make the meal a happy social occasion

recognise what the child likes to eat

be aware of the texture, temperature and the colour of the food

allow the child to eat at her own pace

do not put too much on the plate

Every parent/carer knows that when a child is not feeling happy and secure, she will often find it difficult to eat, and may lose her appetite for a while. Again, a little patience and a willingness to listen to the child's problems usually helps to restore the child's appetite.

Some adults have emotional reactions to the look of certain types of food, so it is not surprising if children do as well. Presenting all food in an attractive way may encourage children to eat foods they normally refuse. Offering small amounts rather than over full plates may also help children to regain their appetites.

CASE STUDY

Gita

Gita is doing her work experience in an Infant school. She noticed that very few of the children ate any fruit or vegetables and knew that this was not healthy. She saw a programme on television where a group of children had been encouraged to eat fruit and vegetables after being shown a video of super heroes who take on wicked General Junk and his junk food junta. They stuff themselves with fruit and vegetables to 'keep their life force strong'. The programme showed that the consumption of fruit and vegetables had increased dramatically.

Gita mentioned this to her supervisor, who discussed the project with the headteacher, and the video was bought and shown to the children.

1 What do you think happened?
2 Do you think the parents should have been consulted?
3 Why should children be encouraged to eat fruit and vegetables?

Cultural factors

We all like the food we know and are used to and we have had the opportunity to taste many flavours from around the world during the last thirty years or so, going abroad on holiday, eating food imported from many countries and eating in local restaurants. In the fifties and beforehand, many of the foods that we take for granted today were not available. We eat foods from many cultures with enjoyment, and our children have the opportunity to taste many different dishes.

Most schools and nurseries provide food from many cultures. This benefits the children by:

- introducing them to new tastes
- helping them to develop an interest in and respect for other cultures
- providing a link between home and nursery/school for some children.

Food from different countries is often healthier and fresher and contains less fat and sugar. For example, a stir-fry would use many fresh vegetables cooked quickly with a small amount of vegetable oil, so as to retain all the vitamins.

Many diets are linked to religious practices. The table on page 123 indicates the main religions, and the foods they do not eat.

You should never assume that because one of the children is from a certain ethnic group that she will necessarily eat certain foods or reject others. The nursery/school will follow the guidelines given by the parents.

Some religions have special days when food is forbidden. This must always be respected and allowance made for the children feeling tired. They may need to rest.

FOOD HYGIENE

Many foods carry germs that grow in warm, moist conditions. Eggs and chickens can be infected with salmonella, a bacteria that can cause food poisoning. Cheeses grow moulds. Milk goes bad, particularly if not kept in the fridge. Raw meat contains many different bacteria and needs to be carefully handled. Food poisoning can be caused by:

- salmonella (germs that usually live in the bowels of humans or animals, or may be found in water polluted by sewage). If food that contains salmonella is cooked thoroughly the germs will be killed and not cause any harm. Care also needs to be taken with personal hygiene. After cleaning a chicken, hands must be carefully washed in an antibacterial soap and all surfaces disinfected
- staphylococcus (germs that may be found in the nose or throat, in boils or septic wounds). If introduced into food, the germs produce poisons that are quite difficult to destroy.
- e-coli, found in the bowel, that may be passed on because of poor personal hygiene
- listeria, found in dairy products that have not been heated to the temperature required to kill the germs (the process of pasteurisation).

When caring for children it is very important that you have very high standards of personal hygiene and an awareness of how to store and prepare food correctly in order to prevent infection. You must be sure that you and the children wash your hands after using the lavatory, handling animals and their equipment, coughing or sneezing, and before preparing and eating food. In addition, you need to wash your hands thoroughly after changing nappies, wiping noses, wiping bottoms and handling raw food. Never touch food if you have been suffering from vomiting or diarrhoea.

Dietary customs

Food	Jewish	Sikh	Muslim	Hindu	Buddhist	7th Day Adventist	Rastafarian	Roman Catholic	Mormon
Eggs	No blood spots	✓	✓	Some	Some	Most	✓	✓	✓
Milk/Yoghurt	Not with meat	✓	Not with rennet	Not with rennet	✓	Most	✓	✓	✓
Cheese	Not with meat	Some	Some	Some	✓	Most	✓	✓	✓
Chicken	Kosher	Some	Halal	Some	✗	Some	Some	Some still prefer not to eat meat on Fridays particularly during Lent	✓
Mutton/lamb	Kosher	✓	Halal	Some	✗	Some	Some		✓
Beef	Kosher	✗	Halal	✗	✗	Some	Some		✓
Pork	✗	Rarely	✗	Rarely	✗	✗	✗		✓
Fish	With scales, fins and back-bone	Some	Halal	With fins and scales	Some	Some	✓	✓	✓
Shellfish	✗	Some	Halal	Some	✗	✗	✗	✓	✓
Animal fats	Kosher	Some	Some Halal	Some	✗	✗	Some	✓	✓
Alcohol	✓	✓	✗	✗	✗	✗	✗	✓	✗
Cocoa/tea/coffee	✓	✓	✓	✓	✓ No milk	✗	✓	✓	✗
Nuts	✓	✓	✓	✓	✓	✓	✓	✓	✓
Pulses	✓	✓	✓	✓	✓	✓	✓	✓	✓
Fruit	✓	✓	✓	✓	✓	✓	✓	✓	✓
Vegetables	✓	✓	✓	✓	✓	✓	✓	✓	✓
Fasting (where not specified, fasting is a matter of individual choice)	Yom Kippur		Ramadan						24 hours once monthly

✓ Accepted   ✗ Forbidden

Adapted from *Nutritional Guidelines*, ILEA, 1985

TASK

Write about two hygiene routines that will help to prevent infection linked with food.

Hygiene routines

The following are important points to note when you are preparing food.

- Wash your hands before and after handling food.
- Keep the kitchen working surfaces, utensils and implements clean.
- Never re-freeze food that has already been defrosted.
- Never store raw meat alongside other food. Keep it well wrapped at the bottom of the refrigerator.
- The freezer should be set at minus 18°C to prevent germs multiplying.
- Sterilise feeding bottles and teats for as long as they are used, as germs multiply very quickly in milk.
- Keep rubbish bins covered and clean.
- Cover any cuts or sores on your hands with a waterproof dressing or wear gloves.

The use of soap and water, fresh air and sunlight will destroy many germs. Using chemical disinfectants, such as strong bleach, to clean surfaces will destroy germs but will be harmful to children and pets, and needs to be stored locked away. Antiseptics are weak disinfectants that prevent the growth of germs but do not destroy them. They can be equally dangerous to children.

Food should always be bought from shops with a good reputation for freshness. The sell-by date should be clearly shown. Raw food that is not going to be cooked should never be touched by anyone's hands, such as salads, cheese or cooked meats. Use a knife or spoon and fork to serve it.

Symptoms of food poisoning can include diarrhoea, vomiting and stomach ache. Babies must see a doctor immediately, and older children after 24 hours if they have not recovered. Children must be encouraged to drink water to replace water loss.

MEALTIMES

Eating is a basic human need and an activity that most people enjoy. Apart from being essential for survival it makes you feel good. Eating around the table is a social activity, a time when relaxed conversations can take place, and news of the day shared.

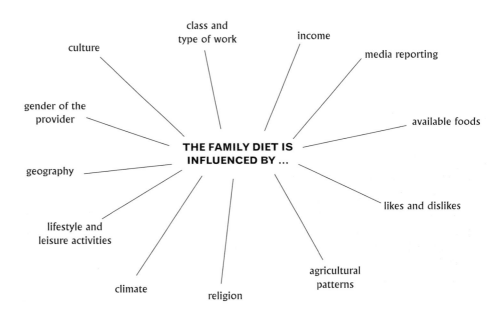

class and type of work

income

culture

media reporting

gender of the provider

available foods

THE FAMILY DIET IS INFLUENCED BY ...

geography

likes and dislikes

lifestyle and leisure activities

agricultural patterns

climate

religion

Children's eating behaviour

Children's eating patterns develop from infancy. The attitude to food of the parents and carers is most important. Adults might show concern and anxiety if a child refuses food, because they worry that the child might not grow and develop well without what they feel is sufficient food. They might feel rejected that the meal they have prepared with such loving care has been refused. The child may discover that whether they eat or not is of very great importance and therefore have a way of manipulating adults.

Your placement will probably provide a range of eating utensils for the children, and they should then become skilled at using chopsticks and knives and forks. 'Table manners' are more important in some schools and nurseries than in others. Remember that some cultures do not have the words in their language for 'please' and 'thank you'.

KEY POINT

Children's eating patterns develop from infancy.

135

Appetites differ in children and are unpredictable. Children know their own hunger signs and it is more sensible to offer smaller portions, and provide more if the child requests it. If children say they are hungry in the middle of the morning, it is wiser to offer them a snack of fruit or raw vegetables, as filling up on milk, bread or biscuits will reduce the appetite for the midday meal.

Children have a shorter attention span than adults. Some find it very hard to sit at the table, and it might be a good idea to allow them to leave the table when they have finished, providing a quiet activity for them so as not to disturb the children who are slower. Let children eat at their own pace.

Some children cause anxiety because they may:

- refuse to eat many foods
- take a long time to eat their food
- refuse to swallow food
- display other poor eating behaviours.

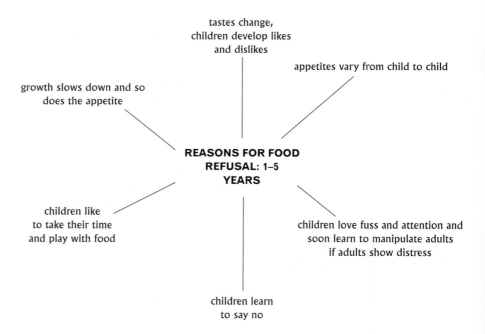

If a child is causing anxiety, make a record of what food is being refused, how she behaves at the table, such as crying, complaining or throwing food, and what food she enjoys. You may see a pattern, such as too many snacks prior to the meal, and be able to resolve the problem. If the behaviour persists after you feel the child has settled in the nursery, and there is no obvious reason, your supervisor will need to involve the parents and discuss how she eats at home.

What do YOU think?
Do you live to eat, or do you eat to live?

Ben

Ben, aged 2½, has recently started to attend a full-time day nursery. The staff have made a good relationship with Ben's mother, and the settling in period has gone well. There appears to be one concern: Ben sits at the table for long periods of time, chewing the same mouthful of food over and over again. He leaves the table with most of the food still on the plate, and the rest still in his mouth, which is later found in various places around the room.

1 Explain why this is a worrying situation.
2 Should the parents be told?
3 Why do you think Ben treats food in this way?
4 How can you help Ben to enjoy his food more?

What do YOU think?

Does your placement involve children in the preparation and clearing away of food?

There is a fashion today for some parents to allow their children to 'graze'. This means eating continually, on demand, and usually walking around with the food. Most childcare and education workers will not be happy with this, and it will have to be discussed with the parents. Children are adaptable, and will probably accept the food rules in your placement.

You can encourage healthy eating habits by:

- letting children help themselves to food at the table
- allowing children to help prepare food sometimes
- encouraging children to set the table and clear it
- talking to children during the meal about the foods
- not making a fuss about accidents at the table, and letting children help mop up the spills
- presenting food in an interesting way, mixing colours, flavours and textures
- making the table look attractive, with a clean cloth and perhaps a small jug of flowers
- encouraging children to try new foods, presenting one new food at a time, when they are not tired or ill
- setting a good example by sitting at the table with the children, and showing your enjoyment of the food
- never forcing children to eat new foods
- never making children finish what is on their plates, or insisting they sit at the table until they do so
- letting children eat at their own pace
- ignoring fussy behaviour and praising hearty appetites.

Food is one of the pleasures of life. Although there are fashions in eating, in the same way as there are in clothes, it would appear that a balanced diet for adults and children and eating in moderation is the healthiest option. In spite of food scares and outbreaks of food poisoning, in this country we have access to a wide range of good food and by choosing carefully we all have the ability to eat well.

✔ TEST YOURSELF

1 Name three macro-nutrients.
2 Name two micro-nutrients.
3 Why do we need to drink water?
4 Name three food groups.
5 List three advantages of breast-feeding.
6 Name three advantages of bottle-feeding.
7 When are babies weaned?
8 Name and describe two special diets.
9 How can we make food attractive to children?
10 Describe four important practices in food hygiene.
11 Name four ways of encouraging healthy eating habits in children.

GLOSSARY

By the time you have finished this chapter you should understand the meaning of the following words:

antibodies   substances found in the blood that fight infection

BSE   bovine spongiform encephalitis, a disease found in cattle that can be passed to people who eat beef

expressed breast milk   milk taken from the breast by hand or pump and given to the baby in a bottle

failure to thrive   children do not grow or gain weight as expected. There may be many causes, some of them physical or medical. It can be found in children who are abused or neglected

fibre   found in plant food. It contains no nourishment but adds bulk to the diet and helps digestion

GMF genetically modified foods, mainly plants, altered by scientists so as to produce more food and be resistant to pests. Not yet proven to be safe

hyperactivity a condition that makes children very active, and unable to concentrate

insulin hormone produced by the pancreas to control the amount of sugar released into the blood stream.

CHAPTER 6

Health and safety

This chapter includes:
- Personal health and hygiene
- Prevention of infection
- Health
- First Aid
- Maintaining a safe and healthy environment
- Glossary

KEY POINT

It is the responsibility of all childcare and education workers to make sure that young children are fit and well, and are protected from danger and disease whilst in their care.

We all need to be healthy and safe, and it is the responsibility of all childcare and education workers to make sure that young children are fit and well and are protected from danger and disease whilst in their care. You will need to be able to recognise possible safety risks (**hazards**) in many places, indoor and outside, whilst travelling in a car or walking down the road. Recognising illness quickly will let you alert parents so that medical help can be sought if necessary.

For further information on the material covered in this chapter, you could consult the following:

Dare, A. and O'Donovan, M., **Good Practice in Child Safety**, Stanley Thornes (Publishers) Ltd, 2000

Your own personal **hygiene**, as well as that of the children, is important, so that you all remain well, and do not pass on any infectious illness through

Does the sight of blood worry you? ▶

poor hygiene routines. Being calm in an emergency and having some knowledge of First Aid will give you confidence if you have to deal with an unexpected crisis.

PERSONAL HEALTH AND HYGIENE

It is particularly important for anyone caring for children to have high standards of personal hygiene, as you may have to carry out personal tasks for the children, as well as teaching them the routines and rules of hygiene.

Personal hygiene means taking good care of your body, establishing routines to wash your skin and hair, cleaning your teeth frequently, washing your hands after using the lavatory and before preparing food, wearing clean clothes, cutting finger and toenails regularly and living in a clean and pleasant environment. This is important for you and for your health and, as someone who is caring for others, you will need to promote cleanliness and establish hygiene routines in the children you will be looking after. In the workplace, it is important that you present yourself as someone who is clean and tidy, not only to avoid giving offence but as a good role model.

The chart on page 142 outlines some areas of personal health and hygiene. Tick one of the three headings against each item.

Most young children need adult help and supervision in their personal hygiene needs. Good standards of hygiene are important to prevent ill health, to increase **self-esteem** and confidence, and to be accepted by others.

Infestation

An infestation is caused by animal parasites that live on and feed from humans. Most children are likely to be affected at some time.

Head lice
Head lice are small insects that live in human hair, close to the scalp where they can bite the skin and feed on the blood. Many children are infested by coming into contact with children who are already carrying head lice. Lice like both clean and unwashed hair. They lay eggs, called nits, close to the scalp and glue the eggs firmly to the hair. You may think the child has dandruff, but if you try to move it you will find the nits are firmly fixed. The first indicator of head lice is the child scratching her head and complaining that it itches. Your supervisor will tell all the parents immediately, and suggest ways of treatment.

Many people now are unhappy with the chemical shampoos and treatments. The current method recommended by many schools is to apply a conditioner to the child's head, and use a nit comb to remove the nits and lice. Regular brushing and combing will discourage lice.

What do YOU think?
Discuss your list with others in the group. Were there many differences? What items are of particular importance when you are caring for children? Can you think of anything else that you would include in the chart on page 142?

What do YOU think?
How would you teach a four-year-old to wash her hands properly?

Personal health and hygiene

	Essential	Desirable	Optional
1. Having a shower or a bath every day			
2. Washing your hands after you have used the lavatory			
3. Cutting your nails every week			
4. Putting moisturiser on your skin			
5. Using a nail brush			
6. Washing your hair at least twice a week			
7. Washing your hands before you prepare food			
8. Taking off your make-up before you go to bed			
9. Not smoking tobacco			
10. Not drinking coffee			
11. Not drinking alcohol			
12. Not taking drugs that have not been prescribed			
13. Washing hands after handling animals			
14. Using a conditioner on your hair			
15. Using a deodorant			
16. Brushing and combing your hair			
17. Washing your feet after exercise			
18. Changing your underclothes daily			
19. Changing your outer clothes every day			
20. Cleaning your shoes			
21. Understanding food hygiene			
22. Checking your body for signs of infestation and infection			
23. Washing your clothes regularly			
24. Using the dry cleaners			
25. Changing your bed linen at least once a week			
26. Cleaning your room thoroughly once a week			
27. Protecting your skin from excessive sun			
28. Wearing appropriate shoes			
29. Covering your mouth when coughing or sneezing and disposing of dirty tissues in a hygienic manner			
30. Disposing of rubbish in an appropriate way, particularly wasted food			
31. Washing up crockery and cutlery properly			
32. Regular check-ups at the dentist			
33. Understanding the principles of safe sex			

Is there anything in this picture that is a danger to health?

Threadworms

Threadworms are small white worms that live in the bowel. They resemble small pieces of white cotton. They can often be seen in the stools when the child uses the lavatory. They come out of the bowel at night and lay their eggs around the child's bottom. This causes severe irritation and the child will scratch herself. If the fingers are then placed in the mouth, the cycle of infestation will continue.

Losing sleep will cause the child to become drowsy during the day and lack concentration. The parents of the child should seek medical advice, as the whole family will have to be treated. Apply the rules of personal hygiene strictly, encouraging careful hand-washing and **disinfect** the potty each time the child uses it. Be alert to the signs in other children.

Fleas

Fleas are small insects that jump from host to host and feed on blood. Fortunately, human fleas are rare in the UK but many children are sensitive to fleas that live on cats and dogs, and a flea bite will leave a red mark that irritates and swells. Animals need to be treated regularly to avoid this problem.

Ringworm

Ringworm is a fungus infestation that may affect the skin or nails. It is seen as a red circle with a white scaly centre. It spreads in increasing circles whilst healing in the centre. The edge is raised into small bumps. On the scalp it will result in bald patches. It causes much irritation. It must be treated by a doctor.

What illnesses can you get from cats and dogs? ▶

Scabies

Scabies is a skin infestation caused by the scabies mite, which burrows under the skin, causing severe irritation. The mites feed on the skin and lay their eggs. Characteristic lines may be seen on the skin. The child will scratch, causing redness and infection. The mites can crawl from one person to another. The child must be seen by a doctor who will prescribe a lotion to kill the mites and eggs.

CASE STUDY

Karen

Karen is enjoying her work experience in a nursery, and building good caring relationships with the children. She picks them up when they cry and cuddles them when they ask her for close contact.

In the second week of her placement, she is horrified to find that she has nits. She tells her supervisor who informs her that there are three children in the nursery who are infested with head lice. The parents have been informed.

1 Should Karen have been told?
2 Do you think that an infestation of nits is a rare or a common event in a nursery?
3 What steps should she take now to get rid of them?
4 How can she protect herself in future?

Ticks

Ticks live on animals, and feed on blood. They are often found on deer. Although rare in this country, if children have been to an area where deer roam, they are at risk from tick bites. These are very dangerous as, if untreated, they can cause Lyme's disease. The symptoms are like a bad dose of flu, but can result in brain damage. Children should be examined for tick bites whilst being bathed, and if found, medical attention should be sought immediately by the parents.

PREVENTION OF INFECTION

KEY POINT

Infection is the most common cause of illness in young children and, if frequent, can cause developmental delay and prevent growth.

Infection is caused by pathogens (disease-producing germs), such as bacteria, viruses and fungi. Infection is passed on by touch, food and water, animals, droplets in the air and through cuts and grazes. Infection is the most common cause of illness in young children and, if frequent, can cause developmental delay and prevent growth. Children can become ill very easily if they are in contact with an infectious illness. It is important that you understand how disease is spread in order to lessen children's exposure to infections.

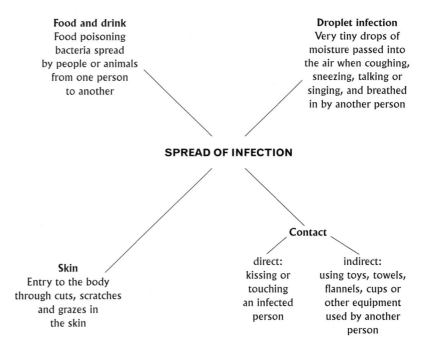

Food and drink
Food poisoning bacteria spread by people or animals from one person to another

Droplet infection
Very tiny drops of moisture passed into the air when coughing, sneezing, talking or singing, and breathed in by another person

SPREAD OF INFECTION

Skin
Entry to the body through cuts, scratches and grazes in the skin

Contact
direct: kissing or touching an infected person

indirect: using toys, towels, flannels, cups or other equipment used by another person

Infection can range from the common cold to more serious infections, such as meningitis. As you gain experience you will find it easier to diagnose the symptoms of illness. If you are caring for a child who suddenly becomes ill the parents must be contacted.

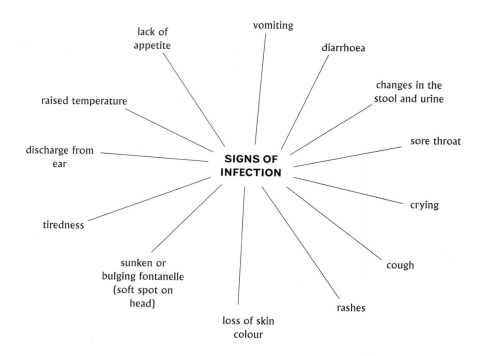

If parents let their children take part in immunisation programmes it will reduce the frequency of childhood diseases.

When you are in your work experience placement:

- make sure that all children wash their hands after using the lavatory, before eating or taking part in cooking activities, or messy play
- play your part in making sure the lavatories are always clean and that soap and paper towels are available
- the eating area should be clean, attractive and free from any spilt food. Serve snacks on a plate and clean up well after meals
- change any child who is soiled or wet at once, with tact and sensitivity. Remember your personal hygiene and use the correct procedure for disposing of nappies and soiled clothing
- regularly wash dressing-up clothes, cushion covers, toys and equipment.
- dispose of rubbish such as dirty nappies or tissues promptly and correctly
- encourage children to cover their mouths if they cough
- teach children to blow their noses with a tissue, and get rid of it correctly
- regularly clean and disinfect floors, equipment, toys and cups
- cover any open wounds on your skin or on a child's skin
- clean up any spilt blood, **faeces**, urine, or vomit with a bleach solution (one part household bleach to ten parts water). Wear disposable gloves
- soak any bloodied clothes or equipment used for First Aid in a one to ten bleach solution for five to ten minutes. Wear disposable gloves
- double wrap all waste that contains body fluids and put in plastic sacks. Check if there are particular sacks to be used.

You may well come into contact with children who have German measles (rubella). If you are a young woman, planning to have a family later in life, check that you are immune to rubella before starting the course. If you have not been immunised and you contract rubella during pregnancy, there is a risk of your baby being damaged.

Those keeping any kind of pet should know about its food and habits, and how to care for it. When you are in your work experience placement, if they have pets there, you should show children how to look after animals, feeding them and cleaning out cages. Good hygiene with pets means that:

- children must be told the importance of washing hands after handling a pet or helping to clean a cage
- children should be discouraged from kissing pets or letting pets lick their faces
- sick animals must always be seen by a vet
- disinfectant should be used to wash floors soiled with animal excreta
- animals foods and plates should be kept and washed separately from those used by humans
- puppies and kittens should be wormed when very young, and before this, children should not handle them. The animals should be wormed again at regular intervals.
- no establishment or family should have a pet that is not tolerant of young children.

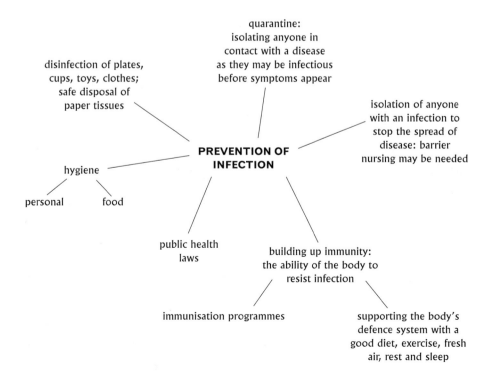

*What other animals
might you find in a
nursery or school?* ▶

HEALTH

The World Health Organisation has stated that 'health is a state of complete physical, mental and social well-being, not merely the absence of disease and infirmity'. It involves children, families and the community and is a positive goal, not just the absence of illness.

You may have a feeling that a child in your care is not very well. You need

TASK

1 What do you understand by the term 'health'?
2 List six factors that influence health.
3 How does our lifestyle affect our health?
4 List six effects of ill health.

care of the
skin and hair

suitable clothing
and footwear

health checks

healthy diet

**MAINTAINING GOOD
HEALTH IN CHILDREN**

emotional stability
and consistent care

toilet training at
appropriate age

safe environment

rest and sleep

exercise and fresh air

to be aware of the most common signs of poor health, so that you can tell your supervisor and take steps to prevent cross infection. The charts below show the most common signs of poor health and the actions to take if a child is unwell.

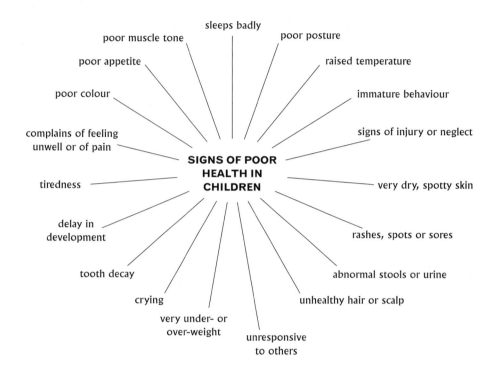

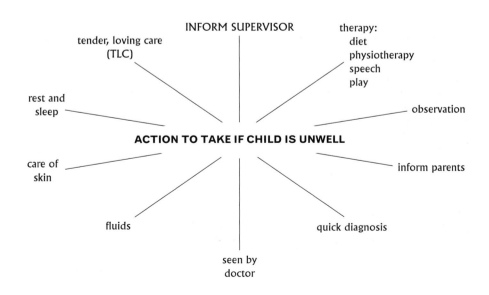

Marvin

Marvin is succeeding on his childcare and education course, in spite of absences for minor illnesses, such as colds and coughs. He attends placement two days a week and finds that he is absolutely exhausted at the end of each day. Some children seem to have continual runny noses and chesty coughs, and are still being taught the basic rules of hygiene.

Marvin is concerned, as before he started the course he rarely had any infectious illnesses, and enjoyed an active social life.

1 Why do you think Marvin is constantly ill?
2 What can he do to protect himself in the placement?
3 What other steps could Marvin take to regain his former good health?
4 Should he discuss this with anyone? If so, who?

KEY POINT

Knowing what to do in an emergency can save life and prevent further injury

FIRST AID

First Aid is the immediate action taken to treat a person who has been injured or has suddenly become ill. Knowing what to do in an emergency can save life and prevent further injury, but it is important to know your limits and do only what you are competent to do. Urgent care requires you to:

- remove the victim from the source of danger
- check breathing and give artificial respiration if necessary
- control bleeding
- place the child in the recovery position if she is unconscious
- protect other children in the setting
- call for help, giving accurate information and, if poisoning is suspected, keep any substance, such as medication or cleaning materials, that might be important in diagnosing the condition. Many hospitals now offer short First Aid sessions, which you might like to attend, before taking a full First Aid course.

Many accidents cause shock in children, and you will need to recognise the signs, which are:

- pale cold sweaty skin
- rapid pulse, becoming weaker
- shallow fast breathing
- restlessness, yawning and sighing

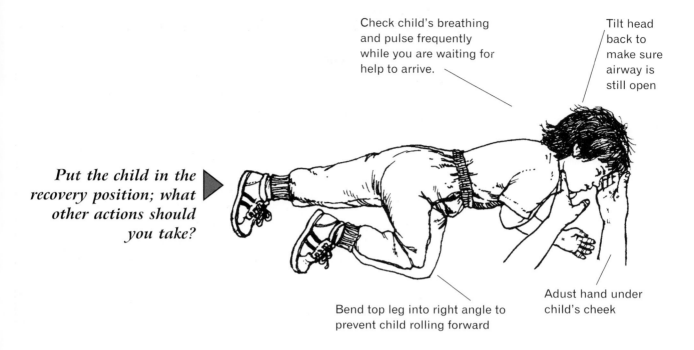

Check child's breathing and pulse frequently while you are waiting for help to arrive.

Tilt head back to make sure airway is still open

Put the child in the recovery position; what other actions should you take?

Bend top leg into right angle to prevent child rolling forward

Adust hand under child's cheek

- thirst
- loss of consciousness.

If you think one of the children is suffering from shock, you should ask your supervisor to summon medical aid.

Concussion is not always easy to recognise. After a bump to the head, a child might be concussed if there is:

- a brief loss of consciousness
- dizziness
- nausea
- mild headache
- loss of memory of events immediately before the accident.

An unconscious child who is breathing and has a pulse should be put into the recovery position to keep the airway clear by preventing choking on the tongue or vomit. Check for breathing and pulse until medical help arrives.

All establishments should provide First Aid boxes and a simple First Aid book. The box should be kept in the kitchen or bathroom, out of reach of the children. The contents need to be checked regularly and replaced as necessary. A First Aid box might contain:

- cotton wool
- bandages in several sizes
- gauze squares in several sizes
- a large triangular bandage
- crepe bandages in several sizes and lengths
- tubular gauze
- surgical spirit
- plasters in several sizes
- surgical tape
- disposable plastic gloves
- safety pin
- small mirror
- tweezers
- scissors
- thermometer.

These lists can vary considerably, depending on the requirements of the Local Education Authority or Social Services. There may be a policy not to include items such as plasters, lotions and spirits that may cause allergies in children.

Emergencies

Not all emergencies involve accidents. Other emergencies might include:

- fire
- gas leaks
- the taking away of a child
- bomb alerts
- outbreak of infectious disease
- a child going missing or getting lost
- unexpected building problems
- violent attacks
- food poisoning
- floods
- blocked drains.

When you are in your work experience you will find policies that exist to deal with some of the above emergencies.

When dealing with any emergency it is essential to keep calm. Panicking will not help you or the children. Understanding the procedures put in place to deal with emergencies and knowing on whom to call for help will lessen any further problems and protect the children. Most establishments have an incident book to record emergencies.

Name four other hazards you might find in the outside play area ▶

MAINTAINING A SAFE AND HEALTHY ENVIRONMENT

Children are the responsibility of the adults who care for them. An accident is something that happens that is not expected, and may be prevented with care and thought. Sometimes accidents occur because the carer is in a hurry, is experiencing stress due to personal problems, or is feeling tired and therefore less alert.

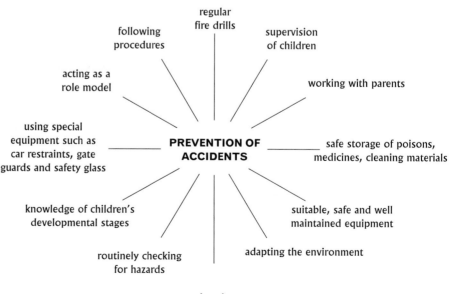

PREVENTION OF ACCIDENTS

- regular fire drills
- following procedures
- supervision of children
- acting as a role model
- working with parents
- using special equipment such as car restraints, gate guards and safety glass
- safe storage of poisons, medicines, cleaning materials
- knowledge of children's developmental stages
- suitable, safe and well maintained equipment
- routinely checking for hazards
- adapting the environment
- education

Types of accidents

The latest figures from the Royal Society for the Prevention of Accidents (ROSPA) and the Home Accident Surveillance System (HASS) show that the most serious accidents happen in the kitchen and on the stairs, and the largest number of accidents happen in the living room area.

Falls

Twenty children die as a result of falls each year, some from windows and balconies, the remainder mostly on stairs. Falls are involved in 42 per cent of all accidents. The worst injuries occur when children fall from a great height or land on something hard, sharp or hot. Most falls result from falling between two levels such as falling out of a pram or falling from a bed.

Burns and scalds

Three quarters of burns and scalds happen to children under 5. Mugs or cups of tea or coffee being knocked over cause most of the scalding injuries. Tea or coffee is still hot enough to scald fifteen minutes after being made and it is therefore not sensible to leave cups of coffee or tea around, or to sit children on your lap whilst you are drinking. Burning injuries are caused from contact with hot surfaces, such as fires or cookers, or by playing with matches.

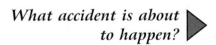

What accident is about to happen? ▶

Cuts

There has been an increase in glass related accidents, because of the fashion for patio doors, large windows and glass table tops. As many as five children might die in one year following an accident with glass. Accidents involving all types of glass account for nearly 40,000 injuries to children a year.

Poisoning

Most poisoning accidents involve medicines, followed by household products and cosmetics. 15,000 children receive in-patient treatment and 43,000 children receive out-patient treatment for poisoning every year.

Other causes

Other accidents may be caused by:

- beads or food in the ear
- dirt in the eye
- choking, mainly on food
- drowning, either in the bath or garden pond
- attacks by family pets
- road accidents involving older children.

CASE STUDY

Miranda

Miranda is 36 and works full-time. Her partner is often abroad on business. She has four children, three of whom are of school age, and a baby of 10 months, who often keeps her awake at night. She employs an au pair, aged 18, who seems to be good with the baby, but often has disputes with the older children, which Miranda has to sort out on her return home.

One evening, trying to meet the demands of all the children, Miranda and the au pair failed to hear the front door open. Nicholas, aged 5, ran over the road to greet a friend whom he saw from the window. A cyclist hit him, and hearing the commotion in the street, Miranda and the au pair ran to his aid, leaving the baby at the top of the stairs without securing the gate. The baby fell down the stairs fracturing his arm.

1 What factors contributed to the events of this evening?
2 How could the accidents have been prevented?
3 What immediate action should Miranda or the au pair have taken after this incident?

TASK

Complete this chart showing the types of accidents you think are the most common for each age group. We have filled in some of the boxes to help you get started.

Type of accident	0–1 yr	1–3 yrs	3–5 yrs	5–7 yrs	7–11 yrs	11 yrs +
Falls	Falling from a bed or sofa					
Burns and scalds						Firework injury
Cuts			Running into a glass door			
Poisoning		Drinking bleach				
Road and car accidents					Not looking when crossing the road	
Suffocation and choking			Choking on a nut			
Electrocution					Playing on a railway line	
Drowning		Falling into garden pond				

This page may be photocopied. © Stanley Thornes (Publishers) Ltd.

Accidents in the home

One child in twelve will be treated for a home accident each year. Half the children are under 4 years of age.

Making sure a home is safe would involve:

- checking each room of the house for obvious hazards
- testing and maintaining all safety equipment, such as gates and smoke alarms
- making sure that all the children's equipment, such as high chairs, pushchairs and prams are clean, have attached harnesses, and are well maintained

How would you make sure a pram was safe for a small baby?

- making sure the garden is safe, clear of poisonous plants, dangerous ponds, and uncovered sand pits. All gardening equipment should be stored safely, and not left lying around.

How many hazards can you spot in this picture?

All child care and education workers working in private homes should use the following check list.

CHECK LIST: IN THE HOME

- Check domestic and play equipment regularly for sharp edges, splinters, and loose pieces. Do not give children under three small playthings, such as marbles or small Lego pieces.
- Toys and equipment should be bought from reputable shops, and not from street markets. Look at the label, and check for the **Kite mark**.
- Make sure the following objects are kept out of sight and out of reach of children:
  - medicines and tablets, which must be kept locked in a high cupboard
  - matches
  - sharp objects, such as knives and razor blades
  - plastic bags
  - household cleaners and chemicals
  - alcohol
  - cigarettes.
- Make sure that safety gates for stairs or doorways are secure.
- Never use baby walkers as there have been serious accidents when using these.
- Do not use pillows or duvets for any child under 18 months.
- Always supervise children in the kitchen where there are many hazards. You must be sure to:
  - turn saucepan handles away from the edge of the stove
  - keep all hot and sharp objects away from the edge of units
  - use short, coiled flexes on electrical equipment

- keep the doors to washing machines, tumble dryers and freezers shut
- avoid using tablecloths that hang down.
- Use a harness fitted to the high chair and see that it is always secured when in use.
- Always supervise children when they are eating or drinking and never leave a baby propped up with a bottle.
- Avoid giving nuts or hard boiled sweets to children.
- Avoid anything around babies' necks, such as anorak strings, dummies on strings, and ribbons on hats.
- Highlight large glass doors with stickers.
- Make sure that the doors leading to cellar, balcony and any unsupervised outside area are kept shut.
- Do not leave a hot drink unattended, and never sit a child on your lap while drinking something hot.

Make sure outside areas are safe. Use the following check list.

- Keep garage and shed doors locked, and keep all equipment and materials locked away out of sight and out of reach of children.
- Secure garden gates and fences so that children cannot get out and people and animals cannot get in.
- Keep children away from water, unless closely supervised.
- Cover sand pits when not in use to avoid soiling by animals.
- Identify poisonous plants and make sure that the children do not go near them. If possible, dig them up.
- Check all outdoor play equipment such as slides and climbing frames regularly for safety.
- Avoid trailing clothes lines.
- Supervise animals when children are in the garden, and put a cat net over a baby's pram.

TASK

You are caring for a six-month-old baby and an active six-year old.
1 Which hazards in the house and in the garden are particularly dangerous for each age group?
2 What safety equipment might you use to prevent these accidents happening?

Name two poisonous plants ▶

KEY POINT

Part of your role is to teach children about dangers, and how to protect themselves.

What do YOU think?

In your group, discuss the best way to teach children under 5 years about the dangers of fire and water.

TASK

Plan a picnic in your local park, with children aged 1, 3 and 6.
What would it be essential to have with you so as to make sure the children were protected and you are prepared for any emergency?

Always be alert to danger, and aware that children need protection. A knowledge of children's development, for example understanding that a small baby is unable to run out of the house, and a child of 10 would not be seriously hurt if she fell off her bed, should allow you to foresee some possible hazards and risks. Understanding a child's personality will help you to predict how she will react to a situation. Part of your role is to teach children about dangers, and how to protect themselves.

Starting work experience

Under the 1974 Health and Safety at Work Act, employers have a duty to provide healthy and safe working conditions. You will, at all times, be supervised during your work experience, but nevertheless be expected to play a part in establishing a healthy and safe environment for the children, colleagues, and yourself. When you start your work experience you need to discover the following information as soon as possible.

CHECK LIST: FIRE

What should you do if a fire breaks out?
Where are the fire alarms?
What type of alarm is used?
How are the children taken from the building?
What exits are used? Under what circumstances?
Where do you meet outside the building?
Where are the registers kept? The children's names need to be checked when everyone is out of the building.
How often do you have a fire practice?
There should be regular fire drills to make sure everyone knows what to do in the event of a fire.

CHECK LIST: ACCIDENTS

What should you do if there is an accident?
What is the policy for recording both minor and major accidents?
Who is responsible for informing the parent/carer of any accident?
Where are the First Aid boxes kept?
Who is responsible for checking the contents?
How often is this done, and is the checking recorded?
What do the First Aid boxes contain?
Do any of the dressings have an expiry date on them?
Who has a First Aid qualification?
Who is the named person to take charge in the event of an accident?
Where is the nearest telephone?

Every accident, however slight, should be reported and recorded in the accident book. Page 162 shows an example of an accident sheet. Ask your supervisor if you can look at the book. You will see that very full details are recorded. This information is necessary as some seemingly minor accidents can result in more serious concerns, and accurate recording can be vital. The accident book may also show hazards that occur regularly. Remember too that parents must be informed of any injury, however slight it may seem and should be asked to sign the accident form.

CASE STUDY

Jordan

Jordan, aged five, chased one of his friends into the lavatory. As he was not taking care, and the floor was wet, he slipped and banged his face against a pipe. He loosened a top front tooth and cut his lip. He was shaken but, as it was playtime, decided to finish his game of 'chase' before telling an adult.

1 Could this accident have been prevented?
2 Do you think Jordan was hurt badly?
3 What would be the first thing the adult should do?

CHECK LIST: OTHER ESSENTIAL INFORMATION

How is medicine stored and given to children? (Not all establishments are prepared to accept this responsibility.)
Do any of the doors exit on to a main road?
Is there a procedure for making sure children cannot get to outside areas without supervision?
Find out the procedure for dealing with the outbreak of infection.
Find out how the outside play area is set up.
Find out how risks from falls and collisions are reduced in and out of doors.

The environment

All children are entitled to a clean, safe, pleasant, caring environment. As a student, you can contribute to this by being aware of hazards. If you have identified a problem or hazard discuss it with your supervisor as soon as possible.

An example of an accident notification form

Parkside School
Accident Notification

Child's Name

Date _ _ _ _ _ _ _ **Time** _ _ _ _ _ _ **of accident**

Place of accident _

Incident –

Staff present

Action taken

Parent informed at the time of accident: ☐ Yes ☐ No

Staff signature

Parent/carer signature

CHECK LIST: HAZARDS

Are any toys or items of equipment damaged or faulty?

Is all the furniture safe and secure?

Are there any electrical points uncovered, or any trailing wires?

Are all electric appliances fitted by trained electricians, with the correct fuses and plugs, and checked on a yearly basis?

Are cleaning substances kept locked away, out of the reach of children?

Are all cleaning products and disinfectants kept in their original containers with contents clearly labelled?

Are all medicines kept locked away, out of the reach of children?

Are there hidden areas outside, where children cannot be seen?

Are electric kettles, and/or mugs of hot fluid used within the reach of the children?

Are there any poisonous plants inside or outside the establishment?

Are all pets in a healthy condition?

Are plastic bags kept out of the reach of children?

Are there any obstructions in corridors and doorways?

Are fire doors left closed, as they should be?

Is there any rubbish or paper lying around?

Is the outdoor play equipment safe?

All safety equipment should meet British Standards and carry the appropriate British Standard mark. All new equipment should meet the British Standard/European CE Safety Standard. Manufacturers' instructions and guidelines for any piece of safety equipment should be kept where they can be referred to easily. All equipment must be used according to the manufacturers' guidelines.

How to maintain a safe and healthy environment

- The room should be aired regularly, and a temperature of 20°C should be maintained.
- Small areas of the room should not become overcrowded or cluttered.
- Organise activities so that noise levels are controlled.
- There should be a clean, soft area where children can rest on pillows or rugs.
- Shut gates and doors properly behind you.
- Use stair gates where appropriate.
- Wear sensible shoes with flat heels for work.
- Wipe spills of water or food at once, and do not allow the children to walk on floors that have been recently washed in case they slip.
- Be careful not to lift anything that is too heavy for you, or allow the children to do so.
- Some activities in the establishment are potentially dangerous. Children working with wood, or cooking, should be closely supervised at all times. With cooking, fire is an obvious hazard. Make sure gas taps are switched

TASK

Fire guards, safety film for glass and smoke alarms are three examples of safety equipment and materials. Make a list of other equipment and materials that are available to make a home or workplace safe for young children.

off, and do not leave tea towels or matches lying around. Use gloves to lift pans, and turn handles away from the front of stoves. Discuss these activities thoroughly with your supervisor beforehand, so that you are alerted to all the risks.

LOW FLAMMABILITY TO
BS 5722

Kite mark – the goods have been made to the correct British Standard

Labels which show that equipment meets safety standards ▶

BEAB Mark of Safety – The goods meet government safety regulations for domestic electrical appliances (BEAB = British Electrotechnical Approvals Board)

E mark – the goods comply with European regulations

- Children should always work and play in well-lit areas.
- Supervise children in outside play areas, and do not allow them to talk to strangers.
- Never allow a child to go home with a person you do not know, until you have checked with your supervisor.

Passive smoking is now acknowledged to be a serious health risk to babies, children and adults. Smoking is no longer allowed in many public places and in all schools and nurseries. If you are a smoker and cannot give it up you will find it difficult getting a job working with children.

All parent/carers want their children to be safe and healthy at all times. This does not happen just by chance, and it takes a great deal of effort to make sure that there are no hazards in the home, garden, nursery and school. Children need to be protected against infection and infestation and care should be taken to reduce accidents and illness.

What do YOU think?
Why will there be rules laid down for collecting children in your work experience placement?

✓ TEST YOURSELF

1   List six important areas of personal hygiene that you should encourage in children.
2   Name three signs of shock in children.
3   Describe four hazards in the outdoor play area.
4   List four emergencies where action needs to be taken.
5   Name four types of accidents.
6   List eight essential items in a First Aid box.
7   List four signs of poor health.
8   List three ways infection is spread.

GLOSSARY

By the time you have finished this chapter you should understand the meaning of the following words:

disinfect	to destroy germs, usually by the use of chemicals. Disinfectant is harmful to body tissue. Boiling also destroys germs
faeces	bodily waste
hazards	dangers, such as long flexes on kettles and splinters in wooden blocks, that may cause accidents.
health promotion	the process of encouraging people to control and improve their health

hygiene concerned with the maintenance of health by promoting clean and healthy practices and routines

infestation invasion of parasites living on or in a human host, such as head lice and threadworms

Kite mark the official mark of quality and reliability on equipment approved by the British Standards Institute

passive smoking being in a smoky atmosphere and having to breathe in other people's smoke

posture a position of the limbs or parts of the body

self-esteem confidence in oneself as a worthwhile person. This is essential to learning and achievement.

CHAPTER 7

The needs of children

This chapter includes:

- Routines
- The needs of the young baby
- Routine care
- Physical care routines for toddlers and young children
- Equipment for the newborn
- Clothing
- Glossary

When working with children, you must understand that there are many needs that have to be met before children are able to grow and develop satisfactorily. You need to learn about development, growth, care and education. Children belong to many different groups, with various values, religions, and approaches to child-rearing.

All children need love and security, stimulation and education, routine physical care and the right to protection. You need to be aware of children's needs, so that together with your knowledge of child development, you will be able to encourage the children's maximum growth and development.

For further information on the material covered in this chapter, you could consult the following:

Dare, A. and O'Donovan, M., ***A Practical Guide to Working with Babies***, Stanley Thornes (Publishers) Ltd, 1998

Beaver, M., Brewster, J., Jones, P., Keene, A., Neaum, S. and Tallack, J., ***Babies and Young Children, Book 2, 2nd edition: Early Years Care and Education***, Stanley Thornes (Publishers) Ltd, 1999

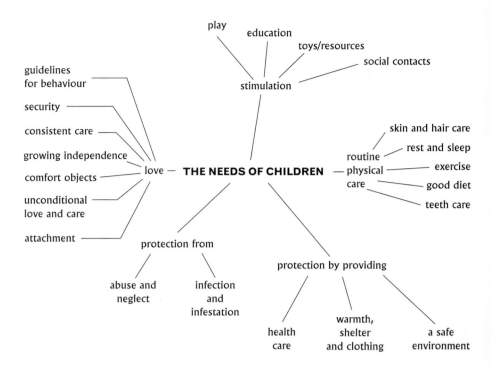

ROUTINES

During your work experience placement you will become aware of the routines carried out each day. Routines refer to regular events, organised and planned within the day, such as hygiene practices, mealtimes, sleep times, exercise and play, and will vary from placement to placement. Much depends on the ages and the number of the children, the type of placement and the views of the team. For example, in a nursery one of the routines might well be rest time for the babies. This would obviously not take place in a school, but the literacy hour would be one of the routines that takes place every day with the five to eleven year olds.

Ideally, routines should follow the same pattern each day, so that the young child feels secure by knowing what to expect. A childcare and education worker who is constantly changing the daily routines, will find the children becoming cross or even distressed. For this reason, your supervisor will need to arrange the routines carefully, allowing enough time for each one. A typical day can be very busy, and there needs to be time built in for unexpected events and for giving 'quality time' to individual children.

THE NEEDS OF THE YOUNG BABY

Any parent who has more than one child will tell you that all babies are different – they have their own personalities, their own ways of behaving

> ## TASK
>
> Think about all your own routines such as your hair care, or exercise. Devise a weekly and monthly chart, showing your personal routines.

and their own needs and wants right from the start. If there are babies in your work experience placement, you will soon find out that some cry more than others, some sleep more than others and some are more sociable than others.

Handling the baby

Children learn about the world around them through the senses: touch, sight, hearing, smell and taste. A newborn baby will very quickly recognise her mother by using all her senses. Because of this, the way a stranger handles a baby immediately communicates either a feeling of security or of threat. You need to be responsive, warm and caring, and this will show in the way you hold and feed a baby.

You should develop a quiet, calm manner when looking after a baby, and make eye contact before attempting to pick her up. Sitting on the floor with very young children obviously shows you understand how threatened they might feel with a stranger towering over them, and you are demonstrating a sensitive approach. Changing a baby's nappy, brushing her hair or helping her to use the toilet are all intimate activities, and preferably should not be carried out by you until you know the child well.

At what age do you think you should aim to make eye contact with a baby?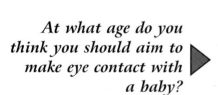

Parents should feel confident that their child will be cuddled and reassured when they are not there. She will feel safe and secure if her needs are met swiftly and responsively. A happy personality and a smiling face are great strengths in a child care and education worker, as unhappiness will communicate itself very quickly to children.

Crying

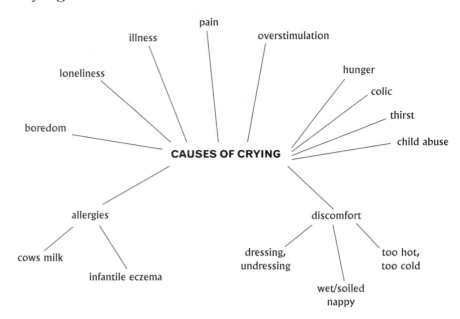

KEY POINT

A baby should never to be left to cry, as it is impossible to 'spoil' a baby by picking her up.

Babies cry because they are hungry, bored, in pain, lonely, cold or hot, or ill. Mothers very quickly learn to recognise the different types of cry, and respond to the differing needs of the baby. You will also soon learn by the cry what need is being communicated and respond appropriately. A baby should never to be left to cry, as it is impossible to 'spoil' a baby by picking her up. Babies vary a great deal in their need to be cuddled and comforted. Some babies seem to enjoy their own company, whilst others prefer frequent human contact. Like feeding, this is an area where the baby will dictate her needs, and the adult will do his or her best to respond suitably.

What do YOU think?

If a baby's crying is ignored what long-term effect might there be on her emotional development?

How long should you leave a baby to cry? ▶

Sharon

Sharon is worried. Her friend Jane, who lives alone, has a 1-month-old baby who seems to be crying most of the time. Instead of picking up the baby and comforting her, Jane ignores her, and leaves the room.

1 Why does this upset Sharon?
2 What might Sharon say to Jane?
3 How might this affect the baby in the long term?
4 What outside sources of help are there for Jane?
5 What could be the reason for Jane leaving the room?

ROUTINE CARE

In the first few months of a baby's life certain routines will have been established. For example, she might be bathed in the morning or in the evening, every day or alternate days. It will have been decided what nappies to use and how frequently to change the baby, what is used to clean her, and how to dispose of the nappies.

Care of the skin

There are some very common skin conditions that are not infectious but nevertheless need careful handling. A trained childcare and education worker will have been taught how to cope with these. To prevent cradle cap (a crusty scab all over the scalp), heat rash and nappy rash, the carer should:

- wash the baby's hair only once or twice a week and rinse it very thoroughly
- look out for any crust on the scalp, and apply olive oil to the crust, washing it off after a few hours
- not allow the baby to become too hot by overdressing her, or leaving her in a hot room with a great many bed coverings
- change her nappy frequently and wash her bottom at each change
- be aware that creams and washing powders can cause allergies
- expose the baby's skin to air at regular intervals during the day.

Bathtime

Bathing a baby should be an enjoyable, rewarding and relaxing time, but there are dangers and potential hazards. A special baby bath can be used for the first few months, or the baby can be bathed in a large bowl kept for the purpose.

What hazards are there in bathing a baby? ▶

Once the baby is bathed in the family bath, it is important that:

- the bath should not be too full
- the cold tap should be run before the hot tap
- the temperature of the water should be checked before putting the baby into the bath
- a non-slip mat should be put in the bath
- the baby should be put in at the end without the taps
- the room should not be cold
- all equipment should be gathered together before the bath
- the baby should never be left alone in the bath.

Bathtime should be fun and an opportunity for the baby to splash, make bubbles, and play with bath toys. She will enjoy the sensation of the warm water against her skin and the freedom of playing without clothes on. If the baby is nervous of the water and becomes upset at bathtime, it is better for her to go without bathing for a while until she is ready to enjoy it than to risk forcing the issue that could lead to a permanent fear of water.

Sleep

TASK

What signs do you look for to show you that a baby is tired and needs to be put into her cot?

Sleeping patterns vary considerably in babies – and, of course, they change as they get older. Your supervisor will find out from the parents the baby's sleeping pattern, and understand the importance of allowing the baby to sleep when she wants to, and not when it is most convenient for the placement.

In your work experience placement, each baby should have her own cot, to prevent infection being spread, and to make sure that the baby can go in the cot whenever she needs to sleep. You will probably want to check on her once or twice during her sleep.

You need to understand the importance of placing a baby on her back to sleep to reduce the risk of Sudden Infant Death Syndrome (cot death). In the past, many babies have died suddenly and without any obvious reason. We now know that by following certain guidelines, the number of cot deaths have fallen. These safety **factors** include:

- cots and prams should meet British Standard Institute safety regulations displaying the Kite marks
- the mattress should be firm and well fitting
- the baby should be placed in the crib or cot with her feet near the end ('feet-to-foot' rule)
- She should never be allowed to overheat by using too many blankets
- She should not be put down to sleep wearing anything with a string or ribbon round her neck
- cot bumpers, pillows and duvets should not be used, as there could be a potential risk of suffocation.

The baby is placed in the correct position in the cot; what else can you do that will help to keep the baby safe?

Health

Prevention of infection

Small babies pick up infections easily, and anyone looking after a baby needs to be aware of this and to be careful when sterilising feeding equipment, making up formula, changing nappies and bathing the baby. Personal hygiene is important, and you must:

- wash hands before preparing food and after using the lavatory
- dispose of dirty tissues and nappies carefully
- cover any cuts on your hands.
- keep the baby's feeding equipment clean and sterilised
- keep rooms clean and well ventilated
- change cot linen regularly or after any accident.

For a very small baby, crowds and over-heated rooms bring the risk of exposure to infection and you will have to be very careful about her environment. As she grows older she will become more able to cope with exposure to germs.

Illness develops faster in a baby than in an older child, and the disease can progress quickly, in some cases becoming life threatening. If you are at all concerned about a baby, you need to discuss this with your supervisor, so that she can contact the parents as soon as possible. Signs to cause concern include:

- a refusal to feed over several feeds
- a rise or fall in body temperature
- noisy breathing and difficulty in taking a breath
- a **convulsion** or fit
- excessive crying that continues despite cuddles and feeds
- a sunken or bulging anterior **fontanelle** (the soft spot on the top of the head)
- a rash
- a persistent cough
- discharge from the ears
- the baby pulling on the ears and crying
- changes in the stools or urine
- a very quiet, pale baby, difficult to wake up, and refusing to feed
- vomiting and diarrhoea
- the baby being very 'floppy'.

Food and nutrition

The giving of food and nourishment is a key part in any relationship with babies. Parents will have their own ideas about how they wish their baby to be fed, when to wean from milk to solids and what type of foods they wish you to offer her. When feeding a baby, make sure that you are holding her close, maintaining eye contact, talking to the baby, and showing an understanding of how to feed and interact with a baby.

> **KEY POINT**
>
> **When feeding a baby, make sure that you are holding her close, maintaining eye contact, talking to the baby, and showing an understanding of how to feed and interact with a baby.**

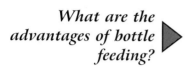

What are the advantages of bottle feeding?

Weaning

Most babies can gradually be introduced to solid food at around 4 months and parents are generally advised to follow the baby's lead, starting to offer baby rice or pureed vegetables when she appears to need more than milk alone. Weaning should not start too early, but if it is left too late it can affect the baby's development.

All mealtimes, especially those for a baby, should take place in a quiet, calm atmosphere, and the baby should be encouraged to enjoy new tastes without ever forcing them upon her.

Play with babies

Babies start to learn and develop from the moment they are conceived. Babies who are very active in the womb often respond to a particular piece of music. It does not have to be classical, just something the mother enjoys. If this is played to a cross baby after the birth, she will usually become calm and go off to sleep. It has been suggested that twins and other multiple births appear to communicate with each other before they are born.

Newborn babies are soon able to recognise the smell, taste, voice, feel and face of the mother and will respond to cuddles and soothing words. In the first few weeks the baby will have received the stimulation she requires through gentle handling and stroking, being spoken to in a soft voice and being fed on demand. As routines become established, there are more opportunities to talk to and play with the baby when feeding, bathing and changing nappies. **Siblings** will enjoy joining in the play.

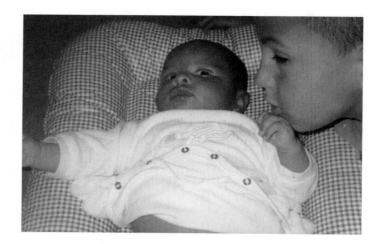

Should you ask siblings to help care for a newborn baby? ▶

There are some safety factors that need to be thought about when providing toys and equipment for babies. You need to make sure that:

- all toys and equipment are clean and are washable to avoid infection
- all toys and equipment are hard wearing so as to avoid accidents from broken edges
- you avoid using pillows and cushions and make sure any plastic bags are stored out of the baby's reach as small babies are easily suffocated
- anything with strings is not near the baby as, if the string becomes wrapped around the neck or other parts of body, the blood supply could be cut off, or the child could be hanged
- there are no heavy toys or objects near the baby
- you always use a harness when the baby is in the pram, or high chair
- you avoid small items that the baby might swallow or choke on.

What three senses are stimulated by this activity? ▶

PHYSICAL CARE ROUTINES FOR TODDLERS AND YOUNG CHILDREN

These include skin and hair care, sleep and rest, exercise, mealtimes, care of the teeth, and hygiene practices, such as hand-washing and toileting. Most small children need adult help and supervision in their personal care needs. Good standards of care are important to prevent ill-health, to increase self-confidence and gain acceptance by other children. The eventual goal is for the children to become independent and care for all their physical needs themselves.

Skin and hair care

The skin has many important functions, including:

- preventing injury to the internal organs of the body
- preventing infection entering the body
- awareness of hot and cold, hard and soft sensations
- producing oil to keep the hair soft, and keep the skin soft and flexible
- controlling the body temperature
- disposing of waste products from the body in sweat
- a role in producing vitamin D through exposure to sunlight, which is important for healthy bone growth.

Too much cleaning of the skin, particularly by scrubbing, removes the **sebum** (oil) and may make the skin dry and cracked.

Childcare and education workers should:

- make sure that children wash their hands and faces before and after handling and eating food
- make sure that children wash their hands after using the lavatory and after messy play
- observe the skin for any rashes or sores
- play a part in moisturising the skin of black children, taking advice from parents
- protect the skin of all children from excessive exposure to the sun, using hats, sun block or high factor sun cream.

Hair varies in colour, texture and style. There can be strong religious and cultural practices linked with care of the hair. Rastafarians, for example, will have long strands of braided hair, tied together. The girls will cover the hair with a scarf and the boys with a hat.

Sleep and rest

Sleep allows the body to rest and recover, so it is important that children are encouraged to rest after energetic physical exercise. Sleep consists of deep relaxing sleep and rapid eye movement (REM) sleep, when we dream.

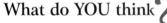

What do YOU think?

In what religions is hair of significance? Why do you think this is?

TASK

Sit with a friend and brush his or her hair, first roughly, not looking, as if your thoughts are somewhere else. Then repeat gently. Change places with your friend and then discuss how you both felt.

TASK

Write down:
1 How might you prepare children for their rest?
2 What particular strategies might you use?
3 Why do you think some parents find it difficult to get children to bed at night?

It is thought that children use REM sleep to make sense of their day, and if they are woken at this time they may become drowsy and confused.

Like adults, children appear to need different amounts of sleep. It is important to find out the sleep routines of babies and children from their parents and efforts should be made to follow this routine. It should be remembered that as the child is having a different and possibly busier day, she might require a rest even if this is against the wishes of the parents, and her sleep needs should be discussed with them.

Some children need to unwind and relax before they are able to sleep, and may need a comfort object, such as a teddy or a piece of blanket, to take with them for their rest. Even if children do not sleep during the day, there should still be a quiet period when they can look at books or just have a cuddle.

Exercise and fresh air

All children need fresh air and the chance to run around during the day. This will:

- increase their oxygen intake
- reduce their exposure to germs and the risk of infection
- increase their exposure to sunlight, for the production of vitamin D
- develop physical skills and co-ordination
- improve **muscle tone** and strengthen muscles
- burn up body fat
- enable them to sleep better
- improve their appetite.

Does your local park have a children's play area? ▶

TASK

Recent studies have shown that today's children are eating less but growing fatter than the last generation. What reasons might parents give for not encouraging their children to take more exercise?

Making sure children exercise every day will help them to establish this as a habit for life and may prevent future heart disease and obesity. Access to a garden is obviously a great help in promoting fresh air and exercise, but even without one, it is possible to take the children to a park or playground regularly. Older children will enjoy many kinds of physical exercise, from swimming and team games to canoeing and gymnastics.

CASE STUDY

Geraldine

Geraldine goes with a group of students from her course on an activity weekend. She enjoys the swimming and the canoeing, but finds it difficult to take part in team games as she gets out of breath very easily. She feels unhappy, overweight and very unfit. She is going on a skiing holiday soon, and is worried that she may not cope.

1 What steps can Geraldine take to make sure she enjoys her holiday?
2 Why is it important to be fit and active when working with young children?

Care of the teeth

Chidcare and education workers play a part in encouraging good dental hygiene. They might:

• encourage children to brush their teeth after meals with a fluoride tooth-paste and using their own brush
• provide a healthy diet, low in sugar, high in vitamins and calcium
• avoid giving sweet drinks, especially in a bottle or on a dummy
• restrict giving sweets to children
• avoid sweet snacks between meals
• provide food such as apples, carrots and brown bread, that has to be chewed.

One of the children may have a dentist appointment in the near future. In partnership with the parents, prepare her carefully, discussing what is likely to happen, perhaps finding a book at the library about visiting the dentist. If you are nervous at the dentist, be careful not to pass any of your fears and anxieties on to any child.

Care of the feet

The bones in the foot are very soft, and can easily become deformed if shoes and socks do not fit correctly. Babies do not need shoes until they are walking outside the home, when they are needed for safety and warmth. Care must be taken to make sure that the feet in Baby-Gros are not too tight and, if socks are worn in the house in cold weather, they should not constrict the foot, and should have non-slip soles as floors can be slippery and dangerous. Stretch socks should be avoided.

Children's feet grow very quickly and a trained shoe fitter should measure the length and width of the foot every three months. Shoes should have an adjustable fastener: for example, a buckle, laces or Velcro. They should be of a natural material, such as leather. Constant wearing of wellingtons or other plastic or rubber shoes make the feet sweat and do not allow the feet to 'breathe'.

Feet should be washed regularly and dried well, particularly between the toes. Athlete's foot (a fungal infection) and veruccas (warts) should be treated immediately. Apart from being painful and irritating these conditions are easily spread. Well-fitting shoes will prevent any blisters or corns forming on the feet.

Toilet training

There are many different theories and methods of toilet training, and child care and educution workers will need to work closely with the parents, to be successful.

To begin with, the child must be aware of the need to use the toilet or potty. Toddlers may know when they are soiled or wet, but are not yet able to realise that they need the potty. They must have enough language to tell their carer that they need to go to the lavatory. Carers should be relaxed and not show disapproval about accidents that will certainly happen. Watching other children or adults use the lavatory will help the child to understand what to do. Pressurising the child too much at an early age can put the child off the idea completely. Becoming dry and clean is easier in warm weather when children can run around without nappies or pants. They can become aware of what is happening when they pass water or have their bowels open.

Once a child is trained, she may still need reminding to use the lavatory, particularly before going to sleep or going out. Accidents can still happen, and you should ignore them, reassuring the child and putting her at ease. Keep some spare pants available.

The needs of the school-age child

School-age children become increasingly independent and the influence of school and their peer group becomes more and more important. While still settling in to school, they may become tired because of the extra long day and the need to concentrate more. They are expected to be more

> **CASE STUDY**
>
> ### Emma
>
> Emma is placed in an Infant School for her work experience. One day, during story time, Jeffrey puts his hand up and asks to go to the lavatory. He leaves the class quickly. When he does not return within ten minutes Emma is asked to see if he is all right. She finds him crying on the lavatory floor. His jeans are soaking wet. He tells her that he could not undo the button of his jeans as it was so tight.
>
> 1 What is the first thing Emma should do?
> 2 What might she do next?
> 3 How might the school try to stop this happening in the future?

independent, taking themselves to the lavatory and dressing undressing for PE. Some children might react by becoming 'babyish' at home, needing help with dressing and toilet needs. This is just a phase, and will soon pass.

At 5 years of age, a child begins to have a world outside her home life. She starts to make her own friends and develop new interests – sometimes ones that her parents do not share. She understands that her parents do not know exactly what has been happening during the day and that it is possible to keep secrets from them.

She may start activities away from home, such as Brownies, music and swimming lessons and sports coaching. She will occasionally spend the night away from home with friends or relations.

From about the age of 8, there is a need for privacy; a child can expect the family to knock before entering her room and she should be allowed to lock the bathroom door. She is developing awareness of the needs of other people, and has more understanding of events within the family. She can cope with all her physical care needs, but will sometimes need help with her homework. She needs her parents and carers to confide her hopes and fears in.

A child's circle of friends will become increasingly important to her as she grows up and her regard for their opinion will start to replace her wish to always please adults.

Children who have a busy day at school need to have their routine firmly structured. Going to bed at a reasonable time, dressing themselves as quickly and efficiently as they can manage, having time to eat a nourishing breakfast, cleaning teeth and combing hair, and being ready on time all takes practice.

What games did you play when you were a junior? ▶

A school-age child appears to be growing up fast but she is still a child, and needs **nurture**. She may have different priorities now, but will continue to want affection and attention.

EQUIPMENT FOR THE NEWBORN

Having a baby is very expensive, but some items of equipment are absolutely essential and should reach required safety standards. Any item borrowed or bought second hand needs to be carefully checked.

For sleeping

A tiny baby can sleep almost anywhere, in a Moses basket, a crib or in the pram. It will not be long before he becomes too big to sleep anywhere but in a cot. This should be sturdy, with bars no more than 7 centimetres apart, and with a waterproof safety mattress that fits the frame, preferably with the option of a high or low position within the cot. Cots with drop sides should have child-proof safety catches.

Duvets and pillows should not be used until the baby is at least 18 months, as they may cause the baby to overheat, and they could cause suffocation. Light blankets and sheets should be used and these can be adjusted according to the temperature.

Remember a baby placed outside in a pram might lose heat quickly on a cold day, and needs to be well wrapped up and not left outside for too long.

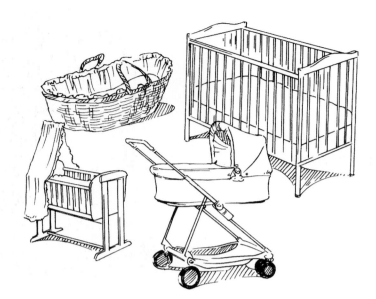

How would you decide which is the most suitable for a baby?

Some parents find it reassuring to fit baby alarms, so that they can hear if the baby cries, and be immediately aware of any distress.

For going out

Babies may be taken for outings:

- in the car
- in a pram
- in a carrying sling
- in a push chair.

All equipment should be of a good standard, kept clean and well maintained. It should carry the British Standard Kite mark, or the European Regulations mark.

All babies and children should be restrained in a special car seat, even if travelling very short distances, and should never be carried on an adult's lap. The very young baby is restrained in a rear-facing seat that supports the baby safely and comfortably.

Many babies fall asleep when in the car. These seats have a handle so that the baby can be carried in to the house without disturbing her. When the baby is about 9 months, a fixed forward-facing car seat should be fitted. All seats should also have harnesses that secure the baby in the seat.

Taking the baby out for a walk is a stimulating experience for her, and she will benefit greatly from the fresh air. She can either be taken out in a pram or a pushchair. Which one is chosen might depend on where the family lives.

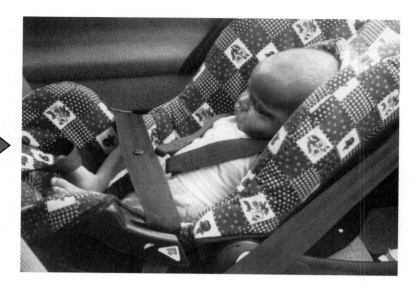

Why should children be restrained in cars? ▶

It is easier to use a pram in a house than in a third floor flat, as prams are much heavier to manoeuvre up the stairs. Harnesses must be used in the pram and the pushchair to prevent the baby falling out and hurting himself. Both must be kept clean, and the brakes checked regularly.

Which would you choose for a baby? ▶

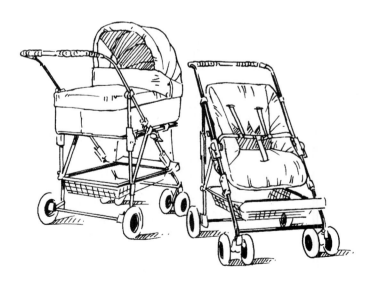

Small babies are often carried in slings by their parents. This allows their hands to be free, and is useful when going shopping. The motion and the closeness to the parent is soothing for many babies, particularly those who are premature. Care must be taken to avoid falls as the baby is vulnerable when being carried like this. People with back problems should not carry a heavy baby in a sling.

Indoor equipment

Little of this equipment is essential for the newborn baby, but is enjoyable for her as she grows older. It is possible to buy:

- a bouncing cradle – a fabric seat used for the first 6 months that allows a baby to exercise and look at her environment
- a baby bouncer – a fabric seat and harness fastened by elasticised straps to the top door frame, that allows the baby to bounce on her toes
- an electric swing – a padded seat and harness that can be set to go slower or faster, and soothes a restless baby into taking a rest
- an activity centre – a frame that is placed over a baby lying on the floor, with attractive rattles and knobs to grasp, that entertains and stimulates the baby to exercise and to reach out and grasp.

Would you choose one of these for a baby? ▶

To prevent cross infection, it is useful to have a changing mat or table.

From 7 or 8 months the baby will need a chair with a harness that allows her to eat at the table with the rest of the family. There are several types available. From about 1 year, a child will be able to use a booster seat placed on an ordinary dining chair. These chairs need to be kept clean and wiped over each time the child has finished eating.

Even the fully breast-fed baby will need a bottle from time to time, for water, for expressed breast milk or diluted fruit juices. The bottle-fed baby will need eight to ten bottles. All bottles will need to be sterilised in a sterilising unit or a large plastic box to prevent infection.

For bathing

A special baby bath is not essential as a large washing up bowl may be used until the baby is large enough at 6 months to use the family bath. A storage box is useful in which to keep all the baby's toiletries.

CLOTHING

Clothing is necessary to keep warm and to protect the body from infestations and injury. Depending on the climate and the season, the clothes you wear will help you to be comfortable and to move freely.

Clothing for the newborn baby

The newborn baby in a centrally heated home, will need:

- 4–6 vests that fasten between the legs, to stop vests from riding up
- 4– 6 Baby-Gros
- nappies.

The newborn baby living in a cold house, will also need:

- 4 – 6 cardigans
- bootees
- mittens
- hats
- a shawl.

All babies will need outdoor clothes. Depending on the season, these would include:

- a coat
- a quilted jacket
- a snow-suit
- woollen hats and mittens
- a sun hat
- socks.

Always keep safety in mind. However attractive some clothes may be, there can be hazards involved, such as:

- ribbons and ties
- loose threads in mittens and booties, that can cut the blood supply to fingers and toes
- buttons that can choke the baby if swallowed
- Baby-Gros where the foot has become too small, and may damage the baby's feet
- clothes without a flame retardant finish.

TASK

It is a bright, warm, sunny summer's day. How would you dress a baby of 6 months, so that she was fully protected?

What do YOU think?

What are the advantages and disadvantages of children wearing school uniform?

KEY POINT

A child who knows she is loved and valued and treated with respect will develop confidence and enjoy the company of others.

Choose clothes that are easy to wash and have some natural fibre in the material. Clothing made from artificial material, such as nylon, can be cold and clammy and can cause overheating in a baby. Stretch clothing, particularly with raglan sleeves, makes dressing and undressing much easier.

Most parents find that the baby grows so quickly, the clothes do not become worn out, and some may never be worn at all, such as clothing given to the new baby that is not suitable for the time of the year.

The toddler

As the child becomes mobile, she should be dressed in clothes that allow comfort and freedom of movement. Dresses are not suitable for toddlers. Keeping in mind the weather, the season and the indoor temperature of the house, the child needs to wear clothes that are comfortably warm, and that wash easily. The independence of the child is encouraged by choosing clothes that fasten with zips, large buttons and Velcro. It will be easier for a boy to see to his own toilet needs if he is wearing loose tracksuit trousers, rather than tight jeans or dungarees. Avoid heavy garments: several light layers are less restricting.

When children outgrow the cot, a bed needs to be considered. Bunk beds save space but young children are at risk of serious injury if they fall from the top bunk, and sides need to be fitted. There is also some concern that children with asthma should not sleep on the bottom bunk as they may inhale the dust and house-mites from the top mattress.

A child who knows she is loved and valued and treated with respect will develop confidence and enjoy the company of others. All parents and carers try to satisfy children's needs, so that they grow up happy, healthy and independent adults.

✓ TEST YOURSELF

1 How should a small baby be positioned in a cot or pram?
2 What signs might alert you to illness in a baby?
3 Why do children need to exercise?
4 Name four functions of the skin.
5 List four safety factors when bathing a baby.
6 Name four pieces of essential equipment for a newborn baby.

GLOSSARY

By the time you have finished this chapter you should understand the meaning of the following words:

allergy   an acute reaction of the body to something eaten, inhaled or touched. For example, peanut allergy or nettle rash

convulsion   a fit caused by unusual nervous activity in the brain. A sudden attack of repeated muscular contractions and relaxation

factors   circumstances that contribute to a result

muscle tone   the constant state of slight contraction in the skeletal muscles that are responsible for posture and movement

nurture   caring for children in a loving way, meeting all their needs

obesity   being 20 per cent or more over ideal weight. It is often linked to lack of exercise

sebum   an oily substance that lubricates the skin

siblings   brothers and sisters.

CHAPTER 8

Working with children

This chapter includes:

- Childcare and education provision
- Talking with children
- Developing relationships with children
- Understanding children's behaviour
- Glossary

When you begin working with young children, you will need to have a good understanding of their emotions, their needs and how children learn. Knowing about childcare and education services will help you understand how the various childcare and education needs of the children and their parents are met.

You will make better relationships with the children if you talk to them every day, and take time to listen to them. As you get to know them, you will start to understand what makes them behave in certain ways, and help them to become independent, sociable people.

Speaking regularly with the children's parents, telling them about the events of the day and listening to their news, will help you to get to know the families and so get to know the children better.

For further information on the material covered in this chapter, you could consult the following:

Hobart, C. and Frankel, J., ***A Practical Guide to Working with Young Children***, 3rd edition, Stanley Thornes (Publishers) Ltd, 1997

Beaver, M., Brewster, J., Jones, P., Keene, A., Neaum, S. and Tallack, J., ***Babies and Young Children: Work and Care***, 2nd edition, Stanley Thornes (Publishers) Ltd, 1999

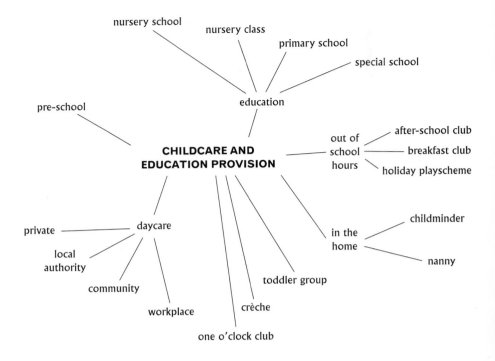

CHILDCARE AND EDUCATION PROVISION

There is a range of childcare and education provision available, depending on the needs of the child and her family, and on her age.

Care at home

Children may be looked after in their own homes by:

- their family, for instance mothers, fathers, grandparents
- nannies
- au pairs
- mothers helps.

They may also be looked after in someone else's home. This could be:

- a relative
- a registered childminder
- a nanny who also cares for another family (nanny share).

Nannies may be qualified or unqualified, experienced or inexperienced. A nanny may live in the family home or care for the children on a daily basis. They may look after children from more than one family. Qualified nannies often have sole charge of the children, whilst the parents are at work. Nannies are not registered with the local authority. Parents should be encouraged to employ a qualified and/or experienced nanny, particularly where there are babies and very young children.

Au pairs are young people, generally from abroad, who live with the family and look after the children for up to thirty hours per week in exchange for board, lodging and pocket money. They will spend part of each day at a language school, so that they learn to speak fluent English. It is unlikely that they will be trained to work with children, and should not be left in full charge without the parents being present.

Mother's helps are usually untrained people employed by families to help with the children and the general running of the house. Normally, one parent would be at home and the children would not be left alone with the mother's help for long periods of time.

Childminders are people who look after other people's children in their own home. They have to be registered with the local authority as a person suitable to care for young children. This involves being checked by the local authority as to health, character and having no criminal record involving children. Childminders are inspected annually to make sure standards are maintained. There is now a recognised qualification for childminders who have succeeded on the Certificate in Childminding Practice course.

Nursery schools

These usually are attended by children from 2 years to 5 years, and staffed by a headteacher, nursery teachers, and childcare and education workers. The children may stay for the morning, the afternoon, or all day, usually between 9 am and 3 pm. There should be one member of staff for every

What makes nursery classrooms fun? ▶

eight children. During their time at the school the children will be encouraged to become independent people, developing physically, intellectually, emotionally and socially, with perhaps more emphasis on intellectual and language development in some schools.

Nursery classes

These usually have the same hours and aims as a nursery school. There may be fewer staff, usually just one nursery teacher and one childcare and education worker for every 25 children. The nursery class will be part of the primary school and will join in many of the school's activities, such as assemblies and end-of-term parties.

The nursery teacher is generally in charge, and the childcare and education worker, plays a most valuable part as a member of the team, reporting to the nursery teacher. The childcare and education worker will be expected to be responsible for the care and health of the children and take part in the teaching. It is to him or her that children will often turn if they are unhappy or have an accident. In a good team, all the staff will work together to achieve the best for all the children and different members of the team will have different responsibilities.

Primary schools

Children are legally required to attend school in this country the term after they become 5 years of age. Many children start school much earlier, sometimes as much as a year early. There are two reasons for this: shortage of nursery places and increased government funding for the number of full-time pupils on the school roll.

No two schools are alike, and may have different beliefs and aims for the children in their care. All state schools will have to carry out the demands of the National Curriculum that tests children's ability in many areas before they move on to junior or middle schools at seven plus.

Special schools

A number of children have needs which call for special education to be provided, either in an ordinary school with support teaching, in a special unit within an ordinary school, or in a special school. The types of disability will include emotional and behavioural problems, moderate learning difficulties, severe learning difficulties, speech and language difficulties, visual and hearing **impairment**, difficulty in moving, and **autism**.

After-school clubs

Recent government funding has led to an increase in the number of after school clubs, which provide care and play opportunities for children after school. The majority of these clubs are held on school premises, and are used mainly by working parents. Eventually it is hoped that all children who require a place should have access to one.

Breakfast clubs

Some schools now offer children breakfast, and allow them to come to school early under supervision. This may be for various reasons:

- there may be a long journey for some children in schools in the country
- parents may work long hours, and have a very early start
- in some areas there may be concern about children coming to school hungry.

Holiday playschemes

Many children of working parents are cared for in the school holidays by playschemes run by the local authority, private establishments or Social Services. These provide various activities including sport, art and craft and outings to interesting places. The buildings and the staff have to be registered by the local authority.

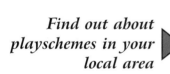

Find out about playschemes in your local area

Daycare

Daycare will usually care for young children from 8 am to 6 pm. The three- to five-year-olds may have a playroom of their own which they may use for some part of the day away from the younger children. The number of staff to children will be about 1:5, and there has to be some extra staff to allow for shift work, staff breaks and annual leave. As the children are there for a long day, and many are under 2, there is more emphasis on the all-round care of the child.

In a daycare centre, some of the staff will be qualified childcare and education workers and others may be experienced staff with little formal training. Other staff may have social work qualifications, counselling diplomas, or some other qualification. As the day is longer, the staff will work shifts, covering the day from 7.30 am to 6 pm throughout the year. Holiday time is less and the hours may be longer but the salary is higher than in a school, the opportunities for promotion are much better and the responsibilities often greater.

What do YOU think?

What might be a good reason for a child to attend a local authority daycare centre?

Local Authority/Social Services daycare centres

The number of places for children in daycare centres will vary from area to area, the towns and cities generally providing more than the country areas. Even so, there are long waiting lists for places, and this country has a poor record of providing inexpensive daycare for babies and young children. There are very few places offered for young babies, mainly because it is felt that most young babies are better cared for in a family setting, either at home or, if this is not possible, with a childminder. Because there is such a shortage of places, these are given to families who have the greatest need. Families will be referred by social workers, health visitors, doctors and other professionals who feel the child will benefit. Some places will be used by Social Services as part of a programme for child protection. When there is an urgent need for a child to be placed in daycare, a place in a private nursery or with a childminder may be used and paid for by Social Services.

Community nurseries

These are usually set up by local community groups with a special interest or need. For example, parents living on a large estate and feeling isolated with their young children, may press for a nursery for the children, and for their own social needs. Again, it might be a group of parents from the same cultural background, who wish their children to be cared for together, maintaining a sense of their cultural identity.

Usually the group will contact the local authority for money and a building, and for help and advice, but they would be independent, and would be run by a management committee of parents and local interested people. Most would employ qualified and trainee staff, sometimes parents helping as unpaid workers.

Because the local authority demands more staff when babies are admitted (usually one staff for every three babies) it is not easy for parents to get a place, even in their own community, for very young babies, unless there is an urgent need.

Why do some people feel unsure about men working with children? ▶

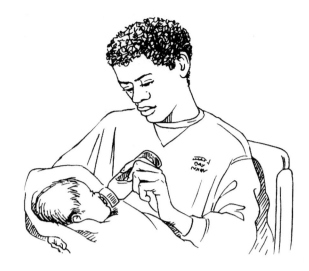

Workplace nurseries

Workplace nurseries might be:

- run by large institutions such as hospitals and universities for their staff and students
- shared by businesses such as banks, manufacturing and television companies for their staff
- set up by a private company.

The nurseries are provided to make sure that companies keep valued and well trained staff. They will have many more young babies, as the mothers return to work after maternity leave. With more women continuing to work whilst their children are very young, there is an ever increasing demand for places.

The hours of the nursery can be very long. Hospital hours have to be covered. Some university courses run in the evenings.

Private nurseries

Recently, many more private nurseries have opened. There are now over seventy nursery chains: these are private nurseries owned by one company, and will be similar in quality of care. Some chains have up to forty nurseries plus holiday playschemes. Most chains plan to expand rapidly. Parents will be paying fees that will cover costs and make a profit for the company.

Pre-schools (playgroups)

Some pre-schools offer full-time daycare, but the majority are run morning or afternoon only, and the parent will choose how often the child will attend; it could be every morning, one or two mornings, or both morning and afternoon sessions every day. A few pre-schools have childcare and education workers with the Diploma in Childcare and Education in charge, and many have staff with a PLA Certificate (a qualification for working in playgroups). The parents are generally involved in the running of the group, both in the day-to-day activities, and in the management. Most pre-schools were started because there was not enough provision for young children in the area. Although originally pre-schools were started mainly for children to learn to socialise and play together, nowadays they offer a full Early Years curriculum.

A pre-school is often held in a building shared by other groups in the community. This means that at the end of each session each user of the hall has to clear away all the equipment, and this can be quite difficult for the staff. It may limit some of the messier activities, such as using clay or painting with their fingers, that should be offered to all under-fives.

As you can see, by the following chart, there are many reasons why parents choose a particular type of childcare provision.

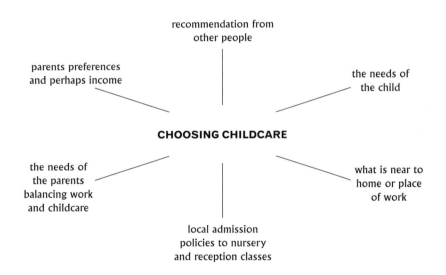

Other services

Crèches
Crèches are places where young children are cared for whilst their parents do other things generally in the same building, or local area. For example, leisure centres, shopping malls and hospitals often provide this facility. Children usually go for a short while, and different children will attend each day.

One o'clock clubs
These are often based in parks and offer play opportunities in the afternoons to children who attend with their parent/carers.

TASK

Your sister has four children aged 8 years, 4 years, 2 years and 6 months. She has recently moved to live near you, and has asked your advice about the care and educational provision in the area, as she wishes to return to work.

What options might you suggest for each child?

In what areas are playbuses important?

What do YOU think?

Some children seem to go to a different activity after school every day of the week. What are the advantages and disadvantages of this?

TASK

Visit your local library and find out what special activities they might have for young children.

Toddler groups

These are held in a variety of places, such as church halls, schools and community centres. Parents and their children can attend a session whenever they choose. It gives young children a chance to play with new toys and equipment, and with other children. The parents have the chance to make friends as well.

Playbuses

Buses or large coaches are converted into playrooms, and then driven with staff to areas where there is little pre-school provision. They offer play sessions to isolated communities.

Toy libraries

These take place in a variety of settings, such as libraries, clinics and community centres, and offer the opportunity to parents and carers to borrow toys for their children. They also provide somewhere for parents to meet and talk together.

Libraries

Many libraries offer story-telling sessions once or twice a week, and some offer art and craft activities in the school holidays.

Leisure activities

There are many activities for children to take part in from a very young age. For example, toddlers can attend classes in music, dance, gymnastics, art and craft, and swimming. Older children can continue with these activities, and add Brownies, Cubs, Beavers, Woodcraft Folk, tuition in a musical instrument, life-saving, sports coaching, martial arts, chess clubs – the list is practically endless.

TALKING WITH CHILDREN

There are many ways of communicating with children, through:

- speech
- **gesture**
- touch
- body language, including eye-contact
- writing
- listening.

Perhaps the most common way of communicating with children is by speaking to them and listening to what they say.

It is now accepted that the achievement of children in schools is influenced by their skill in the use of language. Children who can speak and understand 'book language' achieve well in all areas of the school curriculum. The sooner that children become fluent in both speech and understanding, the better they get on in school and with their friends.

It has also been shown that, whilst most language is learnt in the home, pre-school provision of any sort helps children's language to develop. It gives them the opportunity to talk with sensitive and understanding adults and with other children. It is most important for the carers of under-fives to choose their language carefully, so as to make the most of this sensitive age for learning language.

KEY POINT

It is now accepted that the achievement of children in schools is influenced by their skill in the use of language.

CASE STUDY

Alexander

Alexander is four and a half and has a Spanish mother and a Greek father. There was concern about his language, as he had never been heard to say one word at nursery. His main activity was playing on the mat with the toy cars. He had been at the nursery for nearly a year.

One day, another child took his favourite car away from him. Alexander leapt to his feet, yelling 'P—s off!' The staff and the children cheered, being so delighted that Alexander was now talking.

1 Do you think the staff were right to cheer?
2 What reasons might there be for Alexander's speech delay?
3 How might the staff now encourage Alexander to increase his vocabulary?

To be fluent in two languages is a great advantage in later life, as it will lead to the easier learning of third and fourth languages. Children find it natural to learn a second language in a nursery with good practice, and it is unnecessary to make special provision. Bilingual children who come to primary school without attending a nursery might need additional support. Young children need opportunities to use their home language, and this should be encouraged.

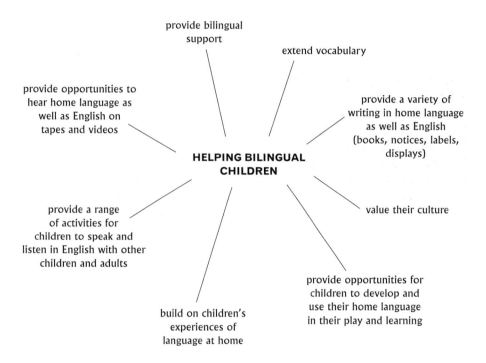

Try not to ask children questions where you know the answer (for example, 'What colour are your shoes?') These are called 'closed' questions. The child will either think you are stupid if you don't know your colours, or else will feel that she is being tested.

Try not to ask children questions that require just one word as an answer (for example, 'Do you like apples?'). These sorts of questions do not extend the children's speech, and are not helpful.

Some of the activities in the nursery lend themselves to adults and children sitting down together, and these times are excellent for making children feel comfortable and relaxed, so that a conversation can take place.

If you want children to carry out a task you must make sure that you say it simply and clearly. Asking a child if she would like to help you clear up might justify the answer, 'No!' The child is not being difficult, but will respond much better if you just ask her politely to do it.

CASE STUDY

Janice

Janice, a student childcare and education worker, who was carrying out her work experience in a pre-school, was heard to say to a group of three-year-olds, 'Before you go outside, I would like everyone to have had his or her snack or drink. Remember to put your coats on, it is cold today. Those of you with hats and gloves, make sure you put them on in the room, before you go outside. And tidy up the room first, I don't want anyone going out before the whole room is clean and tidy.'

1 How do you think the children responded?
2 How could Janice have made her instructions clearer?

Give children time to reply. Do not try and guess what they want to say, and give them the words. Be prepared to really listen to children, as much more can be learnt by listening to them than by taking over the conversation yourself.

Make good relationships with those children who have some speech delay. When they trust you they will speak to you. There are often children in the class who are comfortable speaking only to one other child, or one adult. Respect this, and wait for the child to know you well enough to speak to you.

Reading books and telling simple stories to one or two children at a time not only helps in making trusting relationships, but lets children hear new words. Talking to children whilst playing with them helps to widen their vocabulary.

Do you enjoy reading to children? ▶

Try to speak softly, calmly and clearly to children. Obviously you would never shout, but some people have unfortunately loud and harsh voices. If you are told to speak more quietly, or to calm down, take this as constructive criticism, and listen to yourself on a tape-recorder. You might be surprised at how you sound!

Never correct a young child's speech. Grammatical errors are normal for three- and four-year-olds, and will correct themselves as the child develops. A variety of different dialects are there for us all to enjoy, and who is to say which is the 'right' one, just so long as speech can be understood. If a child has difficulty in being understood outside the family, help from a speech therapist may be necessary.

If a child asks you a question to which you do not know the answer, be honest enough to say so, and discuss ways of discovering the answer together.

Children who use a different language at home to that of the school (bilingual children) will have some difficulty at first in understanding all that goes on around them.

Remember to use music and rhymes with children. Bilingual children, in particular, often feel more relaxed in singing, than they do in speaking.

Try to ignore swearing, and make sure you never use 'bad language' yourself. Young children give up swearing if they get no reaction. Always be positive and polite, avoiding sarcasm or an argument with a child.

DEVELOPING RELATIONSHIPS WITH CHILDREN

Love and mutual trust of the parent and child is the basis of emotional development. This will help the child to make loving and trusting relationships with other members of the family and later with the outside world. A well adjusted child who has had the benefit of loving relationships within the family will be able to take on new situations and challenges with confidence. One of the first challenges may be moving into a pre-school setting without her parent.

When children first start at school or nursery, some of them may find it frightening and distressing. Settling in a new child needs a great deal of planning. Ideally, one or other of the parents will be able to stay for a while during the first week, and this will help the child to feel secure. The youngest babies will probably settle quite easily, but once the baby is 8 months old or so she may feel a great deal of anxiety and distress. The longer the parent can stay, the sooner the baby will feel secure and allow the parent to leave without fuss.

Settling a child successfully into a new situation often needs careful handling. It may coincide with the birth of a new baby and may lead to feelings of jealousy and rejection. Problems within the child's family, such as divorce, unemployment, death or addiction may distress the child and halt their emotional development, causing the child to become more babyish. Understanding the stages of emotional development is a critical factor in making good relationships with children.

You would not have wanted to work with children if you did not very much enjoy their company. Making trusting relationships does not happen overnight. You will need to:

- approach children calmly and quietly
- make eye contact
- be on the same level as young children. If you tower over them they might feel threatened
- try to avoid taking on personal tasks, such as changing nappies, until you know the children well
- be aware of children's body language, respecting when they wish to be left alone.

When children are hurt or upset, most of them want to be comforted. In the majority of establishments, childcare and education workers are encouraged to cuddle the child, but you should check with your supervisor how your work experience placement feels about this.

Some older children take a while to settle in to a new setting. This is partly because of previous experiences and partly due to the personality of the child. It may also be due to the environment, attitudes and behaviour of the carers. The parent staying as long and as often as possible will help a child who is finding it difficult to settle. Once the parent has to go, he or she should do so quickly, as the longer the goodbyes are drawn out, the more distressing it can be for the child. On the other hand, the parent must not sneak out, without the child seeing her, as this can lead to distrust and insecurity on the part of the child.

CASE STUDY

Jerome

Jerome, aged 3, has been in a nursery class for eight weeks. He is still finding it difficult to separate from his mother, and is often found crying by himself in the home corner during the day. He does not relate well to the staff or the other children.

1 Why might this be?
2 What might his parent do to help Jerome?
3 What might the nursery team do to help Jerome and his mother?

Children have many emotional needs and you will play an important part in helping them to develop emotional strengths.

Once the parent has finally left, try to give the child as much of your attention as you can. Provide activities that are known to the child and that do not require too much concentration and effort. Perhaps she could bring one or two treasured toys from home. Check that she has her comfort object with her and that it is available to her whenever she needs it. She may demand cuddles and hugs, and you will need to respond to this. Remember that some children do not like close physical contact with anyone except their mother, and this should be respected. Children have many emotional needs and you will play an important part in helping them to develop emotional strengths.

Why, these days, are some people reluctant to cuddle children? ▶

UNDERSTANDING CHILDREN'S BEHAVIOUR

Behaviour is the way in which a person conducts herself in relation to other people. It is the response to an action. Some behaviour, such as rudeness and defiance is seen as 'bad' or challenging, whilst other behaviour, such as politeness and obedience is seen as 'good'.

Behaviour is learnt through the child watching the people closest to her and the way they react to her, both verbally and non-verbally. Rewards and punishments shape behaviour. The reward may just be praise and encouragement, and the punishment a disapproving look, but it will have an effect.

Barbara

Barbara, aged 5, is being attacked in the playground by two other five-year-olds. Henry, aged 8, Barbara's brother, sees what is going on and rushes to her rescue. He hits one of the children so hard that he makes his nose bleed.

1 Do you think Henry behaved well?
2 What else might he have done?
3 What should the staff say to Henry?
4 What should the staff say to Barbara?
5 What should the staff say to the other two five-year-olds?

Knowledge of the normal development of children will help you to understand what behaviour is acceptable at what age and stage of development. For example, a toddler is not expected to be completely toilet trained, but regularly wetting and soiling pants would be worrying behaviour in a five-year-old.

The children you meet will come from various backgrounds, perhaps from a variety of cultures, with parents who may well have different expectations of their children's behaviour. For example, some parents might explain in great detail to the child what it is she is doing wrong, whilst others might be more of the 'do as I say, not as I do' school. Some parents might have different expectations of boys and of girls, allowing boys to be more physical and active, and expect girls to 'behave like ladies'.

Clive

Clive attends a small nursery. The staff found him to be a delightful child, always happy and helpful, but his habit of never saying 'please' and 'thank you' really upset them. It was clear that this was not expected of him at home.

1 What action should the staff take?
2 Should they insist that Clive says 'please' and 'thank you'?
3 Should they discuss this with Clive's parents?

Factors that influence behaviour

Most of the factors that influence behaviour are family based. This is because behaviour is learnt at first in the family, and the earliest experiences have the greatest influence. These factors include:

- where the child is born in the family, either the oldest, the youngest or in the middle
- siblings
- expectations of the parents
- child-rearing practices
- influence of the extended family, such as grandparents, aunts and uncles
- opportunities for play within the family home
- abuse and neglect
- gender stereotyping, where girls are expected to be quiet and boys allowed to be rude and noisy.

Other events that affect the whole family may also influence behaviour. These might include a death in the family, a new baby, unemployment, divorce or separation.

Other factors are:

- the personality of the child
- the school
- the peer group/friends
- the media, such as watching violent films might encourage fighting
- having a disability
- experiencing discrimination.

What do YOU think?

In what ways might racial discrimination affect a child's behaviour?

What types of programmes do you think children should not be allowed to watch?

Common types of challenging behaviour

Some types of behaviour are so common all children exhibit one or more of them sometimes. Attention-seeking behaviour is one of the most common forms of challenging behaviour. Children need to be reassured that they are loved and cared for, and if they are not given attention, they may seek it by being aggressive, angry, rude, swearing, showing off, and other worrying behaviours.

Temper tantrums

About half of two-year-olds have tantrums regularly, usually when they are with their parents, and very seldom when they are playing on their own or attending school or pre-school. Tantrums happen because children feel frustrated and need to get attention. Tantrums can be quite disturbing to watch, and need to be dealt with in the same way by the carers and the parents. If you see one coming, it is often possible to distract or divert the child. If it is already too late, or you are in a public area and unable to walk away, you will need to hold and hug the child until the tantrum is over. The child may be frightened and needs reassurance.

When the tantrum is over, cuddling the child and talking about feelings in a positive way should reduce further tantrums. It is harmful to slap or handle a child roughly during a tantrum, and even more dangerous to shake her. Equally, giving in to the child and allowing her to manipulate you will increase the number of tantrums. Always report back to parents if the child has had a severe tantrum.

Why do you think this child is having a trantrum? ▶

Jealousy

It is an unusual family that never quarrels, and most children will fight from time to time. A new baby will sometimes cause deep feelings of jealousy from an older child, and this may be shown by aggressive behaviour. Often, rivalry is expressed by quarrelling over toys and attention. In general, children can sort out most of these rows for themselves and unless they are doing serious damage to each other, it is often better to just let them get on with it.

Physical causes of challenging behaviour

Sometimes problem behaviour has a physical cause. Lack of sleep can lead to a child being cross. Hunger can cause some children to lose concentration and become aggressive because their blood sugar level drops. Infection can cause changes in behaviour patterns.

Growing independence

There are some types of behaviour that are to be expected, as they are part of the child's development. Babies starting to crawl need constant watching, and most older children become bored from time to time.

Curiosity

As a baby becomes a toddler there will not be a cupboard that remains unexplored, or a meal that is peaceful and does not have a messy end, as the toddler seeks to feed herself and enjoy the texture as well as the taste of food. Safety factors and constant supervision are of increasing importance as the child's curiosity knows no limits.

Boredom

Children need stimulation and the opportunity to play and learn about the world around them. If they are restricted and frustrated, this will lead to boredom, perhaps resulting in attention seeking behaviour.

Your role with all the children, is to:

- be fair
- be consistent
- understand what behaviour is appropriate for each age group
- have realistic expectations
- give brief explanations as to why you do not accept certain behaviours.

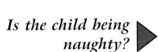

Is the child being naughty?

TASK

You overhear one four-year-old child making a hurtful racist remark to a younger child.

1 What is your immediate reaction?

2 How might you involve the parents?

3 What steps might you take to alter such behaviour?

4 How would you support the younger child?

Managing unwanted behaviour

When children are cared for by more than one person, they will sometimes attempt to play one adult off against another, so it is helpful if both carers and parents follow the same approach. **Consistency of care** helps the child to know what is expected and acceptable. All children need to understand limits set by their parents and carers, as to what behaviour might be tolerated. As children grow older the rules may change, but consistency is still the key for managing behaviour.

Behaviour is not acceptable if it:

- is dangerous, hurtful or offensive to someone else
- is dangerous to the child herself
- will make the child unwelcome or unacceptable to other people
- damages other people's property
- leads to bullying.

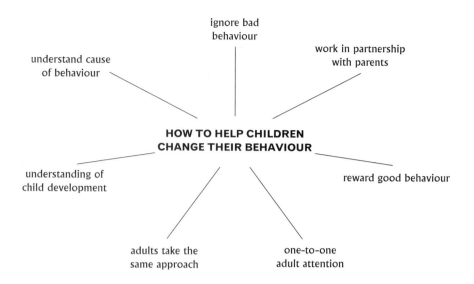

ignore bad
behaviour

understand cause
of behaviour

work in partnership
with parents

**HOW TO HELP CHILDREN
CHANGE THEIR BEHAVIOUR**

understanding of
child development

reward good behaviour

adults take the
same approach

one-to-one
adult attention

The best way to manage unwanted behaviour is to:

- distract her and remove the child from the situation
- restrain her gently during a tantrum until she calms down, and then cuddle her
- grab the child and say, 'No!' if she is in danger
- ignore swear words, as paying attention to them will make the child say them all the more
- say 'No', making sure your whole body shows that you mean it
- not reward unacceptable behaviour by giving the child your attention
- not argue with a child in a tantrum
- show disapproval, and make it clear that the behaviour is not acceptable.
- make it clear that it is the *behaviour* that is not wanted, rather than the child
- explain why the behaviour is unacceptable if the child is old enough to understand
- never smack, shake, bite or humiliate a child
- show affection, and offer cuddles after any incident
- stay calm and in control of yourself.

When children's behaviour causes concern, the question you need to ask is whether this is a normal stage in their development, or whether there is a more serious problem. Most problems sort themselves out in time, and the quarrelsome child becomes charming and manageable.

All the children in your care, whatever their age, need your affection, consistency of care, understanding and an opportunity to play and learn.

✔ TEST YOURSELF

1   Name three types of part-time childcare and education provision.

2   List three leisure activities.

3   Name four points you need to consider when talking with children.

4   Give two examples of closed questions.

5   List two ways a child might be helped to settle in to a new situation.

6   List four factors that might influence behaviour in a young child.

GLOSSARY

By the time you have finished this chapter you should understand the meaning of the following words:

autism describes a condition in which children have difficulty in communicating with others and therefore in establishing relationships

consistency of care all adults caring for a child should follow the same guidelines

gesture moving the hands to convey a message

impairment generally refers to a loss in function, such as being partially sighted, or having some hearing loss.

CHAPTER 9

Providing activities for children

This chapter includes:
- Play
- Practical activities
- The role of the adult
- The curriculum
- Glossary

We all like to play. You probably play games, exercise, dance, paint, sew or knit, go on holiday, visit museums and art galleries, and take part in **passive activities**, such as watching television, going to the cinema and theatre, listening to music and reading. Most adults find these activities stimulating and add to their enjoyment of life. Children need the same opportunities, as it is mainly by play that children learn.

For further information on the material covered in this chapter, you could consult the following:

Hobart, C. and Frankel, J., *A Practical Guide to Activities for Young Children*, 2nd edition, Stanley Thornes (Publishers) Ltd, 1999

Neaum, S. and Tallack, J., *Good Practice in Implementing the Pre-school Curriculum*, 2nd edition, Stanley Thornes (Publishers) Ltd, 2000

KEY POINT

Play is an essential part of children's daily life and promotes all-round development.

PLAY

Children's play has been called 'children's work' and shows adults what they can understand and do. Play is an essential part of children's daily life and promotes all round development. Through play, the child experiences life and learns to understand the world and her place in it.

211

be creative and imaginative

play alongside or co-operatively with other children

communicate

investigate and discover

understand the need for rules

express fears or actual experiences in a safe environment

be happy

PLAY ALLOWS CHILDREN TO . . .

care for others

learn self control

develop and express new ideas

take risks

explore

practise and develop skills

develop concentration

express negative feelings

make sense of the world

learn

share

The baby plays from birth, the first 'toy' being the mother's breast. Play develops through several stages:

- solitary (on her own)
- parallel (playing alongside another child or adult)
- associative play (playing with other children)
- co-operative play, involving planning and games with complicated rules.

Can you suggest other examples for what the children might be doing at the different stages?

The treasure basket

As soon as a baby can sit up on her own, at about 6 months, she will enjoy exploring a treasure basket. This was first thought of by Elinor Goldschmied, and has been used by babies at home and in daycare for the past twenty years.

All the senses can be stimulated by using a treasure basket. The baby is offered a container filled with objects made of natural materials. None of them should be plastic or recognisable as toys, as most of babies' toys are made of plastic, and the treasure basket should be a contrast to this.

About twenty items are needed to excite the five senses, such as:

- a baby mirror
- an orange
- a fir cone
- a piece of pumice
- a small natural sponge
- tissue paper
- small cloth bags containing lavender or cloves
- a new hair brush
- a piece of velvet
- clothes pegs
- a bunch of keys.

What items would be unsafe for a treasure basket? ▶

All the equipment needs to be kept clean, and fruit needs to be replaced before it goes bad. Select items that have no sharp edges. Do not put in any items that are small enough to be put into noses or ears.

A comfortable and safe position for the baby must be found, so that she does not topple over and lose her concentration. She should be allowed to explore the items on her own. You should keep an eye on her from a distance and not talk or interact with her as she plays and explores, as this will interfere with her attention. You need to be aware when she becomes bored, tired or has had enough.

Types of play

There are many different types of play. These include:

- structured play, where the adult chooses the activity, provides the materials and organises the play
- spontaneous play, when the child chooses to play on the spur of the moment
- child-centred play, where the child chooses the activity
- imitative play, the beginning of imaginary play, where a baby copies what she has seen an adult doing, such as waving 'Bye bye'
- domestic play, often in the home corner, such as pretending to make cups of tea and sweeping the floor. This is usually carried out by the pre-school age group, and can be solitary or with other children or adults
- messy play, which often involves exploring materials with the hands or other parts of the body
- play with natural materials, such as sand, water, wood, clay and mud
- imaginative play, which involves creative thought
- repetitive play, where the child feels the need to repeat an activity over and over again, until she feels satisfied
- creative play including art work and model making
- energetic physical play, usually taking place outside
- organised games, which includes ring games and board games, and often have rules.

PRACTICAL ACTIVITIES

All activities should encourage the children's all-round development. Through your knowledge of the children and how they develop, you will be able to plan activities with the children's needs in mind. This will help you to be aware of what is happening and when you need to step in to move the play forward. There will be many occasions when you feel that unstructured and spontaneous activities will be fun for all concerned, and allow children to use their imagination. There are very few activities that do not have some value. You should always be aware of the value of the activities you are planning and preparing.

TASK

Plan a treasure basket. List five items for each of the senses.

KEY POINT

You should always be aware of the value of the activities you are planning and preparing.

For children, passive play such as watching videos is not as valuable as active play in which they take part. That is not to say that there is no place for television, but the child learns more if she watches with an adult, who helps her to understand what is happening and answers her questions. Your supervisor might tape some programmes, such as 'Sesame Street' or 'Blue Peter', and have them available to show the children when they need to relax.

Messy play

Some activities provided for children do not need an adult to direct the children in the use of the materials you have provided. Messy play includes such activities as:

- playing with cooked spaghetti mixed with liquid detergent and colouring
- experimenting with cornflour and water to see if it becomes solid in your hand and liquid on a hard flat surface
- attaching a large sheet of paper to a wall or to a fence outside, and squirting paint in squeezy bottles at the paper
- finger painting, when paints and paste are mixed together, and patterns made in the mixture with the fingers. Older children might like to print their creations
- playing outside with mud and water.

Messy play is enjoyable for all children, but particularly so for the youngest ones.

What do children gain from playing with mud?

CASE STUDY

Monica

In her nursery work experience placement, Monica has been asked to supervise a group of children doing finger painting. She mixes the paints and glue, and puts out sheets of paper for those who wish to print their art work.

Unfortunately, she has forgotten to place a bowl of soapy water and some cloths nearby, so that she can quickly clean up any spills and the children can take the worst of the paint off their hands before washing properly in the bathroom. After ten minutes, the paint is everywhere – on the floor, on the curtains, on the chairs. The supervisor goes ballistic.

1 Who was mainly at fault?
2 How can Monica put the matter right?
3 What should she do next time she is asked to supervise an activity?
4 How should the supervisor have reacted?

Messy play is one of the best activities for intellectual development, as children use their imagination and creativity in planning and producing this work. Their concentration span is often extended in well thought out and enjoyable activities. Different materials encourage them to explore and experiment and this in turn leads to an understanding of design and technology. Mathematical and scientific ideas may be learnt. It is an emotionally satisfying and enjoyable activity.

Play with natural materials

Water

Water cannot be destroyed and is always available. Children can bang and splash it without harm. Some children will enjoy using any tools provided and finding out about floating and sinking, whilst others might enjoy playing with water on its own, finding it a soothing and relaxing experience. Playing with water links home with school or nursery, as children are used to playing in their bath or at their parents' sink. Children learn that water comes in many forms: as snow, rain, steam, and ice, and is essential for life.

Sand

You might see children using sand for the first time in your placement as most parents would not provide sand at home although some might have sand pits in their gardens.

Dry sand is relaxing to play with. A great deal can be learnt with the use of various tools. It is not suitable for very young children, unless closely supervised, as they tend to throw it around and get it in their eyes and hair as well as eat it.

Wet sand is suitable for all age groups. It can be used for modelling, and can be combined with blocks and cars and other small toys to stimulate the imagination. It will lend itself to many experiments. Making patterns and marks in sand is linked to early reading and writing.

Mud

Once children are mobile, most of them find out about mud quite quickly, and should be allowed to play with it outside freely if suitably dressed. The garden should be free from chemicals, and records should be checked to make sure the children are protected against **tetanus**. It is one of the most enjoyable of natural materials for young children and is free and readily available in every garden. Mud can be mixed with water, and children can

---

TASK

Your supervisor in the pre-school has asked you to fill the water tray.
What should the temperature of the water be?

1 Name six things you could put in the water to extend the children's play.
2 How might you protect the children from getting wet?
3 Name two hazards to do with water play.

CASE STUDY

Jasmine

Jasmine is placed in a day nursery for her work experience placement. One day, she is out in the garden, where a group of toddlers are making mud pies. They are getting dirty and are very much enjoying playing in the mud. All of a sudden, Jasmine sees one of the toddlers put a worm into his mouth.

1 What is the first thing Jasmin should do?
2 Would it have been an emergency if the worm had been swallowed?
3 How might the parents be told?
4 Could this situation have been prevented?

217

watch it dry out to go back to being dry soil. Small animals, such as worms and ants, found in the mud give interest and pleasure to children, who often need to be persuaded to return them to the garden.

Modelling materials

Plasticine, dough and clay are all used for modelling. Plasticine is a useful manufactured material and is good for developing manipulative skills, and for making models with older children. It is much cleaner and less messy than other modelling materials and is often familiar to children from their play at home. It can get hard very easily and needs storing in a warm place.

Dough can be made in many ways and presented to children in a range of colours, and the children will enjoy helping to mix it. By adding other ingredients, apart from the flour and water, different kinds of elasticity can be achieved. Salt should always be added as a preservative, and it will also make sure that children do not eat it. Dough should appear attractive, have enough elasticity without sticking to surfaces or fingers, and should last for at least a week in a sealed plastic container, kept in a cool place. Playing with dough is a relaxing, soothing social activity, and is one often chosen by children when settling in to the nursery. When playing with dough a shy child is often encouraged to take part in a conversation, as the experience helps relaxation.

Clay is not usually played with at home. It is very messy and needs the adult to have a relaxed attitude to the amount of mess it can make, otherwise some of the value of the material is lost. It is suitable for children who are upset or angry, as it can be bashed about, handled harshly and will go back to its original form. It can be used very wet, and is then soothing and enjoyable.

TASK

Experiment with different dough recipes using various flours, ingredients and colours. Make a note of the recipe you find most successful.

You might like to involve the children in making dough with you whilst in your placement.

What preparation is needed before letting children play with clay? ▶

Cooking

From a very young age, children enjoy watching and helping adults prepare and cook food. From this, children learn about food hygiene and balanced meals, how to make choices in the supermarkets for taste and value, and where different foods come from.

It is possible today to buy food from all around the world, and by using recipes from various countries children learn about a range of cultures in a most enjoyable way. Children and parents from different ethnic groups feel valued and respected when an important part of their culture is recognised.

'Cooking' covers a wide range of activities, from making a sandwich to producing a complicated meal. It is important that the children do as much as possible for themselves, being involved from the preparation stage through to sharing the food.

By helping to plan the activity, children gain shopping skills, such as making lists, choosing ingredients and handling money. Listening to and following instructions aids concentration. Cooking helps children learn many mathematical, scientific and technological concepts. It gives them an understanding of healthy eating, home safety and hygiene. Recipes and labelling show the importance of reading and writing in a practical way. Knowledge of foods from many cultures will be gained, and children from the age of 6 years might begin to follow recipes from a book.

Older children should be encouraged to cook, so that they may be able to prepare simple foods for themselves and their families.

What recipe would you use with a group of six-year-olds? ▶

Imaginary play

Imaginary play follows imitative play. Babies from a very early age imitate adults in games of 'peek-a-boo', waving goodbye and copying actions. Later, children do not need an adult in front of them, but will start to use their memory, pouring out imaginary cups of tea and pretending to eat non-existent food.

At around 2 years, children start to take on roles. One will be the 'mummy', and another the 'daddy', and this will gradually extend to include the baby, the big sister, the childcare and education worker, and even a visiting aunt. As children become older, they will pretend to be other people they know or characters from books and television, such as superheroes. Providing dressing-up clothes often stimulates the imagination of the children. It is best to give children clothes that can be used in many different ways.

For some children, acting out a role can help them come to terms with problems, through pretending to be someone else. A child who is constantly listening to adults quarrelling may find it helpful to pretend to be one of those adults, and have some say of her own. This type of play can give you an insight into possible difficulties at home, but take care, as the child could be acting out what she has seen on the television the night before.

A child waiting to go into hospital will find it very useful to pretend to be a patient, as a way of expressing emotions and fears. Some children, who may be withdrawn or shy, may still have difficulty in talking about their feelings. Puppets or a toy telephone can be a great help here. Ready made puppets should be introduced cautiously, as small children can be afraid of a toy that seems to have a life of its own. As children are small and defenceless, they enjoy acting out roles of superheroes, such as Power Rangers. It makes them feel powerful and strong, and is a boost to their self-esteem.

Children play with dolls in different ways at each stage of their development. Once babies start to walk, they will use the doll as any other object, just holding onto it anywhere (usually the feet) and dragging it after them. At about 2 years, some children will start to cuddle the doll, treating it more as a baby, particularly if there has been a recent birth in the family. This doll might come in for some very hard knocks! A little later on, children enjoy bathing dolls, washing their hair, dressing (but mainly undressing) them and taking them out for walks in a pushchair. At about 5 years, groups of children might play with several dolls, having pretend tea parties or schoolrooms. Many girls start to collect dolls, such as Barbie, and there is often competition in the collecting of their clothes and equipment. Some boys might have dolls, such as Action Man, but rarely collect them in the same way. Graded dolls and dolls' clothes help children understand the ideas of small, medium and large. Small scale models of people, animals, vehicles, dolls' houses, and tea sets are often used in imaginary play.

TASK

Make a cloak from a piece of material gathered at one end with elastic.
Do you think boys and girls would play with it in the same way?
If not, why not?

TASK

What equipment and clothing might you put in a home corner to help;
1 a four-year-old who is about to go into hospital?
2 a two-year-old whose mother is expecting a new baby?

What do YOU think?

What do you think might be the feelings expressed in play by a three-year-old, who has just had a new baby brother?

KEY POINT

All children should be offered the chance to paint and draw when they feel like it.

Should you ask this child what her picture is about? ▶

Domestic play, such as making pretend cups of tea or using a broom, is a link with home, and very comforting to the insecure child, or a child experiencing a new situation. Domestic play often takes place in the home corner in the pre-school.

Imaginary play lets boys take on what are seen as female roles such as the mother or the ballerina, whilst girls can be fathers and fire-fighters.

Older children learn drama in school. This follows on from role play, and is a subject that most children enjoy. Some shy children find it easier to express themselves when acting out a part, and more outgoing children benefit by working co-operatively together to produce a play that might be seen by others. Drama helps self-esteem and confidence in all children.

Painting and drawing

All children should be offered the chance to paint and draw when they feel like it. Very young children have a limited amount of language, so spontaneous drawing and painting is a way in which they can make their feelings known. Children may be reluctant to paint if adults insist on questioning them about their work, suggest additions to the painting, and want a title for every painting or drawing.

What do YOU think?

Do you think schools and pre-schools should encourage children to take home every piece of art work that they make? Why do you think this happens? What do you think happens to the art work?

Adults interpreting children's paintings are quite often wrong. Children love to do all-dark one-colour paintings at some stage in their development – this does not mean that something terrible has happened to them that they wish to forget! Understanding what stage of development children might have reached through looking at their paintings is interesting, and there are many books on this subject.

Creative art activities

There are some activities that encourage creative thought on the part of the child, but are generally adult directed. For example, junk modelling and printing depend on the materials provided by the adult.

If children are allowed to use their own ideas, creative art activities will stimulate their imagination and encourage their creativity. Carrying out these activities will help social development by the children sharing materials, taking turns, and develop language skills as the children have to understand instructions and ask questions. From the age of 5 years, many activities will link in with the technology curriculum.

Children usually work in small groups with an adult supervising, and sometimes the whole class is involved as part of a topic. The following list of suggestions for creative art activities is not a full list, by any means:

- printing with vegetables, fruits, sponges, Lego bricks, leaves and string using paints, inks and dyes; hand and foot prints and toy cars can also be used
- junk modelling using all shapes and sizes of cartons, containers, pots and odds and ends, using different types of glue, paste, Blu-tack and sticky tape
- painting, making butterfly prints, drip paintings, paintings in different shades of one colour, marble painting, oil painting, sugar painting, bubble painting, straw painting and making patterns
- collage, using paper of all kinds, such as tissue paper, sweet papers, postcards, magazine pictures and foil; other manufactured materials such as polystyrene chips, pieces of fabric, bottle tops and straws; and natural materials such as leaves, sand, twigs, seeds, shells, bark, wood and shavings. Pasta and pulses can be used, but as with printing with food, some placements might feel this is not suitable, as there are many people in the world who do not have enough to eat
- older children may be encouraged to draw objects, plants or animals in a realistic way.

Bricks, blocks and construction sets

A bag of bricks is the most valuable piece of equipment that any child can have from the age of 1 year onwards, as so much can be learnt. Bricks can be built up, knocked down, banged together, used to build cities and space stations.

What natural materials could a child use for printing? ▶

How would a two-year-old play with these bricks? How would a group of school-age children use these bricks? ▶

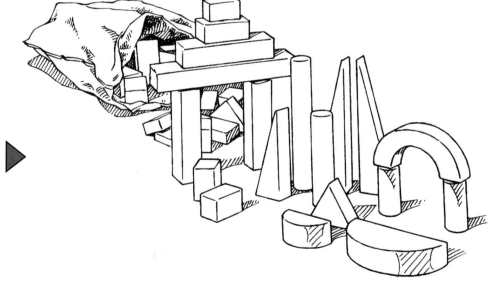

Blocks can be hard and made out of wood or plastic, they can be soft and made from rubber, cotton or foam, they can be brightly coloured or in natural wood – but they are all construction toys and are there to build with.

223

At first, children will play on their own, building a tower of bricks, and enjoying knocking it down again. This leads on to four-year-olds planning small and large constructions together, playing co-operatively and imaginatively.

There are very many types of construction sets on the market, the best known being Lego. Most children will know Lego from home, and it is probably the most adaptable of the construction toys. Younger children will find Duplo (the large scale version) easier to put together. Children from 5 years upwards, enjoy Meccano, the wooden and the plastic types being easier to manage than the metal, which is made for older children.

Building with bricks is a first-hand experience of three-dimensional objects and encourages creative thought and problem solving.

Music, sound and movement

Music is a familiar part of everybody's life. Some people think that babies respond to music in their mother's womb. It seems to have a calming effect.

From a very young age, babies will respond with enjoyment to a wide range of musical sounds. Lullabies are often used to soothe babies to sleep. As children grow older, their musical taste is formed by outside influences, particularly those of the family, the culture they are born into, the media and their peers.

It seems entirely natural to move in response to rhythm, and children and adults from all cultures enjoy moving to music and dancing. Experimenting with musical instruments helps children hear the sounds and they become able to tell which instrument is making the sound. Singing helps their language development. In some classrooms and homes, singing or rhyming is quite natural, and carries on between the children and adults as a way of normal communication.

Why do young people enjoy music? ▶

Puzzles and simple games

Jigsaw puzzles are familiar to all young children, and create an excellent home/school link, as children feel relaxed and safe doing jigsaws. They are usually done alone although children may do the large floor puzzles with other children.

Jigsaws range from simple inset boards for the youngest children, to very complicated puzzles for adults. Sometimes children will choose easy puzzles when they are feeling the need for reassurance, and at other times will enjoy the challenge of more difficult ones. Jigsaws should be checked regularly, as it is important that no pieces are missing, particularly for the younger children, as this spoils the pleasure of completing a task satisfactorily.

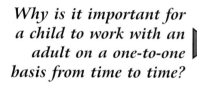

Why is it important for a child to work with an adult on a one-to-one basis from time to time?

Board games similarly come in varying degrees of difficulty. Most are not suitable for the under-fours as the children will not yet know how to take turns. They may get upset at having to wait and spoil the game for others. Most games for young children are a variation of 'Ludo' or 'Snakes and Ladders', whilst older children enjoy more difficult games such as 'Cluedo' and 'Monopoly'.

Card games, such as 'Snap', 'Go Fish', 'Pairs' or 'Sevens', are enjoyed by children of 4 years upwards. Older children might play 'Gin Rummy', 'Canasta' and 'Whist', but these days often play card games such as 'Free Cell' and 'Solitaire' on the computer.

Doing jigsaw puzzles and playing sorting and matching games helps children to find similarities and differences and so are valuable early reading activities. Card games encourage memory and quickness of thought. Concentration, logical thought, reasoning and perseverance are necessary for all these activities.

Activities that help manipulative skills

Children enjoy threading beads and cotton reels, and again these are graded in order of difficulty, the younger children finding the larger beads the easiest. Pegboards and mosaic pieces help children to make patterns, as do sewing cards, where children are asked to sew in and out of holes with a lace or a threaded needle.

Books and stories

Enjoyment of books and stories usually starts in the home and will continue throughout life. A love of books is probably the main reason children become readers.

Young children in particular, derive great pleasure in being told stories. These can be tales from the storyteller's past, or stories where the listener becomes the centre of the tale. Being told or read a story is delightful and relaxing. Many parents read to their child just before settling her down to sleep, and she will enjoy the attention of a loved adult.

> **KEY POINT**
>
> **A love of books is probably the main reason children become readers.**

CASE STUDY

Rani

The teacher in the nursery class is called away to speak to a parent. She is in the middle of reading a story to a group of four-year-olds. She asks the student, Rani, to take over from her.

Rani starts to read the story, but feels very uncomfortable. The childcare and education worker is in the room, listening to her. The children become restless and she finds it difficult to keep their attention.

The teacher returns to the room, and Rani rushes out. She bursts into tears outside the classroom.

1 Should Rani have been asked to take over reading the story?
2 Could she have refused?
3 Why do you think she found reading to the children so difficult?
4 What should she do to gain confidence in reading to the children?

Poetry for older children will enlarge their vocabulary and let them know that it is all right to express their feelings. Older children might be encouraged to write their own poems. For younger children comic verse is a good introduction. Rhyming that is repeated is most helpful to children with limited language skills. For all children poetry can, like books, open up a world of fantasy and imagination.

Being able to read gives a child independence. Understanding how a character in a book feels helps a child to understand her own feelings. Being able to read gives a child self-esteem and a sense of achievement. Books and stories encourage concentration, extend the child's knowledge of the world and stimulate the imagination.

Books should always be available to the children and, ideally, an adult should always be there to read to them if required. Children enjoy reading on the floor, and books should always be within reach. They should be kept in good condition, and children taught at a young age to treat them with respect. Children who damage books should be encouraged to help in mending them.

A full range of books needs to be available. The books should reflect our multicultural society, with stories from countries around the world and some books in the home languages of the children in your placement. Great care must be taken to avoid stereotyping when choosing books, whether it is in the area of race, religion, class, age, disability or gender. All books should show the various culture and family patterns in a positive way, together with stories showing children with disabilities and girls in strong roles.

> ### KEY POINT
> **Being able to read gives a child independence.**

> ### KEY POINT
> **Books should always be available to the children.**

Should small children be allowed to handle books? ▶

The suitabilty of the book or story needs thinking about. The youngest children will be content with stories about familiar events, such as shopping and bedtime, and some simple tales that are happily resolved about other children and animals. As children's experience of stories is extended, longer books about imaginary events can be read, but always be careful not to frighten the children. Young children's imagination is very vivid, and fairy stories can be terrifying, as they often deal with tales of rejection, death and separation. Monsters and witches should be left for an older age group, and even then not all children feel comfortable with fantasy tales, as they may still have difficulty in telling fact from fiction. The way that you read stories has a good deal of bearing on how much the children will enjoy them. You should choose stories you enjoy reading and telling, and you will need to be familiar with the story you are going to read.

Reading sessions are sometimes held in your local library. Older children should be encouraged to join the library, and the younger ones should visit from time to time.

Books are available from the library to help children who are having to deal with problems in their private lives, such as hospitalisation, parental separation, bereavement and so on.

Information technology

Because of the growing importance of computers you will probably come across them in your work experience placement. You may have a Personal Computer (PC) at home, and be familiar with the multi-media skills required. It is likely that you will have access to computers at your college or school, and you should take full advantage of any training offered.

Some nurseries and schools will have state-of-the-art equipment and software, whilst others have older machines, but in most schools the children will be offered the opportunity to use them. They will bring into the school or nursery a variety of experiences, some being very familiar with the computer from home, whilst for others it may be their first opportunity to use the equipment. Those of you who are not confident in your use of computers will be learning alongside the children. An interested and positive approach is best, and if you feel anxiety you must try not to communicate it to the children.

Some people have suggested that using computers at a very young age may not be all that suitable, as there are many other social and physical skills to be learnt, and computers can be isolating and time-consuming. No child should be encouraged or allowed to spend long periods of time at the computer.

In a number of areas, homework centres are being set up, where older children can use the Internet or word process their work. Using computers helps concentration and problem solving. It can be used as a tool for gaining language and number skills.

TASK

Name the five most popular books in your work experience placement. Why do you think these are the favourites?

CASE STUDY

Mel

Mel is in an Infant School, working with six-year-olds. Three times a week the class visits the IT room, where several computers have been set up. Mel has been asked to help any child who finds it difficult to use a computer. She dreads these sessions, as she has not admitted to her supervisor that she has never been able to come to terms with computers, and the children are all much better than she is.

1 What steps can Mel take to feel more competent?
2 Should she discuss her problem with her supervisor?
3 Who else might she talk to?

As with videos and television, it is the way the computers are used with the adult that results in a satisfactory activity that extends the children's learning.

Outings

Children with whom you are working will have a wide variety of different experiences, and this will include their knowledge of the outside world. Some children are quite familiar with airports and holidays abroad, some may be lucky enough to enjoy different weekly outings with their family. Others may come from families where there is no money for the extra luxuries of transport and admission charges and the adults have little energy to take their children to new places and enjoy new experiences with them.

In the pre-school setting, it is not necessary to travel long distances. A walk to the park to feed the birds, to the letterbox to post a letter (and await its arrival at the nursery the next day), to the supermarket to shop for cooking ingredients or to the station to watch the trains arrive and leave are all exciting experiences. A walk in the local park, armed with a bag to collect interesting items, may become the basis of a display for pre-schoolers. However broad their experience, children do not often have the opportunity to go for a walk at their own pace and to have questions patiently answered.

As children become older, outings can become more structured, and they can include a visit to a swimming pool, a local farm, a zoo, a building site, the market place in the local community and concerts in church halls. In London the Tate Gallery is quite suitable for five-year-olds to give them their first opportunity to look at modern art. The Science Museum has a sensory area for young children, where they can take part by pressing buttons, playing with water, and constructing buildings. By 7 or 8 years most children are ready for visits to all museums and art galleries, as long as the outing is kept quite short, and they do not try and see too many things.

Some schools and daycare centres may take all the children, staff and parents on a grand annual outing to the seaside or a theme park. Whilst very good for staff/parent relationships, it is difficult to give the children the same individual attention as you would try to do on a less ambitious outing.

On occasion, an outing may be planned that involves older children in staying away overnight. This may be the first opportunity for some children to experience being away from family and local friends.

Outings are a useful way to introduce a theme or project to a class of older children, to link with the National Curriculum. All outings need careful planning, safe and sensible supervision, and care to make outings suitable to the ages of the children.

If there is an outing planned whilst you are in your work experience placement, you should not be asked to take on any responsibility that you are not happy with. Permission from the parents must always be given in writing before any child goes on an outing.

Outside play

Nearly every activity that takes place in the house or in the classroom can equally well be taken outside if the weather permits. Some activities can only take place outside, and it is to these that this section refers.

Why do children enjoy playing outside? ▶

A safe outside play area is great for young children, to exercise and let off steam, to practise their developing physical skills and to build self-confidence. Fresh air and exercise adds to good health. A safe outdoor play area gives children the freedom to investigate and explore their environment. Very young children, who are not used to playing outside, and live in a flat, may find the garden too large and frightening at first, but when their self-confidence has developed they will soon enjoy being outside.

An adult needs to be outside with the children to make sure it is safe. What is provided will influence the quality of the play. Traditional games may be organised, either by the children, or by you, such as 'What's the time, Mr Wolf?', 'Hide and Seek', and 'Ring-o'-roses'.

The resources you might find in a well equipped playground or garden might be some large equipment such as:

- a climbing frame, planks, metal A-frames, barrels and a slide
- large covered containers for natural materials, such as sand and water
- benches for sitting on
- large cardboard cartons, wooden and plastic crates, tyres, tree trunks; cubes with holes
- trampolines, ladders, tunnels, drainpipes, plastic guttering, pieces of hosepipe.

In the outside area, there might also be:

- large brushes and pails filled with water for 'painting' paving stones and walls
- a patch of ground for growing flowers and quick growing vegetables, gardening equipment such as trowels, small forks, watering cans and flower pots, and a bird table
- a place for playing with mud.

The most popular resources are the:

- bicycles, scooters and other wheeled toys, which can be used by more than one child, such as carts and porters' trolleys
- toy pushchairs and push-along toys.

Small equipment is also found, such as pulleys, ropes, brushes, rubber rings, bats, balls and beanbags, blankets and magnifying glasses. It is fun to use chalk outside, but some placements feel it may lead to children writing graffiti.

Playing outside releases energy and it is an opportunity to make more noise. It stimulates the appetite and helps food to digest. It helps the circulation of blood and oxygen in the body, promotes sleep, and helps the body fight infection. It leads to healthy skin, as well as developing muscle tone, manipulative skills, balance and control. Children develop skills, such as:

- stopping and starting
- running, hopping, and skipping

What are the benefits of outside play? ▶

What do YOU think?
If your work experience placement does not have a large outside area, how would the staff make sure that the children get enough fresh air and exercise?

- digging and planting
- climbing and swinging
- pedalling and steering
- crawling through and under equipment.

Children share toys and tools and work together, take responsibility for sharing space, and begin to understand the rules of outside play and games. They learn to respect living things.

The garden is a stimulus for all the senses and an opportunity for many play experiences. Children must be dressed according to the weather, protected against the sun as well as the rain.

THE ROLE OF THE ADULT

Adults supervising children's play and practical activities have an important and sensitive role to play. They need to be aware of the value of all activities to the children's development and learning, and plan and prepare them thoroughly. There should be enough material provided for the entire group to take part in the activity.

There has to be enough space for the children, and they should have the chance to do the activity if they want to. Young children should never be forced into doing an activity if they do not wish to. On the other hand, a child who refuses at first, might well want to join in later on.

There is also the question of enough time. It is obviously not sensible to start a creative art activity that will take about an hour or more, just before the dinner break. You will also have to fit in with the time that your supervisor has given you.

All activities need to be supervised for safety reasons. Even playing with water can lead to a slippery floor and an unnecessary accident. Other activities, such as woodwork, cooking and outside play, have obvious built-in hazards, and need to be carefully planned and closely supervised. If there are small babies or toddlers in your work experience placement, even more care must be taken. Small beads or broken Lego bricks need to be put out of the way, to avoid choking accidents. Scissors, needles and knives should never be used or left lying around near babies.

All the activities you plan need to be suitable and accessible to all the children in your care. All the resources you use need to be checked so that they promote positive images of all cultures, and both genders. If you are not careful, you will find boys dominating the outside play, whilst the girls take over the home corner. This is not acceptable, and you may need to make sure that all children take part in all activities. If you have children with disabilities in your placement, you must make sure that they can take part.

Whatever the activity, the adult is there as a resource, to provide materials, time and space, and to take part when necessary. For example, in imaginary play, the adult should only take part if invited, whereas in cooking the presence of the adult is essential, in providing support, instructions and supervision.

Whenever you provide an activity, having prepared and planned it well, and carried it out, you will need to think about the learning and development of the children, and how you might do it even better next time. Talk to your supervisor about what you have done, and be prepared to accept constructive criticism. Even if something goes disastrously wrong, you will have learnt from it, and it is not the end of the world!

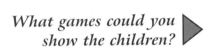
What games could you show the children?

THE CURRICULUM

The curriculum can be described as the experiences, opportunities and activities that are offered to the children in your work experience placement, to help them to learn and develop. Some of these activities you might help to prepare and plan.

Early learning goals

In the last few years, there have been more children in pre-school education, and the government is putting in place a national childcare policy in which it is investing large sums of money. It is expected that by working to early learning goals, children will reach the level of learning required by the time they leave the reception class. This is known as the foundation stage.

The areas of learning include:

- language and literacy
- mathematical development
- creative development
- personal, social and emotional development
- knowledge and understanding of the world
- physical development.

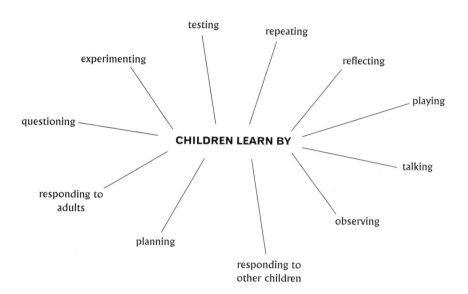

Baseline assessment

This was introduced into schools in September 1998. Children are assessed during their first seven weeks of primary education. The assessment must cover language and literacy, mathematics, and personal and social development. The assessment schemes vary from school to school. The aim of baseline assessment is to allow the teacher to find out about each child's knowledge and abilities, in order to plan for each child's learning. It will also help the school to measure and monitor children's progress from when they enter school.

The National Curriculum

If your placement is with children of 5 years and over in school, you will need to be aware of the National Curriculum. This is laid down by the Department of Education and Employment, and must be used by all schools. The National Curriculum is divided into attainment targets that state what each child should achieve at certain ages. These are known as Key Stages. Key Stage 1 is for children 5 to 7 years old and Key Stage 2 is for children 8 to 11 years old. At each Key Stage, children are expected to do a series of Standard Assessment Tasks (SATS).

In a school, everything you take part in will have an educational aim. You will need to keep in mind the development of the whole group as well as individuals, and to be aware of the standards that the children need to reach. From 5 years onwards, all children will learn language and mathematics daily during the literacy and numeracy hours (see page 237).

Children learn from everything they do. Everything you see in your placement will contribute to the learning outcomes, whether it is:

- preparing and sitting down to eat a leisurely meal with the children
- involving them in domestic tasks, such as clearing up, shopping and gardening
- going for a walk in the park
- all the play activities you plan, inside and out of doors
- any routine carried out by you and the children, that you are describing and talking about with them.

All activities and experiences for children should be suitable for their stage of development. You should think about:

- the child's current stage of development
- what the child can already do
- what she has achieved so far
- the child's interests and preferences.

Children develop at different rates and it is not helpful to compare children with one another. Learning outcomes should not be seen as the only goals for children. Many children are capable of much more and of much wider learning.

All research has shown that close partnership between teachers, carers and parents encourages children's learning and development.

KEY POINT

Children learn from everything they do.

TASK

Plan an outing to a supermarket with two children. What will they learn from this outing?

✓ TEST YOURSELF

1 Name three different types of play.
2 Give three examples of play using natural materials.
3 Give two examples of how to encourage imaginary play.
4 Name four objects children can use for printing.
5 Describe three activities to encourage fine manipulative skills.
6 Name three places you might visit with nursery age children.
7 Name three pieces of equipment that might be found in the outside play area.
8 Name two of the early learning goals.

The Literacy Hour at Key Stage 1 (60 minutes)

4 Reviewing, reflecting upon and consolidating teaching points and presenting work covered in the lesson.

1 Shared text work: a balance between reading and writing, e.g. reading a 'big book' and asking questions encouraging the children to think about the meaning of the story.

Whole class approx **10 mins**

Group and independent work (4 to 6 children in a group, they may work in pairs) approx **20 mins**

Whole class approx **15 mins**

Whole class approx **15 mins**

3 Independent reading, writing and word work while the teacher works with at least two ability groups each day on guided text work. Children are taught to work independently. When reading, all the children have copies of the same book.

2 Focused word work: teaching early reading and writing skills e.g.:
- understanding that words go from left to right
- understanding that there are spaces between words
- recognising letters and words
- recognising sounds of letters
- recognising sounds or words that rhyme
- recognising punctuation.

The Numeracy Hour at Key Stage 1 (45 minutes)

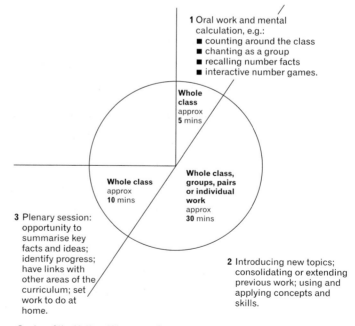

1 Oral work and mental calculation, e.g.:
- counting around the class
- chanting as a group
- recalling number facts
- interactive number games.

Whole class approx **5 mins**

Whole class approx **10 mins**

Whole class, groups, pairs or individual work approx **30 mins**

3 Plenary session: opportunity to summarise key facts and ideas; identify progress; have links with other areas of the curriculum; set work to do at home.

2 Introducing new topics; consolidating or extending previous work; using and applying concepts and skills.

Copies of the National Numeracy Framework and the National Literacy Framework can be obtained from DfEE Publications, P.O.Box 5050, Sudbury, Suffolk CO10 6ZQ. Telephone: 0845 60 22260 to obtain free copies.

GLOSSARY

By the time you have finished this chapter you should understand the meaning of the following words:

immunisation artificial protection against illnesses such as polio and diphtheria, often given by injections

passive activities activities like television that involve watching and not taking part

spontaneous on the spur of the moment. Not structured

tetanus an illness sometimes known as lockjaw. It affects the central nervous system. Can be prevented by **immunisation**.

Succeeding in your work experience placement

This chapter includes:
- Preparing for work experience
- The first visit
- Settling in
- The role of your supervisor
- Developing a professional attitude
- Assessment in placement
- Communication skills
- Glossary

KEY POINT

Having the opportunity of a work experience placement will help you to decide if working with children is the career for you.

During your course you will be given a work experience placement, where you will have the chance to practise all those skills you have learnt in college. Some of you will be in your placement regularly throughout the course, whilst others might have a block placement of three or four weeks at the end. You will be supervised at all times, and not expected to be left on your own, or to make decisions about the children. If you decide to go on to a professional training course in childcare, you will be given more responsibility and expected to show more initiative. Having the opportunity of a work experience placement will help you to decide if working with children is the career for you.

For further information on the material covered in this chapter, you could consult the following:

Hobart, C. and Frankel, J., *A Practical Guide to Working with Young Children*, **3rd edition**, Stanley Thornes (Publishers) Ltd, 1999

All placements are chosen by the college because they offer you the opportunity to work where there is good practice and experienced qualified staff. It would be very unusual for you to be allowed to select your own placement.

PREPARING FOR WORK EXPERIENCE

Before you start your work experience placement, your tutor will give you full details including the address, telephone number and the name of your supervisor, and the organiser or headteacher. In many colleges, there may be a visit before you start, and it will be up to you to find the most convenient and quickest route from your home to the placement. First impressions count and are remembered so it is worthwhile taking some time to prepare yourself for your first visit.

KEY POINT

People often remember their first impression of you.

Appearance

Your appearance should be neat, and you must be careful with your personal hygiene. Your hair should be tidy, your nails short and well cared for, your clothing non-restricting, and your shoes flat and comfortable so that you able to take a full part in the children's day. For example, unsuitable clothes would be high heels and smart clothes that you are afraid of getting dirty. On the other hand, torn or very shabby clothing is equally inappropriate. In some areas, jeans are unacceptable wear in schools.

People often remember their first impression of you, and it is on this that further judgements may be based.

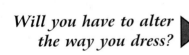

Will you have to alter the way you dress?

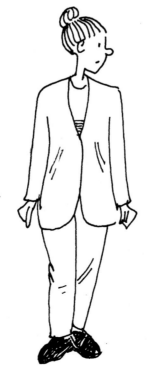

Jennifer

Jennifer takes pride in her extremely long nails. She spends a great deal of time polishing them and wears large rings to show them off. She visits her work experience placement for the first time, and is upset when the supervisor tells her that it is not a good idea to have such long nails when working with young children.

1 Why are long nails unsuitable when working with children?
2 What action should Jennifer take?

What do YOU think?

Do you feel uneasy when you meet people for the first time? Do you have any ways of coping with this?

KEY POINT

With thought and preparation you can show your supervisor right from the start that you are a well-organised and reliable person.

TASK

What was your first impression of the work experience placement? Write down a few notes and check if they stayed the same by the time you completed the placement.

If you feel very nervous, try some relaxation exercises, take some deep breaths, and start your visit with a smile on your face and a cheerful and eager expression. Be sensitive to the atmosphere in the room, and aware that supervisors may have many demands on their time and attention.

With thought and preparation you can show your supervisor right from the start that you are a well-organised and reliable person, and you will stand a very good chance of success. Arrive a little before the expected time, and seek out the headteacher or organiser to let him or her know that you in the building. Take with you some personal information, such as your past experience with children, other qualifications and interests, and the name of your next of kin to contact in any emergency. Whenever going into placement, you should have with you a pen and a small notebook as you may wish to write down any information you are given, or the details of events or activities that you may be involved with.

THE FIRST VISIT

Although an appointment will have been made for you with the placement, the supervisor may be busy with the children when you arrive. Be prepared to sit down with a small group of children and quietly enter into any activity they may be doing, until such time as the supervisor is free. Introduce yourself clearly, and listen carefully to any information that your supervisor gives you. Make sure before leaving the building that you have the correct telephone number.

What to look for during the visit

You will need to know how many children are on the register, and how old they are. In some areas, there may be children from several cultural backgrounds, and perhaps some who do not speak English at home. Some children may come part-time, and some may be full-time. Note how many adults were there in the room.

Have a look at the building you will be working in. It may be purpose-built, or converted from an old house. The room may be spacious, or rather cramped. The outside play area may have grass, flowers and trees, or it may be a rectangle with a hard surface and no planted area at all. Are the children allowed to play outside whenever they want to?

CHECK LIST: THINGS TO FIND OUT FROM YOUR SUPERVISOR

What time do I need to arrive in the morning?

What time can I expect to leave in the afternoon?

What room will I be working in?

What breaks will I have?

Will I have to pay for any meals?

Is there a booklet about the placement that I can take away and study?

How large is the staff team, and what are the names of the other staff members?

Is it possible for someone to give me a tour of the building?

How many children are there in the room in which I will be working? How many boys are there, and how many girls?

Are the children part-time or full-time — or some of each?

Do any of the children have any health or diet needs of which I should be aware?

What are the cultural backgrounds of the children? How many different languages do they speak?

Are there any clothing restrictions for staff?

The local environment

When you leave, take some time walking around the environment. See what sorts of homes most of the children live in. They might be living in blocks of flats or in houses with gardens. There may be shops and markets nearby. The placement might be rather isolated, or there could be parks and a community centre and easy access to public transport.

You will find that the mix of the children, the suitability of the building, and the pleasantness or otherwise of the environment in which the children live may well have a bearing on their behaviour and their ability to concentrate when in placement. A large airy room and a beautiful garden with grass and trees will make for a calm atmosphere among staff and children. An interesting and exciting environment will lend itself to many outings and visits within the community.

SETTLING IN

Having started your work experience placement, you will find it easier to make good relationships with the staff team if you take on as full a part as possible in all activities, showing enthusiasm and a willingness to learn. They will see you as a reliable and enthusiastic member of the team and this will be recorded in your final report. Finding out the information on the following check list will quickly help you to find your way around the building and settle in to the placement.

CHECK LIST: FINDING YOUR WAY AROUND

Where are the staff lavatories?
Where is the staff room?
Is there a room that can be used if a member of staff is unwell?
Where can you eat in the building?
Are you able to buy food in the placement?
What hours are you expected to work?
You should make sure that the placement knows who to contact should you be unwell or have an accident.

Do you find it easy to socialise with groups of people? ▶

CASE STUDY

Siobhan

Siobhan is on work experience placement in an Infant School. She enjoys being with the children but is very shy when she has to talk to adults. She sits in the staff room away from other people, reading a book and not taking part in any conversation. She hopes no one will notice her or ask her any questions. Her hair falls over her eyes as she sits huddled in her chair.

1 What might Siobhan be thinking about, as she sits in the staffroom?
2 Is there any help she can get, to overcome this problem?
3 If she finds it so difficult to speak with adults, is she on the right course?
4 How might you help any children who are shy, so that this does not become a lifetime habit?

243

Working with the team

After a day or two, you will be ready to take part in the general routine of the day, being sensitive to the needs of the placement and of the children. The following chart shows you the activities that will be included in your day.

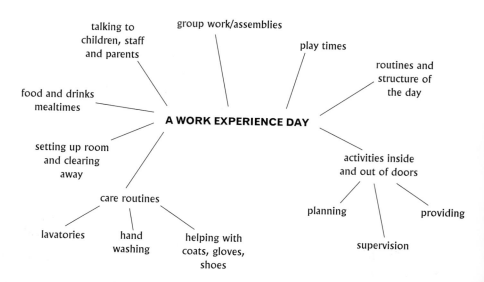

TASK

Using this chart of the activities in your work experience day, how is the day organised in your placement?

Many students find it useful to keep a notebook to write down questions they need to ask, and activities in which they have taken part. Arrange a time each week with your supervisor to discuss your progress and any difficulties you may have come across. At the end of each day you will need to find out what is expected of you the following day.

Your work experience placement will have set **procedures and policies**, such as equal opportunities and health and safety policies. You will need to know fairly quickly the procedures for reporting accidents, dealing with emergencies, fire drill and settling in, and the arrangements for the collection and delivery of children. A fuller list can be found in Chapter 11 (see pages 288–9).

Taking part in the social life of the placement is very important. Try to arrange to use the staff room at breaktimes, so that the staff can see that you think of yourself as one of them. You may find it intimidating at first, but with a little effort on your part you will soon relax and become a full member of the team.

Being reliable

You should always be punctual, arriving at least half an hour before the children. If you find you might be unavoidably late, make sure you telephone and let the placement know. If you should be ill, and unable to attend the placement, you must telephone as soon as possible, and keep in touch on a daily basis, so that they will know when to expect you back.

As you gain in confidence, you will make good and lasting relationships with children and colleagues, and enjoy every minute of your time in your placement.

CHECK LIST

(After one week in placement)
Are you arriving at the expected time?
Have you attended every day?
Have you telephoned if you have been absent or late?
Do you know the names and ages of most of the children?
Do the children know your name?
Do you know the names and the roles of all the staff team?
Have you used the staff room?
Have you enjoyed being with the children, looking forward to every day?
Do you have a clear understanding of what is expected of you in the placement?

Do you enjoy being with small children? ▶

THE ROLE OF YOUR SUPERVISOR

When you arrive at your work experience placement, one of the staff will have been appointed as your supervisor. He or she will be an experienced qualified member of staff who will:

- act as a role model in his or her practice
- show you around the placement
- introduce you to the children and the staff team
- explain the policies and procedures of the placement
- describe the routine of the day
- outline what you will be expected to contribute
- help you with any difficulties you might have
- monitor your progress and keep you informed on how you are performing

- be in touch with your school or college
- write your report
- help you succeed.

Your supervisor will not expect perfect practice as you are in the process of learning, and you must try not to feel threatened or distressed if he or she criticises your work or behaviour. Constructive criticism should always be helpful, as it should include plans to help make you progress. Make sure you discuss anything you feel unhappy about with your supervisor. The supervisor who tells you your good points and fails to tell you where you might do better is not helping you to succeed.

Sometimes students feel unhappy in their placements and have great difficulty in settling in. If this is true of you, ask yourself the following.

- Have you been there long enough to give it a chance?
- Are you sure you would settle in more easily somewhere else, or have you perhaps made the wrong decision about working with children being the job for you?
- Are you sure you know what the problem is?
- Have you discussed any problems with your supervisor, or kept them to yourself?
- Do you think too much is being asked of you?
- Do you find there is not enough to do?
- Do you feel very much on your own, and not included in the staff team?

If you cannot find an answer to your anxieties and unhappiness, talk it over with your tutor. If he or she feels there are real grounds for you not settling in, it may be decided to find you another work experience placement.

DEVELOPING A PROFESSIONAL ATTITUDE

To act professionally means that there is a responsibility to respect the rights of the people with whom you work. This is particularly important for those working with young children, as the children are often unable to tell you what they need.

Becoming a professional person is not something that happens overnight. With the help of tutors and supervisors you should regularly assess your knowledge, skills, behaviour and attitudes. This will be a gradual process, and you will receive support and encouragement from tutors and your supervisor.

The professional person working with young children will have made progress in three areas: knowledge, behaviour and attitudes.

Knowledge

During your course, both in college and in placement, you will be gaining knowledge. You will be learning about the physical, intellectual, language, emotional, and social development of children. This will make you sensitive to their needs and so help you to work well with children.

Knowledge plays an important part in preventative work, for example identifying children who are at risk of abuse and in need of protection. You will need to know the procedure for referral to make sure these children are safe. Although you may not be directly involved as a student, your supervisor will explain the procedures to you.

Knowledge is never at an end. A professional person is one who goes on after qualifying to update himself or herself regularly by attending courses, reading professional journals and always being ready to question and challenge in a thoughtful and constructive way.

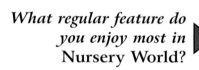

What regular feature do you enjoy most in **Nursery World?**

Behaviour

During your placement time, your motivation, enthusiasm and commitment will be continually assessed. You should show a positive attitude towards your work, and become aware of your role and responsibilities, reaching a clear understanding of what you can and cannot do in the placement. Good behaviour covers a number of areas that we shall look at one by one.

Attendance and punctuality

You must attend your work experience placement regularly, and be punctual.

At the end of your placement, your supervisor will be commenting on your reliability, in particular your time-keeping. This may be an important point in progressing in a childcare and education career.

Communicating with others

How clearly you speak and the ways in which you talk to children, parents and other professional people will show them that you are a caring, knowledgeable and sensitive person, and able to express your ideas clearly. Your body language should show that you are interested and motivated. Shrugging your shoulders and sulking is no substitute for expressing calmly and clearly your point of view over a disagreement. Maintaining eye-contact with children and adults will help good relationships.

Your ability to accept and act upon constructive criticism forms part of your professional development, and even when you are a qualified childcare and education worker, you will need to look at your work with others in the team, and be able to offer and accept suggestions for improvement.

Responsibility

The well-being and safety of the children in your care has to be your main priority, and at no time should you behave in a way that might put them at risk. No person is perfect in all respects, so understand and acknowledge your limitations. Do not feel forced to take on responsibilities when you feel that you have not had the necessary theory and training to carry them out successfully. If, for example, you are asked to assess children's reading and do not feel you have had enough experience, tell your supervisor that you are not ready to do this, but would be willing to do something less demanding instead.

Confidentiality

Your placement will have on record much confidential information about the children and their families. The amount of information told to you will depend on what is necessary to meet the needs of the child, help you to work within the team and to gain deeper understanding of working with families. All information that you receive, whether written or spoken, is strictly confidential. You should never share it with your family and friends. Even your college tutors will not want you to tell them the surnames of the children that you work with in your placement.

If you feel parents or carers want to confide in you, remind them that you are still a student; it may be more correct for them to discuss the problem with your supervisor, or another member of staff. If they wish to talk only to you, ask their permission to give the information to the supervisor. If children confide in you, you must treat such confidences seriously, and may well need to talk to your supervisor. Never promise children that you will not pass on information that they give you. Sometimes to keep quiet means that the child might be at risk.

KEY POINT

The well-being and safety of the children in your care has to be your main priority.

What do YOU think?

With a group of friends, discuss how you would cope with a gossiping parent. Would you tell your supervisor the gossip? Could it be of benefit to the family being discussed? If something serious is being talked about among the parents, such as abuse, should you keep quiet or pass it on to your supervisor, or to your tutor, or to anyone else?

CASE STUDY

Lauren

Amelia, aged 4, confides in Lauren, the student, that her mother is having a baby. Lauren is surprised, as she knows that Amelia's father is in prison. When Amelia's mother arrives to take her home, Lauren congratulates her on her pregnancy in a loud voice. Amelia's mother looks very embarrassed. Lauren realises that she has made a mistake.

1 What mistake has Lauren made?
2 How can she try to put it right?
3 Should she discuss it with the supervisor?

Other professionals

In your work experience placement, you may come into contact with people from other professions. A speech therapist might visit, whose role would be to help children who have language difficulties, and find it difficult to express themselves. You may be in contact with health visitors, who visit local families in their homes. Social workers may be supporting a family in your placement, and will want to know how a child is progressing. Educational psychologists play an important part in helping a child who is causing concern, and will assess his or her development and behaviour.

Attachment

Be careful about allowing children to become too attached to you. It is very flattering to have young children clinging to you, but remember that you are only in placement for a short time, and cannot provide the continual comfort and care that is sometimes needed.

Opinions

If you have strong religious or political views, work experience is not the place to declare them. You may wish to raise some issues in the staff room or at college, but it is unprofessional in front of the children and their parents.

Attitude

It will be expected in your placement that you show awareness and understanding of the total needs of all the children, parents and team members, regardless of race, class, culture, religion, disability, gender or age, both individually and in groups.

Never show favouritism or special treatment towards some children in preference to others but always show respect and interest in the customs, values and beliefs of all the children with whom you are involved. This will help you to provide children with positive images of themselves and each other. Make it clear that you will not take part in gossip about children or their families.

In some work experience placements, there may be times when you are unsure what to do, and feel you are just standing around feeling awkward and uncomfortable. The following list, adapted from a handout prepared by the tutors and supervisors at West Thames College might give you some ideas.

48 things to do when there's nothing to do

1 Tie up any loose shoe laces
2 Wipe any runny noses
3 Hang up aprons lying on the floor
4 Pick up equipment on the floor
5 Take part in outside play
6 Sharpen pencils
7 Put the tops on felt pens
8 Tidy books
9 Do the washing up
10 Read with the children
11 Play with the children
12 Check the lavatories are flushed
13 Check there is soap and towels in the bathroom
14 Check there is sufficient lavatory paper
15 Tidy up the home corner and the dressing-up clothes
16 Sweep up any sand on the floor
17 Mop floor around the water tray
18 Make sure you know how to play the table top games
19 Prepare fruit for snack time
20 Talk to the children
21 Feed the pets
22 Wash toys and dolls
23 Pick coats up from the floor
24 Check toys and equipment for safety
25 Sort pencils and pens into the right pots
26 Check jigsaws for missing pieces
27 Water the plants
28 Wash the aprons
29 Mend the dressing-up clothes
30 Check the spare clothes cupboard and tidy
31 Get to know the children

32 Learn to spell the children's names correctly
33 Learn correct pronunciation of their names
34 Make sure you know the policies and procedures of the establishment
35 Make sure you know the routines of the establishment
36 Learn names of all the staff
37 Cover boards ready for new displays
38 Make sure you know the computer games
39 Check the cassette tapes with the story books
40 Know the fire drill
41 Read some of the books in the book corner
42 Invent a game for the children to play
43 Collect resources for the sand and water areas
44 Check the home corner – can you think of anything else that could be used there?
45 Clean tables and chairs
46 Sort out lost property
47 Clean up easels and paint pots
48 Ask staff if there is anything you can do to help them

ASSESSMENT IN PLACEMENT

The work experience placements are chosen by the college as suitable work models for students because they offer good practice in caring for and educating children. For this reason, it is your supervisor who will be responsible for assessing your progress, not only in your reliability and commitment, but also in your growing awareness of what it means to be a team member.

Visit by tutor

It is one of the responsibilities of your tutor to visit you in your work experience placement, by arrangement with your supervisor. The main reason for the visit is to discuss with the student and the supervisor how you are getting on. You may wish to talk about any problems you are having with your tutor first, and he or she will help you to think about how you can tell your supervisor during the visit. This is part of your learning, as when qualified you will have to discuss difficulties with colleagues and try to sort out problems in a positive professional manner.

Often the use of a check list aids a three-way discussion between student, tutor and supervisor by making sure that all good points are noted whilst showing where progress is needed. An example of a work experience placement monitoring form is shown on page 252.

Tutor visit form

Date of Visit	Name of Candidate		Name of Placement	
		Unsatisfactory	Improving	Satisfactory
Professionalism:				
attendance				
punctuality				
knowledge of safety procedures				
Relationships:				
with children				
with team				
with parents				
Communication:				
speech				
listening skills				

Areas of strength

Areas for progress

Comments from candidate

Action plan

Candidate Signature

Supervisor Signature

Tutor Signature

If problems are identified and discussed openly, you should be able to state your point of view, and at the same time be prepared to accept fair, constructive criticism. At the end of the discussion it should be clear what you need to do to put right the problem and make progress. For example, a student who is constantly late will need to either get up earlier, or look again at the journey to the placement.

Your performance in work experience will show you whether or not you have chosen the right career. If the college work is a struggle but the placement a joy, in the end you are likely to succeed as you will be highly motivated to work very hard. If you find working with the children difficult and often boring you will come to the conclusion yourself that you have made a wrong career choice, and your tutors will guide you on to a more suitable course

<table>
<tr><td>KEY POINT</td></tr>
<tr><td>Your performance in work experience will show you whether or not you have chosen the right career.</td></tr>
</table>

COMMUNICATION SKILLS

An ability to communicate well with others in the workplace is a vital skill. Communication means:

- speech
- writing
- listening
- body language (including gesture and touch).

Speech

There is no better way of communicating than talking with people. This helps build relationships which using memos, faxes and e-mail can never do. Always speak clearly, slowly and with expression, particularly when in formal situations, or when the information is important. You will be using speech in informal day-to-day conversations, with your friends and colleagues and with the children. From time to time you will be using speech to give instructions to others, and at other times using it in public, for example at staff meetings. Try to present one idea at a time, and make sure that it is understood before continuing.

The drawbacks to using speech as a method of communication is that you have to make a quick reply without thinking first. Speech is generally not so precise as written language, and it is unlikely that you will keep a copy or record. Be aware of your listener's background, knowledge and feelings, and what your ideas will mean to him or her.

Some people communicate better with speech than in writing, but it may be the other way round. You will need both skills to be an effective childcare and education worker.

Writing

A childcare and education worker has to be capable of communicating information, ideas, directions and requests in writing and this will take many different forms. When writing for your own information, for example, a daily diary, a list of things to remember, or a note to remind yourself to bring in certain objects for the home corner, you can record this information in whatever way is useful to you.

When writing informally to others in your placement, you might decide to use memoranda (memos). See below.

Memo

To   All members of staff

From   Philippa Harris

Date   5. 5. 2000

Subject   INSET day 9.6.2000

The INSET day will start at 9 a.m in the Learning Resource Centre. We will be looking at child protection issues. I will circulate an agenda in advance.

A memo as shown above is a short informal note with a message put across as simply and clearly as possible. It must show:

- whom it is to, and copies (cc) to anyone else
- whom it is from
- the date
- the subject.

It can be handwritten or typed, mailed or e-mailed. It should be initialled and dated at the bottom. There is a danger that some organisations may use them instead of speaking directly to colleagues. Too many memos may result in people not bothering to read them properly.

Whatever you are writing, remember to:

- be clear about why you are writing
- use short sentences, that get across your exact meaning
- check the spelling and the grammar
- keep a copy. Use a black pen as this will photocopy well.

- be as neat and legible as possible. The word processor is a great help.
- date all **correspondence**.
- stick to the facts and be **objective**.

Answering the telephone

In your work experience placement you may find yourself having to take telephone messages (see below). When recording a telephone message, remember:

- whom the message is from, and his or her telephone number
- whom the message is to
- date and time call was received
- the subject of the actual message
- your name, as the taker of the message.

Telephone Message

To Lisa

Date/Time 10.15   8/9/00

From Julie Conway   (020) 8474 1682

Message Julie won't be collecting Abraham this afternoon. Her partner will be coming instead. She says you know him.

Taken by Frances Curtis

The above memo is an example of a written telephone message.

People use different voices on the telephone, and the one you use to chat to your friends may not be suitable at work. As there is often some noise on the line, speak very clearly, a little more slowly than usual, and do not allow your voice to drop at the end of the sentence. Give the name of your placement, your name and your role. If taking a message for someone else, repeat the message to make sure you have heard correctly. If making a call immediately say who you are and where you are from, and make sure that you are speaking to the person to whom you wish to talk. Be clear about the purpose of your call. Personal calls should not be made from your work experience telephone unless there is an emergency.

Remember always to be polite — you may not be seen, but you will be heard.

Why are listening skills important for carers? ▶

CASE STUDY

Cheryl

Cheryl is on placement in a busy Nursery School. She goes into the school office to take in some dinner money, and the telephone is ringing. After a while, she thinks she should pick it up and take a message. Two boys come into the office, and start a fight over a football. The person on the telephone has a very quiet voice, and Cheryl is too shy to ask the caller to repeat himself. She is distracted by the boys, and when she puts the phone down she realises that she has no idea who has rung, who the caller wanted to speak to and only remembers that the message was urgent.

1 Should she leave the room and forget about the call?
2 Should she dial 1471 and try to find out who called, even if it makes her look silly?
3 Should she confess all to her supervisor?
4 How should she have handled the situation at the time?

Can you ignore interruptions? ▶

Listening skills

When working with people it is as important to develop your listening skills as well as your speech. Being a 'good' listener does not come naturally to everyone. You need to listen carefully to others, concentrate, look interested and not interrupt, never finishing sentences for the speaker. This is especially true when listening to children, who may take longer to put over their ideas than adults. Give them time. Ask questions if you need more information.

Remember that in some circumstances you may not be listening properly. If you are worried or upset about something you may not be able to concentrate. Other noises or movements in the room may distract you.

Listening is a positive activity, and therefore the good listener does not relax when listening but has to understand and think about what is being said in order to make a correct reply. It may be necessary to let them see that you are listening carefully by use of sounds such as 'Uhuh' and 'Mmm', which show interest and understanding.

KEY POINT

Listening is a positive activity.

Body language

Remember that your body is sending out messages at the same time as you are talking and listening. To be effective, all messages should be the same but sometimes communication is spoilt when body language differs from what is being said. Think about:

- your posture
- eye contact
- facial expression
- energy level
- position of your feet and legs when sitting
- personal space
- touching others.

For example, whilst talking to a colleague, positive body language would show you looking at each other, smiling, and leaning towards each other. Negative body language would be yawning, looking or turning away, looking at a clock or watch, going off into a daydream and missing cues.

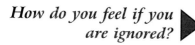

How do you feel if you are ignored?

Meetings

Meetings range from the very formal to the informal, and during your work experience you may go to both. Your colleagues, your supervisor or the notice board will tell you about meetings. You will need to find out who goes, what is usually discussed, where and when the meetings are held, how long they last, and whether they are formal or informal.

Formal meetings

All meetings are different but there are some things common to all, such as agenda, minutes and matters arising, and the opportunity to raise any other business at the end of the meeting. Meetings can be large or small but there will usually be a chairperson and someone to take the minutes (notes of what is said and what is decided).

The agenda of the meeting should be given out in advance, and sets out what is going to be talked about. For the more formal meetings the agenda has a standard form, noting apologies for absence, minutes of the last meeting, and matters arising from them. This is then followed by the items to be discussed at the meeting, and finishes with any other business and the date of the next meeting.If the group meets regularly, minutes of the last meeting are sent out with the agenda. Written minutes should be:

- brief, but with enough detail to let anyone not at the meeting understand what was discussed, what decisions were made, and what action was decided
- a true record of what took place
- taken in note form, but written up in complete sentences, using the past tense.

When attending a formal meeting:

- prepare yourself well by reading the agenda and minutes if they are available
- think what you can add to the meeting, and what you might wish to gain
- if you want to speak, wait until there is a pause, and always address the person who is chairing the meeting.

Public speaking

Public speaking includes:

- speaking up at staff meetings
- presenting information to other students
- attending a public meeting in your community.

When preparing what you want to say, think about to whom you are talking, the purpose of your talk, what you wish to get across, and how you are going to present it. Remember to speak clearly and slowly so that the audience has time to take in what you are saying. You might try practising in a mirror or before a friend, so that you are aware of any irritating mannerisms, such as using too many gestures, or twiddling your hair.

Points to remember are:

- realise that most people are nervous when talking in public
- concentrate on the task, remembering that you are trying to give a message
- take your time

Do you know how to operate an overhead projector (OHP)? ▶

- remember to speak your words more clearly for a larger audience
- if you forget your words, pause, take a breath, remember what you want to say and carry on
- read up about some relaxation techniques.

Communicating your thoughts to others, whether in speech or in writing, or by your body language is an essential part of the work of the childcare and education worker, and you should try to continually improve your performance in these areas. Practise helps, and you should take any opportunity you are offered to become more skilled.

Most students thoroughly enjoy their work experience placements, and you should, too, as long as you are well prepared and committed.

✓ TEST YOURSELF

1   Name three ways of preparing yourself for your work experience placement.
2   Name three things you need to find out about during your first visit.
3   Why is it important to be punctual?
4   Name four things for which the supervisor is responsible.
5   What does confidentiality mean?
6   What information must you record when taking a message on the telephone?

GLOSSARY

By the time you have finished this chapter you should understand the meaning of the following words:

correspondence communication in writing. This could be letters, memos, notes and so on

objective judging something in an impersonal way, and not allowing one's feelings to be involved

policies and procedures statements, often in writing, about guidelines for carrying out certain acts dictating good practice. For example, for fire drill, accidents, collecting children, equal opportunities and so on.

Finding employment

This chapter includes:
- Career choices
- Looking for a job
- Succeeding at interview
- Settling in
- Glossary

Working with young children will give you a choice from a large range of job opportunities.

Working with young children will give you a choice from a large range of job opportunities. The course has given you the experience and knowledge to decide whether or not a career in childcare and education is for you. If you have decided not to work with young children, you will still have gained knowledge and skills that will be useful in other jobs and you will find these very useful when you become a parent yourself. At the beginning of this book, we have described courses available to you to become a professional qualified childcare and education worker. Having completed your Caring for Children Award, you would be able to apply for a job as a trainee Nursery Assistant, or as a Playworker, working always under supervision and working towards a National Vocational Qualification Level 2. NVQ Levels 2 and 3 would let you apply for the main jobs open to childcare and education workers, at the start of their career. Any of the jobs described below will help newly qualified childcare and education workers to gain good basic practice putting their knowledge and skills to good use.

For further information on the material covered in this chapter, you could consult the following:

Hobart, C. and Frankel, J., *A Practical Guide to Child-care Employment*, Stanley Thornes (Publishers) Ltd, 1996

CAREER CHOICES

Working alone

Nannying

Many young people will look for employment as a nanny in a private family. You would be expected to provide full care for the children of the

What do YOU think?

What are the main advantages and disadvantages of being a daily nanny?

family, and often take charge of the children on your own if both parents work. Occasionally two families will join together to employ a nanny. You may work with a family and live in their home (residential), or you can be employed on a daily basis.

Working in a private family can offer useful and valuable experience. This can be a comfortable and exciting life, but in the long term offers little in the way of career prospects. You may feel isolated working on your own with children and it can be more difficult to keep in touch with current ideas and good practice. It is important that you keep up to date with new ideas in childcare and education.

It is sensible to work in this country, gaining experience and skills, before looking for work abroad. Certain countries are more dangerous for women on their own than others, so do seek advice and try and learn the language of the country before you go. America is one place where you know the language, and there are trustworthy agencies that may offer you a job, such as Au Pair America.

If you want to work outside the European Community you must find out whether you need a work permit; you will almost certainly need a visa. It is intended in the European Community that all professional and educational qualifications will eventually become accepted in any European country, so it should become easier to get a job in Europe.

Make sure that wherever you go, you are registered with a respectable and well known agency, and that you have enough money for emergencies and for a return flight.

What special hazards are there by the sea? ▶

What do YOU think?

As they are already parents, some childminders seem to think it unnecessary to seek training for their job, although there is now a special qualification available to them. Do you agree with this, and if so, why?

Mother's help

Before you start your childcare training, you might like some experience of working in a family. As an untrained person, you would be expected to do some housework for all the family, not just the children, and even if called a nanny, you would be a mother's help. Sometimes the term 'au pair' is loosely applied to this kind of employment.

Childminding

The Children Act, 1989 stipulates that anyone caring for children under 8 years in their own home for payment for more than two hours in any day must register as a childminder. This is a growing area of employment, with more and more mothers wishing to return to work after taking maternity leave. Your local authority will have to carry out certain checks before registering you. Although the majority of childminders do not hold a qualification, some training is clearly an advantage and courses leading to a childminding qualification are now in place. This choice of career often appeals to more mature people who have children of their own and a home that has enough room for several children.

Working in a team

You may prefer to work as part of a team of people.

Education

Many childcare and education workers, searching for their first job, will try for a job in a school. This will often be working with pre-school children, in a nursery class or a nursery school, either within the state system or in an independent school. Some local authorities employ childcare and education workers in infant schools, working with children from 5 to 7 years.

If you work in a school with three- to seven-year-olds, you will be part of a team usually headed by a teacher. A great deal of experience is gained working in a school as part of a team, and this will stand you in very good stead in any later career that you might choose. You will be expected to contribute to the curriculum and to the team, to do observations and make assessments of the children, and to work with parents.

Nursery schools may be part of the local authority provision, or may be owned privately. In a state school, your pay and conditions of service will be the same as anyone else in a similar job with similar experience in your local authority. In the private sector, wages and conditions may vary from school to school.

Most schools are interested in providing regular in-service training for staff, and you will need to ask what your school will provide for you.

Many children with disabilities are educated in ordinary schools, but those with more severe disabilities may be educated separately in special schools. Childcare and education workers are employed as part of a **multi-disciplinary** team, which will include teachers, physiotherapists, speech therapists, social workers, nurses and doctors. As well as helping with the children's learning, you will be expected to understand and meet the children's physical needs. In some circumstances, you may be involved in lifting and moving children. Training will be given for this.

Would you like to work with children with disabilities?

TASK

Find out as much as you can about the work of a physiotherapist and a social worker.

There are schools for children with physical disabilities, such as hearing and vision **impairment**, and for children with **cerebral palsy**. There are schools for children with learning difficulties and for those with emotional and behavioural needs. Caring and educating children with disabilities is often physically tiring and emotionally stressful, but offers a great deal of job satisfaction. This type of work gives childcare and education workers more responsibility than many other jobs in education.

Daycare

Daycare includes care and education provided for children of working parents and care and education provided by Social Services for families where some professional support is needed. Daycare is different from education in that children may attend from a very young age and the day offered may start early in the morning and finish late in the evening.

The different types of daycare are:

- Social Services provision, such as family centres and day nurseries, provided by the local authority
- workplace provision, provided by the employer

- community nurseries, possibly set up by parents with grant aid
- nurseries, run by companies to a certain standard, often referred to as 'chains' or franchises
- private nurseries
- university and college nurseries
- voluntary sector nurseries, often run by charities such as Save the Children.

Many daycare centres concentrate on caring for all the needs of the child rather than the emphasis on learning found in schools. This is to be expected as the day (and the year) is longer, and the children are often much younger, although daycare managers realise that education is very important, and teachers are often employed to work in day centres. There are more career opportunities for qualified experienced staff in daycare.

CASE STUDY

Caroline

Caroline is 17, and has just finished her CACHE Foundation Award in Caring for Children. She sees an interesting job advertised in a magazine for a group leader in a daycare centre. She completes the application form and is upset when she receives a letter saying she has not been chosen for interview.

1 Why do you think Caroline was not considered suitable to interview?
2 Should Caroline have discussed this application with anyone? If so, who?
3 For what type of job should Caroline have applied?

Pre-school groups

These may be run by the Pre-school Learning Alliance (formerly PPA), local authorities, or by groups of parents. They are often run for half a day, although some may run all day. Parents often help on a rota basis, and may be involved in the management. The age range is from 2 to 5 years. Childcare and education workers may be employed to organise the groups.

Crèches

There is a growing area of work for childcare and education workers in crèches set up in supermarkets, clinics, hospitals, airports, sports and leisure centres and shopping centres, where parents can leave their children with qualified staff for a short period of time. They work with children from babyhood through to primary school age. The work is varied, as some days there are very few children, and on others there may be up to the numbers allowed. It is not possible to know in advance the ages of the children using the crèche.

List three reasons why parents use daycare ▶

The growth in leisure and tourism world-wide has resulted in opportunities in working abroad, such as in tour operators' holiday places, in crèches on luxury liners and in summer camps at home and abroad.

Playwork

Playwork describes working with children from 5 to 15 years in a number of different settings. They range from adventure playgrounds, play centres, breakfast clubs, after-school clubs, and holiday playschemes to projects for children with disabilities.

The role of the playworker is to provide a safe, secure place that lets children play and explore the environment, providing the necessary materials for enjoyable play. The adult will only get involved when not to do so might lead to a dangerous situation. A playworker will need to understand thoroughly the value of play.

Hospitals.

Opportunities for working in hospitals can occur in either the National Health Service or in the private sector. You might be employed helping the mothers care for their newborn babies, either on the post-natal ward or in the special care baby unit. The children's wards of large hospitals may provide education or play for children. Some hospitals have special assessment units, where the **observation skills** and the understanding of developmental needs of children by the childcare and education worker are especially valued.

Would you enjoy working in a hospital? ▶

What do YOU think**?**

What disadvantages would there be to working part-time? Why might you want to work part-time?

Working part-time

Not everyone is looking for a full-time job. It might suit you to start your career either by seeking a permanent part-time post, or working on a temporary or casual basis. This could be either through an agency or becoming part of a 'bank' of workers. It is possible to job-share, that is to hold a permanent full-time post which you share with another person.

Other areas of employment

We have listed the main areas of work. It is still possible to be employed in residential homes, particularly those for children with disabilities, although nowadays as many children as possible are being looked after in their own home with some help for the parents, or fostered in other families.

Job opportunities are constantly changing. An example of this is the recent development of childcare and education workers working alongside health visitors in clinics in health centres. Some local authorities are now employing childcare and education workers in **respite schemes**, set up to allow families a break from caring for children with disabilities.

Applying for employment or for a place on a course of further training requires careful planning, preparation and organisation. You will need to understand the stages of the application process, and approach it with the same enthusiasm and skills as you do in all your work. It is a very valuable exercise to consider your strengths. After completing the CACHE Foundation Award in Caring for Children you might like to fill in the chart on page 269 which should help you to see what you have to offer at this stage of your career.

Self-appraisal before employment

	Assessment of ability			Any comment from placement report
	low	medium	high	
Professional skills				
attendance				
punctuality				
working in a team				
Communication skills				
writing				
talking				
listening				
Personality				
sense of humour				
flexibility				
cheerfulness				
enthusiasm				
outgoing				
leadership				
able to take direction				
able to respond to criticism				
maturity				
staying power				
Experience with				
babies 0–1 yrs				
children 1–3 yrs				
children 3–5 yrs				
children 5–7 yrs				
children 7–12 yrs				
Experience in				
– daycare				
– education				
– a family				
– other				
Commitment to				
equal opprtunities				
anti-discriminatory practice				

LOOKING FOR A JOB

There are many ways of looking for a job. This can take a long time. You might find a job:

- through a private **employment agency**
- by answering individual advertisements
- from reading professional journals and newspapers
- through a friend
- by writing letters to employers, on the off chance they might be able to employ you.

It is useful to keep a record of your job applications, listing each job you apply for, the date of application, the interview date and the reply. Always keep paper work in a safe place, keeping copies of any forms that you send away. It is likely that you will apply for a number of jobs as you finish your training, and keeping a childcare job search record (see pages 271 and 272) will help you to be clear about the progress of each application.

Preparing your curriculum vitae (CV)

Many employers will ask for a curriculum vitae (CV) and you should be ready to send yours when it is requested.

A curriculum vitae is a Latin term meaning the course (or story) of your life. It has come to mean that area of your life that you have spent in work and education, and of other experiences and interests that may be looked at as useful by a future employer.

If your CV (see the example on page 273) is on a word processor, you will find it easier to alter it when you need to. Whilst being totally honest, you should match your particular strengths and experiences to the job for which you are applying. Remember that you may well be asked to answer questions on your CV at interview.

Remember the following points.

- The CV should be typed, and presented tidily on white A4 paper.
- Some people think that an imaginative and unusual presentation will make more of an impression. It may, but it could put off as many people as interest others. Ask friends, colleagues or tutors what they think.
- Spelling and grammar must be correct (have it checked).
- Keep it brief. It should be no more than two pages long.
- Use spaces to emphasise points and make sections stand out.
- Get a tutor or friend to check it for any mistakes. It may be clear to you but muddled to an outsider.
- Update it regularly.

Childcare job search record

	1	2	3	4
Job title				
Employer's name & address Tel no.				
Type of establishment Age range				
Where advertised Date seen Closing date				
Type of response Date				
Details received Date				
Completed application returned date				
Copy taken				
Date application acknowledged				
Result Date				
Interview Date				
Outcome and date				
Comments				

Childcare job search record

	1	2	3	4
Job title	Nursery Assistant Trainee	Play Scheme Worker		
Employer's name & address Tel no.	Acorns Nursery 11 High Rd. Bristol BS13 6AB 01234567	Social Services Civic Centre Holby HO2 3AZ 06789234		
Type of establishment Age range	Private Nursery 2–5 yrs	Social Services Play Scheme 6–13 yrs		
Where advertised Date seen Closing date	Local Paper 29.2.00 30.3.00	Avon Evening News 1.3.00 27.3.00		
Type of response Date	Letter of Application 3.3.00	Phonecall 3.3.00		
Details received Date	Job description App' form Person spec. 8.3.00	Application form 6.3.00		
Completed application returned date	16.3.00	16.3.00		
Copy taken	✓	✓		
Date application acknowledged	20.3.00	22.3.00		
Result Date	Interview 11.4.00	Interview 4.4.00		
Interview Date	20.4.00	9.4.00		
Outcome and date	not offered post 21.4.00	offered 2 weeks at Easter 9.4.00		
Comments	12 people interviewed. I dried up in interview – could not answer many 2's. Nervous	Accepted. Can apply for summer scheme. Useful experience		

An example of a curriculum vitae

Mary Jones
26 Queen Street
Bath
BA33 6EM
Tel: – 01722 12345

Date of birth 4.4.83

I am a responsible and confident person. I am hoping to follow a career in Childcare and Education by achieving National Vocational Qualifications.

Personal strengths

I am:
- enthusiastic
- highly motivated
- able to work under pressure
- very patient

I have:
- good communication skills
- the ability to work in a team

Education and Qualifications

School

Walter Mitty Comprehensive
Broom Street
Bath BA33 24T

GCSE results

D English Language
E Art and Design
C History
E Maths

I attended school from Sept 1994 to July 1999.

College

Tamworth College of FE
Wellington Road
Bristol
BS22 6AB

Qualifications

CACHE Foundation Award
in Caring for Children

I attended college fromSeptember 1999 to July 2000. During this time I successfully completed a Nursery School Placement working with children from three to five years.

Work experience

Sainsbury plc
Weston Green
Bristol
Avon
Oct 1999

I work as a Saturday sales assistant. My duties include: serving customers, using a computerised till, stacking shelves.

Prior Hope Nursery School
Weston High
Bristol
BS22 9AC

Placement with children aged 3–5 years 1 day a week for two terms, three week block placement in May 2000. Duties included
- working with children
- playing a part in the nursery team.

Interests

In my spare time I enjoy swimming and going to aerobics. I also enjoy karate. I like to read historical novels. When I qualify as a childcare and education worker I would like to travel and work abroad.

Referees

Cynthia Johns, Tutor
Tamworth College of FE
Wellington Road
Bristol BS22 6AB

Mike Read, Deputy Head
Walter Mitty School
Broom Street
Bath BA33 24T

Your basic CV should include:

- personal details
- education and qualifications
- work experience and career history
- personal interests and hobbies.

Personal details

This should include your name, address to which you wish letters to be sent, telephone number, and your date of birth.

Education and qualifications

Start with the highest qualification. Make sure that you list your qualifications clearly, spacing them well apart. It is not necessary to include any failures unless there is a large time gap on your CV. If you did not finish a course, put 'course discontinued'. If you failed a course, you may wish to explain briefly why. If you have overseas qualifications, you should note their equivalent UK level. If you have been on any relevant training programmes, you might feel it a good idea to list them. First Aid and Food Handler's certificates would be appropriate.

Work experience and career history

Start with your most recent job, because if your future employer has many applications to read, he or she will probably just skim through your CV, and the last job should be the most relevant. Each period of employment needs to be clearly separated, with the month as well as the year. You should include full-time, holiday and part-time work, both paid and voluntary. It is unnecessary to give addresses of your past employers, but you should include the dates of employment, job title, and duties and responsibilities undertaken. Details of your work experience either in school or college should be stated in this section.

It is important to match the description of your experience to the job for which you are applying. Describe briefly what you did in each post, and note any achievements or successes. Remember that only you can outline your skills, so you do not need to be modest. Be brief and to the point. This is the most important part of your CV, so work on it and get advice from your tutors.

Personal interests and hobbies

This should be a fairly short section of the CV, perhaps more useful for the younger person who has not yet had the opportunity to develop a career. You need to show yourself in the best possible light, so only list those hobbies that make you look interesting, active and enthusiastic, and which might be of use in the job. Any interest showing team involvement or **initiative** would be useful to list. Indicate in some hobbies whether you watch or take part, as just putting 'cricket' would not be enough.

Other relevant details

This section might include a driving licence, the fact that you do not smoke, knowledge of other languages, swimming or life-saving certificate, and computer skills.

A CV usually ends with the names and addresses of two people who would be willing to act as **referees** and write a reference for you. You should put their occupation or job title. Always ask their permission before giving their names.

Covering or accompanying letters

Most employers, when asking you to fill in an application form, will also want a covering letter (see example on page 276). This should be handwritten, neat, and well spaced. If your skills in letter writing are not of the highest, you will find several books in your library to help you. The type of paper you use and the neatness of your handwriting will give an impression of your personality and ability.
The letter falls into three sections:

- who you are, and why you are writing
- what you are offering
- what you hope to get in reply to your letter.

It should be short and to the point. It should mention the job for which you are applying and quote any reference number. You should show you understand what the job involves and that you have some knowledge of the age group and type of setting. Give your reasons for applying for the job and show the employer where to look for the most important information on your CV. Match your skills and achievements to the job requirements, saying why you feel you are suitable for this job and what you are offering them rather than what you expect to gain. Say when you are available for interview. The letter should show interest and enthusiasm.

Telephone technique

You may be asked in an advertisement to telephone a named person. Give yourself time when doing this and make sure you are not going to be inter-rupted. Try to use a private phone rather than a pay phone, and have the advertisement by you when you ring. Speak slowly and clearly, stating where you saw the advertisement, your reason for interest in the job, and your name and full address, including the postcode. If you are applying for a job as a nanny (or even, perhaps, for a job with a small private nursery), the telephone conversation might turn into a short-listing interview. Make sure that you have your CV with you, so that you can answer any questions clearly. You may wish to make some notes yourself, so have a pencil and some paper with you.

Once you have made your telephone call, you will be sent an application form, a job description, the person specification and possibly some infor-mation about the place, together with details of any equal opportunity policy. All papers should be read carefully before you try to fill them in.

An example of an accompanying letter

32 Bridge Street
Bath
BF2 8QP

28 October 2000

The Manager
The Town Nursery
75 Pembroke Square
Bristol
CT3 6CH

Dear Sir/Madam,

I am writing to you to apply for the position of Nursery Assistant that I saw advertised in the Bristol Evening News on 26 October.

I have just successfully completed the CACHE Foundation Award in Caring for Children and am looking for a job with young children. From your advertisement, I understand that you offer training linked with NVQ to your employees. This of interest to me as I wish to take a professional course but cannot afford to do so without employment.

As you will see from my CV I completed three weeks' work experience at the Toddle Inn nursery near you. I enjoy this age group very much. The manager of the nursery, Miss Bunn, has said she will give me a good reference.

I believe I would work well in your nursery and would be a hard working member of staff. You could interview me at any time and I look forward to hearing from you.

Yours faithfully,

Henrietta Beecroft

Henrietta Beecroft

What do YOU think?

How many forms have you filled in during the last six months? Did you find them easy to complete, or did you need some help?

The application form

There may well be instructions enclosed with the form as to how to complete it, and you must read these carefully. You may be asked not to send a CV as the form will ask for all the information needed. The first thing to do is to photocopy the form, so that you can practice completing the copy first. Answer all the questions on the form, and use a black pen, so that it can be photocopied clearly.

You will be asked to give the names and addresses of two referees. If you have never worked, you may give the name of your college or school tutor. If you have had a particularly successful placement, your supervisor may be happy to write you a reference. You must check with any referee that he or she is prepared to write a reference for you.

When you have carefully completed the application form, and without Tippex or crossing out, make a photocopy before sending it off. You will be questioned on your answers and it is sensible to take the copy with you when you are interviewed.

CASE STUDY

Justin

Justin has been in care most of his life. He has just completed the Level 2 Certificate in Childcare and Education with very successful placements. He very much wants to work with young children and hopes to eventually work in a children's residential home. He has applied for thirty jobs and has not yet been chosen for interview.

1 Give some reasons why he may not have been successful in getting an interview.
2 With whom should he discuss this?
3 What other ways might Justin use to find employment?

Person specification/job description

Most jobs will enclose a job description/person specification (see page 279) along with the application form. The person specification will spell out the qualifications, skills and experience needed for the job. This will help you to see if you are suited to this particular job. The job description will explain the purpose of the job, and the duties and responsibilities involved.

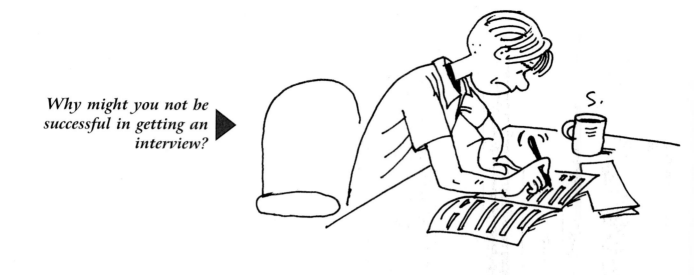

Why might you not be successful in getting an interview?

What do YOU think?

What questions would you want to ask at a job interview?

SUCCEEDING AT INTERVIEW

This stage of finding work is possibly the most nerve-wracking and worrying part. You feel at your most exposed and vulnerable. Being well prepared will help you to become confident and so succeed.

If you are offered an interview, remember to do the following.

- Reply at once, confirming that you will be able to be there on the given date. If you are unable to attend, telephone at once, explaining why, and stating that you are still interested in the job. If you decide that you do not want this job, you must let the employer know at once that you will not be coming for an interview.
- Make sure you know exactly where the interview is being held. Plan your journey there, and time how long it takes.
- Read all the information you have been given about the job, and try to work out some of the questions you may be asked. Common questions are: 'What are your strong points?', 'What are your weak points?', 'Why did you apply for the job?' Be truthful, but positive, relating all your answers to the job.
- Read through what you have put on your application form and your CV, and think about any questions that may come out of them, for example gaps in employment, or why you did not sit your exams.
- Think up some questions that you might like to ask about the job.
- If you know someone who is already working in a similar job, you might ask him or her about interview experiences.

An example of a job description and person specification

PARKSIDE SCHOOL

JOB DESCRIPTION

TRAINEE NURSERY ASSISTANT

Responsibilities

1. To take guidance from senior staff in providing quality care for the children in accordance within the policies of the school.

2. To relate appropriately to parents, carers and other professionals.

3. To undertake the training and asasesment provided by the institution.

Duties

1. To care for the children and meet their needs in respect to their physical, emotional, social and intellectual development.

2. To participate with the team members in the care of the nursery environment.

3. To liaise with colleagues in furtherance of the schools' provision, become a member of the nursery team, attending and participating in meetings.

PERSON SPECIFICATION

1. Candidates should be able to demonstrate a sensitivity to the needs and interests of children.

2. Candidates should be of good character and be able to provide two references as evidence of this.

3. Candidates should be educated to the level which will allow them to participate in the training.

4. Candidates should not have a criminal record.

5. Candidates should have an appropriate self-presentation during the working day.

6. Candidates should be in agreement with all of the nursery's policies, in the short term in particular with the policy of "EQUAL OPPORTUNITIES".

7. Candidates should be in good health.

8. Candidates should be able to communicate to a level which makes it possible to perform successfully in the workplace.

- Think about what you are going to wear. Wear neat clothes in which you feel comfortable, and avoid too much make up and jewellery.
- You may be invited to a pre-interview visit. Jump at the opportunity, as it not only shows how keen you are, it also gives you a chance to get to know the staff, the children and the building.

Before the interview

Having arrived safely and in good time, tell someone at the reception desk or general office that you are there. You may have time to look around the building. While you are waiting, have a look at the notice boards, be aware of the children and the noise levels, and get a feel for the atmosphere of the place. Find out where the lavatory is, in case you suddenly feel the need! Take a book or magazine with you, as you may have to wait. Obviously, you know not to smoke on the premises, and you should make sure that you have eaten before you leave home.

Take copies of your application form and CV with you, together with the job description, the person specification and any other information. You should take the originals of any certificates of qualification or education with you. Allow them to be photocopied, but make sure you take them home. Try to relax, take some deep breaths before entering the interview room, and think positively.

The interview

Enter the room in confident way, looking cheerful and relaxed. You will be asked to sit in a particular place. There may be two or more people in the room. There may be a short time spent on small talk, trying to put you at your ease. The person chairing the interviews should introduce you to the people on the interview panel and the plan of the interview will be explained to you.

The first questions may be personal to you, concerning your CV, experience and education. Equal opportunity means that all candidates are asked the same questions. To put you at ease, the first question may be a very general one, asking you to talk about your childcare experience, so have your CV in front of you as a reminder. Another question usually asked will be to do with equal opportunities. You will probably be asked what you think you can offer and your reasons for applying for the job.

Answer all questions fully and honestly. Take your time to think about what you are going to say, and do not allow yourself to be hurried. Remember you are showing the panel how lucky they are to have the opportunity of employing someone with your skills, initiative and enthusiasm. When asked why you are applying for the job it will show you in a better light if you tell them how well suited you are, rather than just replying 'Because the money is better' or 'I live next door'. If you do not understand a question, ask the questioner to reword it.

TASK

List the reasons why an understanding of equal opportunities is important to the childcare and education worker.

What should you never do at an interview? ▶

Whatever questions you are asked, the way that you answer is nearly as important as what you say. You need to sound relaxed, confident, positive and polite. Keep your cool even if the questioning becomes uncomfortable. The other candidates will be given the same questions.

Once all questions have been asked of you, it will be your turn to ask some questions. Have the ones you have prepared on a piece of paper in front of you, and ask them if the answers have not already become obvious. There may well be something else that you now wish to ask. The first question should be about the job. The following are some examples.

- What are the roles of the other people in the team in which I will be working?
- What in-service training will be available to me?

Having asked your questions, the interview will end, and you will be thanked for coming. You may be asked whether you are a serious candidate for the job, and would you accept it if it is offered to you. A few candidates opt out at this stage. Remember to thank the panel for interviewing you as you leave the room.

Body language

Whatever type of interview you attend, your appearance and speech will tell the panel a great deal about you. Your body language will also convey messages, for example, sitting with your arms folded will show that you are nervous and defensive. What you say should fit with your body language, otherwise the employer will be very confused and perhaps not believe what you are saying.

TASK

Working with a close friend, give a two- to three-minute talk on a subject that interests you. Ask the friend to record your body language.

Remember:

- when you enter the room, put your belongings away from you, stand up straight, walk slowly into the room to help you stay calm, and use a firm, not limp handshake
- make yourself comfortable as you sit down. Sit back in the chair, and try to relax
- look pleasant and attentive
- do not be over-friendly with the interviewer. Call them by the names they have given you
- look at people when replying to a question
- do not put your hand across your mouth
- if your hands are shaking, keep them out of sight, and do not accept a drink
- listen intently to any questions, showing respect to the interviewer.

Decision time

You may be offered the job subject to satisfactory references and a medical examination. Well done! Before making a decision you need to think about:

- the starting date
- the salary and any pay increases
- the travelling time and cost
- is there a trial period?
- what in-service training will you be offered?
- are the **conditions of service**, regarding hours of work, holidays and sickness arrangements fair and satisfactory?
- did you feel comfortable with the people?

Contracts and the law

A sample Contract of Employment is shown on pages 283. Your contract should include the following information:

- job title
- identity of the employer and the employee
- the starting date of employment
- details of pay
- holiday entitlement, public holidays and rates of holiday pay
- details of normal hours of work, and overtime arrangements
- place or places of work.

An employer must also be able to provide the following information for you:

- details of any pension schemes
- period of notice required
- sickness arrangements, and sick pay

An example of a contract of employment

PARKSIDE SCHOOL
CONTRACT OF EMPLOYMENT

Between ....
of
....
....
....
and

PARKSIDE SCHOOL
Address
Telephone No.

Line Manager: Head of School
Post Title: Nursery Assistant

1. Remuneration
Your salary will be based on an hourly rate, calculated on qualifications, experience and role in the organisation. This salary to be reviewed annually and paid monthly in arrears.

2. Hours of Work
This is a proportional full-time appointment. Attendance times will be arranged to accommodate the satisfactory operation of the nursery but will generally be between the hours of 7.45 am and 6.30 pm.
You will be expected to attend the school for work-related activities out of hours to a maximum of one evening per week, for which time in lieu will be made available.

3. Training
You will be expected to participate as both a member and a provider of staff training and development where appropriate and will be expected to maintain a high standard of professional practice at all times.

4. Place of Work
You will work at one of the schools owned by the partnership.

5. Probation and Notice
The contract is subject to six months probationary period in accordance with normal employment law.
One month's notice will be applicable on either side, however the school will be entitled to terminate the contract without notice in the event of serious misconduct or negligence on your part.

6. Holiday Entitlement
You are entitled to the following leave to be arranged with the line manager.
10 days plus Bank holidays in the first year.
This will be increased by 5 days in each subsequent year to a maximum of 20 days.
Further unpaid leave is negotiable for individual reasons.

7. Confidentiality
Except in the course of your professional duties under the contract you will not during or after the termination of your employment disclose to any person or organization any information which comes into your possession during the course of your employment relating to the school, its business or clients without first gaining the permission of the nursery owner/manager or the parties concerned.

8. Dress Code
Employees are expected to wear the designated uniform shirt and appropriate trousers or skirt and sensible shoes. Dangling jewellery and earrings are not allowed and no rings except plain bands.

SIGNED ON BEHALF OF THE SCHOOL

....
Head of School

I accept the appointment of Nursery Assistant.

....
Nursery Assistant   Date

- a finishing date for fixed term contracts
- details of disciplinary and grievance procedures
- the health and safety policy
- any other details that the employer wishes to make clear. This may include training expectations, equal opportunity policies and so on.

Criminal background check

You will be asked to complete a form to arrange a criminal background check. This is now required for any person working with children under the age of 18 years. You must declare any conviction, however long ago or whatever type of sentence you received.

Preparing for an interview in the private sector

You have been given an appointment for an interview as a mother's help, and you need to check that you are clear about the time and date of the interview, and have the correct address. Remember to let a friend or relative know where you are going, and at what time. You have to be careful. You may even wish for someone to be with you in the house or place of interview, and wait outside until you are ready to leave.

> **TASK**
>
> Pretend to be a mother's help coming for an interview. A friend can ask you questions, and another friend can make notes and give you feedback.

Why is it important to take someone with you in a situation like this?

Tracey

Tracey replied to an advertisement in her local paper for a post as nanny to two children working abroad. The money was good, and the conditions of employment sounded excellent. She was invited to attend an interview at a nearby hotel.

When she arrived she was sent up to a room, where two men were waiting. It became clear that interviewing a nanny was not the first thing on their minds. Fortunately, she realised this quickly, and managed to leave the room without further involvement, but felt shaken and distressed by the experience.

1   What steps should she have taken to protect herself before the interview?
2   What steps should she have taken to protect herself during the interview?
3   What steps should she take after this experience?

The interview

In most instances, this will take place in the informal home setting, with just one person, or at most two. The children may well be around, and most parents would be anxious to see how you relate to the children, so even though you may be nervous, make sure you do not ignore any member of the family.

When talking to the parent, see that you are sitting comfortably, and feeling as relaxed as possible. Listen carefully to what you are being asked. Take your time to consider each question put to you, and answer honestly and positively. Try not to be put off if notes are being taken or recordings being made; this will only be to help the person remember your good clear answers, particularly if he or she has several people to interview.

Most interviews will contain some of the following questions.

- What is your past childcare experience?
- Can you supply at least two references that can be followed up?
- What interests you about this particular job?
- Are you in good health?
- Do you enjoy housework?
- Can you cook?
- What are your views on: play, food and mealtimes, activities, toilet training, managing behaviour, rest, exercise and sleep?

What do YOU think?

Name some of the problems that may occur between you and the parents.

If offered the job, disappointments often occur on both sides because certain difficult issues have not been adequately discussed, and people enter into a contract with different expectations. It is worthwhile spending quite some time at the interview, as each family is unique, and you want to make quite sure that you will fit in well.

Most importantly, trust your instincts. You will know right away if you feel on the same wavelength as the family, and if you like the children.

The contract

When you have come to a decision, it is sensible to ask for a contract, so that there are no misunderstandings. Employers have to give an employee a written contract of employment after fourteen weeks. Both employer and employee should sign this document.

SETTLING IN

Everyone is nervous and anxious before starting any new job. You know how important first impressions are, and you will arrive punctually, wearing suitable clothes, willing and eager to learn and to fit in with the family or the team.

Wherever you work, you are aware of the importance of professional behaviour and attitudes. You know that you will be reliable and punctual, contacting your employer if unavoidably delayed or sick.

Anyone working with individual children or with groups of children is expected to:

- make sure the children are safe and well
- be sensitive to the individual needs of the children
- regularly speak with parents, respecting their greater knowledge of the child
- keep their line manager informed
- take part in staff meetings and training
- make sure there is equality of opportunity for all children, respecting and valuing each child as an individual.

Every team member should know what they are trying to achieve and what they are expected to contribute. The line management system should be clear, and each member will understand their own responsibility. The whole team will be involved in decision making, and all the members will feel their opinions are valued.

> ### KEY POINT
> Every team member should know what they are trying to achieve and what they are expected to contribute.

CASE STUDY

Clara

Clara has recently started working in a private day nursery. In the room in which she works there are two other members of staff who have worked together for many years. They seem to go out of their way to exclude Clara from their conversation and day-to-day decision making. Clara has become so unhappy she is thinking of leaving.

1 Would the unhappy atmosphere affect the children in the room?
2 Why would it not be sensible for Clara to leave?
3 How might she resolve the problem?
4 With whom should she discuss this problem?

To become a successful team member:

- accept your fair share of the workload, and always be willing to help when asked
- you need to work co-operatively with the whole team, not allowing personality clashes or feelings of dislike to get in the way of your work
- ask for help and advice when necessary
- respect colleagues privacy. Do not ask questions about other people's private lives and always keep confidences
- be aware of the working environment and respect other people's feelings with regard to temperature, light and noise
- repay promptly favours given to you. For example, if someone changes a shift to suit you, be willing to do the same for them
- try to support colleagues at all times, and be quick to give credit where it is due. Never criticise a team member publicly or in their absence
- be ready and willing to take part in activities outside your working hours whenever possible
- make a contribution to the team by keeping up to date with your reading
- give extra support to colleagues who are under stress or unwell
- always be reliable and punctual.

You will have met some members of the team at the interview. You now need to get to know the other members and, of course, the children. You may be lucky enough to have a 'mentor' allocated to you, who will be responsible for giving you information on policy and procedures, and be willing to spend time with you on a regular basis to discuss any concerns you or the team may have.

What skill does a mentor need? ▶

What do YOU think?

You have been given the task of cleaning the rabbit hutch for the past six months. You feel this is unfair. How would you express your feelings to your line manager?

If you have to find everything out for yourself, you might find this checklist useful.

CHECK LIST: THINGS TO FIND OUT

- the names and roles of each member of the team
- the names and dates of birth of the children
- the layout of the building and where to find the staff room, the medical room and the lavatories
- the daily, weekly, termly and yearly routines
- which children have special needs, for example those with chronic illnesses such as asthma or diabetes, or those with speech delay or learning difficulties
- where the First Aid box, the accident book, the register and the telephone are
- fire drill procedure
- the storage of equipment, inside and outside.

Once you can find your way around, and you know about the day to day running of the setting, you will need to find out about policies and procedures.

CHECK LIST: POLICIES AND PROCEDURES

- the Equal Opportunities Policy and how it is put into practice
- the Health and Safety Policy and the procedures that are in place
- the policy identifying illnesses that bar children from coming to school/nursery
- the policy on the procedure to be followed if there is a serious accident or a child becomes ill

- the procedures on the reporting of suspected child abuse/neglect
- procedures for the management of children with behaviour problems
- procedures for bringing and collecting children
- the admissions policy and settling in procedures
- the policy regarding the food eaten on the premises
- the policy regarding the involvement of parents
- the procedure to follow if everyone has to leave the building quickly
- opportunities for in-service training
- times and days of regular staff meetings
- methods of recording information about the children
- arrangements for outings
- arrangements for giving medication, when necessary.

Remember, all employees have certain basic rights:

- protection under Health and Safety Legislation
- protection from discrimination on grounds of race or gender
- protection from discrimination or dismissal for Trade Union activities
- equal pay for work of equal value
- time off on full salary for ante-natal appointments
- access to medical reports concerning employment.

When working in an establishment, you need to be clear about your role, and the role of others in the team, as the safety and well-being of the children may depend on this. Accept that you will be working under the direction of others, who will give you tasks to do. Instructions are generally spoken. Listen carefully, and make sure you understand what you are being asked to do. If anything is unclear, you must ask for an explanation.

Working with children is a fulfilling and worthwhile profession. The training can be the foundation of a very satisfying professional career.

> ## KEY POINT
>
> **Working with children is a fulfilling and worthwhile profession.**

✓ TEST YOURSELF

1 Name four career choices open to the childcare and education worker.

2 Name two ways of finding employment.

3 What is a CV, and what information does it give?

4 Name three things you should do when preparing to be interviewed.

5 Name three things that have to be in a contract of employment.

6 Name four qualities that will help you become a successful team member.

7 Name four policies found in all childcare and education establishments.

GLOSSARY

By the time you have finished this chapter you should understand the meaning of the following words:

employment agency a business that will find employees for employers

cerebral palsy a condition resulting from brain damage, usually during pregnancy or at birth, affecting the part of the brain that controls movement

conditions of service statement in a contract of what the employee is entitled to in the areas of pay, holidays, hours of work and so on

initiative being aware of what needs to be done, and doing it without being told. For example, mixing fresh paints when some colours have run out

mentor someone who takes responsibility to help and support another person, often a new member of staff

multi-disciplinary team a number of people with different qualifications working together

observation skills professional skills of how to look at children in an objective way and record this information using various techniques

referees people prepared to write to say that you are suitable for a certain job

respite schemes help provided by local authority and voluntary groups to let parents of disabled children have a rest from providing continuous care.

Appendices

APPENDIX 1

Developmental norms 0 to 16 years

	Physical development – gross motor	Physical development – fine motor	Social and emotional development	Cognitive and language development
At birth	Reflexes: ■ Rooting, sucking and swallowing ■ Grasp reflex ■ Walking reflex ■ Moro reflex If pulled to sit, head falls backwards If held in sitting position, head falls forward, and back is curved in supine (lying on back), limbs are bent In prone (lying on front), lies in fetal position with knees tucked up Unable to raise head or stretch limbs	Reflexes: ■ Pupils react to light ■ Opens eyes when held upright ■ Blinks or open eyes wide to sudden sound ■ Startle reaction to sudden sound ■ Closing eyes to sudden sound	Bonding/attachment	Cries vigorously, with variation in pitch and duration
1 month	In prone, lifts chin In supine, head moves to one side. Arm and leg extended on face side Begins to flex upper and lower limbs	Hands fisted Eyes move to dangling objects	Watches mother's face with increasingly alert facial expression Fleeting smile – may be wind! Stops crying when picked up	Cries become more differentiated to indicate needs Stops and attends to voice, rattle and bell
3 months	Held sitting, head straight back and neck firm. Lower back still weak When lying, pelvis is flat	Grasps an object when placed in hand Turns head right round to looks at objects Eye contact firmly established	Reacts with pleasure to familiar situations/routines	Regards hands with interest Beginning to vocalise

continued

Developmental norms 0 to 16 years

	Physical development – gross motor	Physical development – fine motor	Social and emotional development	Cognitive and language development
6 months	In suspine, can lift head and shoulders In prone, can raise up on hands Sits with support Kicks strongly May roll over When held, enjoys standing and jumping	Has learned to grasp objects and passes toys from hand to hand Visual sense well established	Takes everything to mouth Responds to different emotional tones of chief caregiver	Finds feet interesting Vocalises tunefully Laughs in play Screams with annoyance Understands purpose of rattle
9 months	Sits unsupported Begins to crawl Pulls to stand, falls back with bump	Visually attentive Grasps with thumb ad index finger Releases toy by dropping Looks to fallen objects Beginning to finger-feed Holds bottle or cup	Plays peek-a-boo – can start earlier Imitates hand clapping Clings to familiar adults, reluctant to go to strangers – from about 7 months	Watches activities of others with interest Vocalises to attract attention Beginning to babble Finds partially hidden toy Shows an interest in picture books Knows own name
1 year	Walks holding one hand, may walk alone Bends down and picks up objects Pulls to stand and sits deliberately	Picks up small objects Fine pincer grip Points at objects Holds spoon	Co-operates in dressing Demonstrates affection Participates in nursery rhymes Waves bye bye	Uses jargon Responds to simple instructions and understands several words Puts wooden cubes in and out of cup or box

continued

Developmental norms 0 to 16 years

	Physical development – gross motor	Physical development – fine motor	Social and emotional development	Cognitive and language development
15 months	Walking usually well established Can crawl up stairs frontwards and down stairs backwards Kneels unaided Balance poor, falls heavily	Holds crayon with palmar grasp Precise pincer grasp, both hands Builds tower of 2 cubes Can place objects precisely Uses spoon which sometimes rotates Turns pages of picture book	Indicates wet or soiled pants Helps with dressing Emotionally dependent on familiar adult	Jabbers loudly and freely, with 2–6 recognisable words, and can communicate needs Intensely curious Reproduces lines drawn by adult
18 months	Climbs up and down stairs with hand held Runs carefully Pushes, pulls and carries large toys Backs into small chair Can squat to pick up toys	Builds tower of 3 cubes Scribbles to and fro spontaneously Begins to show preference for one hand Drinks without spilling	Tries to sing Imitates domestic activities Bowel control sometimes attained Alternates between clinging and resistance Plays contentedly alone near familiar adult	Enjoys simple picture books, recognising some characters Jabbering established 6–20 recognisable words May use echolalia (repeating adult's last words, or last word of rhyme) Is able to show several parts of the body, when asked Explores environment energetically
2 years	Runs with confidence, avoiding obstacles Walks up and down stairs both feet to each step, holding wall Squats with ease. Rises without using hands Can climb up on furniture and get down again Steers tricycle pushing along with feet Throws small ball overarm, and kicks large ball	Turns picture books pages one at a time Builds tower of 6 cubes Holds pencil with first 2 fingers and thumb near to point	Competently spoon feeds and drinks from cup Is aware of physical needs Can put on shoes and hat Keenly interested in outside environment – unaware of danger Demands chief caregiver's attention and often clings Parallel play Throws tantrums if frustrated	Identifies photographs of familiar adults Identifies small world toys Recognises tiny details in pictures Uses own name to refer to self Speaks in 2- and 3-word sentences, and can sustain short conversations Asks for names and labels Talks to self continuously

Developmental norms 0 to 16 years

	Physical development – gross motor	Physical development – fine motor	Social and emotional development	Cognitive and language development
3 years	Competent locomotive skills Can jump off lower steps Still uses 2 feet to a step coming down stairs Pedals and steers tricycle	Cuts paper with scissors Builds a tower of 9 cubes and a bridge with 3 cubes Good pencil control Can thread 3 large beads on a string	Uses spoon and fork Increased independence in self care Dry day and night Affectionate and co-operative Plays co-operatively, particularly domestic play Tries to please	Can copy a circle and some letters Can draw a person with a head and 2 other parts of the body May name colours and match 3 primary colours Speech and comprehension well established Some immature pronunciations and unconventional grammatical forms Asks questions constantly Can give full name, gender and age Relates present activities and past experiences Increasing interest in words and numbers
4 years	All motor muscles well controlled Can turn sharp corners when running Hops on favoured foot Balances for 3–5 seconds Increasing skill at ball games Sits with knees crossed	Builds a tower of 10 cubes Uses 6 cubes to build 3 steps, when shown	Boasts and is bossy Sense of humour developing Cheeky, answers back Wants to be independent Plans games co-operatively Argues with other children but learning to share	Draws person with head, legs and trunk Draws recognisable house Uses correct grammar most of the time Most pronunciations mature Asks meanings of words Counts up to 20 Imaginative play well developed
5 years	Can touch toes keeping legs straight Hops on either foot Skips Runs on toes Ball skills developing well Can walk along a thin line	Threads needle and sews Builds steps with 3–4 cubes Colours pictures carefully Can copy adult writing	Copes well with daily personal needs Chooses own friends Well-balanced and sociable Sense of fair play and understanding of rules developing Shows caring attitudes towards others	Matches most colours Copies square, triangle and several letters, writing some unprompted Writes name Draws a detailed person Speaks correctly and fluently Knows home address Able and willing to complete projects Understands numbers using concrete objects Imaginary play now involves make-believe games

continued

Developmental norms 0 to 16 years

	Physical development – gross motor	Physical development – fine motor	Social and emotional development	Cognitive and language development
6 years	Jumps over rope 25 cm high Learning to skip with rope	Ties own shoe laces	Eager for fresh experiences More demanding and stubborn less sociable Joining a 'gang' may be important May be quarrelsome with friends Needs to succeed as failing too often leads to poor self-esteem	Reading skills developing well Drawings more precise and detailed Figure may be drawn in profile Can describe how one object differs from another Mathematical skills developing, may use symbols instead of concrete objects May write independently
7 years	Rides a 2-wheel bicycle Improves balance	Skills constantly improving More dexterity and precision in all areas	Special friend at school Peer approval becoming important Likes to spend some time alone Enjoys TV and books May attempt tasks too complex to complete	Moving towards abstract thought Able to read Can give opposite meanings Able to write paragraph
8–12	Movements well co-ordinated Physical skills improving Takes part in team games with enjoyment Swims	Skills constantly improving Drawings become more complex	Friendships become more important Independence increasing More understanding of self	Concentration improves Able to read fluently Can write a story May think scientifically Able to play complex games such as chess
12–16	Hormonal changes Puberty Skin changes Growth spurts Body hair develops Girl: menstruates breasts develop hips broaden Boy: facial hair develops voice deepens growth of penis and testes	Skills develop depending on interest and practice, for example playing guitar Nintendo games, model making	Mood swings May rebel against authority Interest in sex begins May experiment with different identities	Adolescents start to think about the future and if motivated will use all their intellectual ability to achieve their educational goals

APPENDIX 2

✓ TEST YOURSELF

Test yourself with these multiple choice questions and answers.

1. Proteins are essential for
   a. growth and repair
   b. eyesight
   c. energy
   d. hearing
2. Kosher food is eaten by
   a. Muslims
   b. vegetarians
   c. Jews
   d. Hindus
3. What is the most common cause of death in children aged 1 – 5 years?
   a. accidents
   b. cancer
   c. cot death
   d. infections
4. Which professionals are responsible for the health care of children?
   a. geriatricians
   b. dieticians
   c. paediatricians
   d. physiotherapists
5. Which of the following is not an infestation?
   a. threadworms
   b. chicken pox
   c. scabies
   d. head lice
6. If a child has touched a hot iron, what is the first course you would take?
   a. send for medical aid
   b. apply antiseptic cream
   c. hold the hand under cold running water
   d. apply a dry dressing
7. A three-year-old refuses to eat lunch. What is the best way to deal with this?
   a. make her sit at the table until she eats it
   b. do not make a fuss about it
   c. play a game with her to get her to eat it.
   d. change the meal to something she likes

8. Which of the following is essential if children are to enjoy a paddling pool?
   a. constant supervision by an adult
   b. attractive equipment
   c. enough space to move in
   d. sunny weather

9. If fire breaks out in a nursery, what is the first thing the staff should do?
   a. call the fire brigade
   b. close all the windows
   c. get the children out of the building
   d. try to put the fire out

10. What would you expect a child from a Hindu family not to eat?
    a. eggs
    b. beef
    c. fish
    d. sweets

11. Which of the following foods is the best source of iron?
    a. green vegetables
    b. milk
    c. white bread
    d. oats

12. Which of the following is not a natural material?
    a. mud
    b. wood
    c. clay
    d. Plasticene

13. A book corner in a nursery should never be used for
    a. a story session for a large group
    b. a singing session
    c. a place for a child who is not behaving to sit on her own
    d. a place for an ill child to rest

14. A child with coeliac disease must not eat
    a. glucose
    b. gluten
    c. protein
    d. fat

15. Play is essential to children because it
    a. keeps them busy
    b. stops them fighting
    c. prevents boredom
    d. helps them to learn

16. Gross motor skills can be stimulated by
    a. threading beads
    b. riding a tricycle
    c. building with bricks
    d. doing a jigsaw puzzle

17. Most children will be able to tie their own shoelaces by the age of
    a. 3 years
    b. 4 years
    c. 5 years
    d. 6 years

18. An 18-month-old comes to the nursery with a comfort blanket. The childcare and education worker should
    a. ask the parent to take the blanket home
    b. tell the child he will not need it
    c. keep the blanket in a drawer in case it is needed
    d. allow the child to keep it with him

19. Outside play is important for children because it stimulates
    a. gross motor skills
    b. the imagination
    c. the intellect
    d. all of these

20. In which year was the Children Act passed by Parliament
    a. 1800
    b. 1999
    c. 1989
    d. 1993

21. Raw meat should be stored
    a. on the bottom shelf of a refrigerator
    b. in a container in the kitchen
    c. wrapped in a cool place
    d. on the top shelf of a refrigerator

22. Which vitamin cannot be stored by the body?
    a. A
    b. C
    c. D
    d. K

23. When a child first starts at nursery, should the parent/carer
    a. leave immediately
    b. stay until the child is settled
    c. stay for the first day
    d. stay for five minutes and then go without saying goodbye

24. Which of the following childcare courses is a Level 2 course?
    a. Foundation level award in Caring for Children
    b. Certificate in Childcare and Education
    c. Diploma in Childcare and Education
    d. Developing Childminding Practice

25. Which of the following pieces of equipment are essential when starting a course?
    a. ruler
    b. briefcase
    c. pens
    d. computer

26. What piece of clothing is the most suitable for a three-year-old boy at nursery?
    a. jeans
    b. dungarees
    c. jogging bottoms
    d. a suit

27. Newborn babies should be placed in the cot
    a. on their side
    b. on their tummy
    c. on their back
    d. upside down

28. A child can hop on one foot when she is
    a. 1 year
    b. 18 months
    c. 3 years
    d. 4 years

29. CV stands for
    a. career volunteer
    b. curried vegetables
    c. childhood vitamins
    d. curriculum vitae

30. The main reason childcare and education workers should be punctual is because
    a. they are part of a professional team
    b. they get their money stopped if they are late
    c. they will be given the most boring jobs if they are not on time
    d. they will get a good reference when they leave

31. An extended family consists of
    a. mother and child
    b. parents and children
    c. parents, children, grandparents, aunts, uncles and cousins
    d. stepparents and children

32. What is the most suitable outing for toddlers?
    a. the zoo
    b. the park
    c. a museum
    d. a theme park

33. Which religion celebrates Divali?
    a. Islam
    b. Judaism
    c. Hinduism
    d. Catholicism

34. If you wanted all day care for a toddler would you choose
    a. a Primary School
    b. a pre-school

c. a nursery class

d. a childminder

35. The British Standards Institute symbol for safety is
    a. a bite mark
    b. the Kite mark
    c. a triangle
    d. a bird

36. Which item of equipment is essential when using a computer?
    a. a monitor
    b. a printer
    c. a scanner
    d. a comfortable chair

37. A child playing alone is an example of
    a. parallel play
    b. associative play
    c. co-operative play
    d. solitary play

38. Collage means
    a. sticking materials on paper
    b. bubble painting
    c. junk modelling
    d. playing with water

39. Which person is not a member of the nursery class team?
    a. the childcare and education worker
    b. the teacher
    c. the student
    d. the dinner lady

40. You should respond to a crying newborn baby by
    a. picking the baby up and cuddling her
    b. leaving the room for ten minutes to see if she stops
    c. telling her to stop in a firm voice
    d. putting more covers on her

ANSWERS TO QUESTIONS ON PAGES 297–301

1. a.
2. c.
3. a
4. c.
5. b.
6. c.
7. b.
8. a.
9. c
10. b
11. a.
12. d.
13. c.
14. b.
15. d.
16. b.
17. d.
18. d.
19. d.
20. c.
21. a.
22. b.
23. b.
24. b.
25. c.
26. c
27. c.
28. d.
29. d.
30. a.
31. c.
32. b.
33. c.
34. d.
35. b.
36. a.
37. d.
38. a.
39. d.
40. a.

Glossary

allergy an acute reaction of the body to something eaten, inhaled or touched. For example, peanut allergy or nettle rash

antibodies substances found in the blood that fight infection

anti-discriminatory practice making sure that no one is discriminated against, that all resources, language and behaviour in the school/nursery are appropriate

assertive dealing with difficult situations in a calm and non-threatening way whilst putting over your point of view

associative play playing with other children

attachment feeling affection, often devotion to another, which is always returned, and is often between parent and child

autism describes a condition in which children have difficulty in communicating with others and therefore in establishing relationships

bibliography list of books and articles that you have used in your work

body language where your face and the way you use your body show what you are thinking, without having to talk

bonding becoming emotionally attached to one person, and usually describes the attachment of the mother to the baby and of the baby to the mother

BSE bovine spongiform encephalitis. A disease found in cattle that can be passed to people who eat beef

catalogue a way of storing information about books and resources, usually alphabetically

cerebral palsy a condition resulting from brain damage, usually during pregnancy or at birth, affecting the part of the brain that controls movement

child-centred play the child chooses the activity

chronic illness longstanding conditions continuing over a period of time, such as diabetes and asthma

class one way of looking at a society is to put people into different groups according to their education, job, accent, income and housing

comfort object an object, often a blanket or a soft toy, which a child carries around as a comforter, and usually takes to bed with her

concepts ideas and theories

conditions of service statement in a contract of what the employee is entitled to in the areas of pay, holidays, hours of work and so on

confidentiality keeping to yourself information about children and their families

consistent care children should be cared for in a way that does not change very much, and is the same each day, so that the child feels safe and secure. When the child is very young there should not be too many changes in carers

constructive criticism criticism that helps you to improve your work, and that you are expected to accept

convulsions fits caused by unusual nervous activity in the brain. A sudden attack of repeated muscular contractions and relaxation

co-operative play involving planning and games with complicated rules

correspondence: communication in writing. Could be letters, memos, etc.

cradle cap a crusty brown scalp, seen in babies, which can be dry or greasy

creative play play which uses the imagination, including art work and model making

developmental norms normal development as recognised by doctors and scientists. Patterns of development that most children follow in sequence

diabetes the body is unable to produce insulin, the hormone that controls the amount of sugar released into the bloodstream

disinfect to destroy germs, usually by the use of chemicals. It is harmful to body tissue. Boiling also destroys germs

distraction hearing test a hearing test carried out at 7 months. A baby sits on someone's lap while a person in front of them distracts her attention, and someone behind makes a number of sounds. The baby's awareness of these sounds is noted

domestic play often in the Home Corner, such as pretending to make cups of tea and sweeping the floor. This is usually carried out by the pre-school age group, and can be solitary or with other children or adults

employment agency a business that will find employees for employers

epilepsy a condition caused by the disruption of electric impulses in the brain that might lead to having a fit

ethnic groups refers to racial groups

expressed breast milk milk taken from the breast by hand or pump and given to the baby in a bottle

faeces bodily waste

failure to thrive children do not grow or gain weight as expected. There may be many causes, some of them physical or medical. It can be found in children who are abused or neglected

feral refers to animals in the wild, often cats that have been left to die. On occasion this has happened to children who have been cared for by animals

fibre found in plant food. It contains no nourishment but adds bulk to the diet and helps digestion

fontanelles soft spots in the baby's skull before the bones join together

footnotes notes at the bottom of pages

gesture moving the hands to convey a message

GMF genetically modified foods, mainly plants, altered by scientists so as to produce more food and be resistant to pests. Not yet proven to be safe

Guthrie test routine blood test carried out within days of birth on all babies in the UK

habitat a natural environment

hand-eye co-ordination the way that sight and hands are used together to complete a task, for example threading a needle

hazards dangers, such as long flexes on kettles and splinters in wooden blocks, that may cause accidents

health promotion the process of encouraging people to control and improve their health

hygiene concerned with the maintenance of health by promoting clean and healthy practices and routines

hyperactivity a condition that makes children very active, and unable to concentrate

imaginative play play that involves creative thought

imitative play the beginning of imaginary play, where a baby copies what she has seen an adult doing, such as waving 'Bye bye'

immature behaving or speaking in a younger way than one would expect for the age

immunisation status a record showing how many immunisations a child has had

immunisation artificial protection against illnesses, such as polio and diphtheria, often given by injections

impairment generally refers to a loss in function, such as being partially sighted, or having some hearing loss

index what is contained in a book, in alphabetical order

infestation invasion of parasites living on or in a human host, such as head lice and threadworms

initiative being aware of what needs to be done, and doing it without being told. For example, mixing fresh paints when some colours have run out

insulin hormone produced by the pancreas to control the amount of sugar released into the blood stream

Kidscape an organisation founded to prevent child abuse and neglect

Kite mark the official mark of quality and reliability on equipment approved by the British Standards Institute

lone parent (may also be referred to as "single parent") one person living alone with his or her children

manipulative skills all skills that require the hands

masturbation playing with the genitals to achieve sexual pleasure. A common practice in children of both sexes, causing no harm to health or development

media the means by which news is spread. It could refer to television, radio, newspapers, magazines, the Internet and so on

mentor someone who takes responsibility to help and support another person, often a new member of staff

messy play often involves exploring materials with the hands or other parts of the body

milestone a significant event in the development of a child, for example cutting the first tooth or learning to read

motivation what makes you want to succeed or achieve

multi-disciplinary team a team of professionals with different skills working together with a common aim

multiple birth the birth of two or more children being born at the same time. This is more common today because of fertilisation treatment

multi-racial society a society that includes many races

muscle tone the constant state of slight contraction in the skeletal muscles that are responsible for posture and movement

NSPCC the National Society for the Prevention of Cruelty to Children, a charity that helps protect children from abuse and neglect

nurture caring for children in a loving way, meeting all their needs

obesity being 20 per cent or more over ideal weight. It is often linked to lack of exercise

objective judging something in an impersonal way, and not allowing one's feelings to be involved

observation skills professional skills of how to look at children in an objective way and record what you see, using various techniques

parallel play playing alongside another child or adult

paramount of the utmost importance

parental responsibility the rights, duties, powers, responsibilities and authority, which by law a parent of a child has in relation to the child and his or her property

passive activity an activity like television that involves watching and not taking part

peer group friends

plight a desperate state, often used to describe the state people are in who are suffering from famine, earthquakes, flood or homelessness

policies and procedures statements, often in writing, about guidelines for carrying out certain acts dictating good practice. For example, for fire drill, accidents, collecting children, equal opportunities and so on

positive images developing an environment that shows all children in a positive way, shown in posters, dressing up clothes, books, equipment and reflected in the attitude of the staff

posture a position of the limbs or parts of the body

prejudice a set of beliefs, usually strongly held, that leads to discrimination against a particular group

professional working in a way that shows you have the knowledge, behaviour and attitudes that show in good practice. It also means being reliable and keeping confidences

psychology study of the behaviour of an individual

puberty the shift from childhood to adolescence, involving many changes in the body and in mood swings

redundancy loss of employment due to a business closing down or cutting down on staff. There is often a payment to the employee

referees people prepared to write to say that you are suitable for a certain job

regression a child showing behaviour more suited to an earlier stage of development for example, if there is a new baby in the home, the older child might start sucking his thumb and wetting the bed. An ill child might prefer toys and puzzles suitable for a younger child

repetitive play the child feels the need to repeat an activity over and over again, until she feels satisfied

resource books books used to help you in your work

respite schemes help provided by local authority and voluntary groups to let parents of disabled children have a rest from providing continuous care

role model a person looked to by others as a good example in a particular situation

role playing a part

sebum an oily substance that lubricates the skin

self-esteem confidence in oneself as a worthwhile person. This is essential to learning and achievement

siblings brothers and sisters

socialisation the way the family, at first, and later other people influences the child to behave in an acceptable way

society the customs and organisation of a community

solitary play playing by oneself

spontaneous on the spur of the moment. Not structured

stereotype generalisations about a particular group for example, believing that all boys are more aggressive than girls

stimulation/stimulus a situation or action that needs a response. For example, the smell and sight of dinner will make a hungry child run to the table eager for her food

structured play the adult chooses the activity, provides the materials and organises the play

supervisor a qualified person who will support you in placement, assess your progress and write a report

taboos a practice forbidden and regarded as totally unacceptable by any society

tetanus sometimes known as lockjaw. It affects the central nervous system. It can be prevented by immunisation

three-dimensional an object having length, width and depth, such as a cube as opposed to a two-dimensional object that only has length and width, such as a photograph or a drawing

Index